Brexit

KEY ISSUES IN MODERN SOCIOLOGY

Key Issues in Modern Sociology series publishes scholarly texts
that give an accessible exposition of the major structural changes
in modern societies. These volumes address an academic audience through their
relevance and scholarly quality and connect sociological thought to public issues. The
series covers both substantive and theoretical topics as well as addresses the works
of major modern sociologists. The series emphasis is on modern developments in
sociology with relevance to contemporary issues such as globalization,
warfare, citizenship, human rights, environmental crises, demographic
change, religion, postsecularism and civil conflict.

Brexit

Sociological Responses

Edited by William Outhwaite

ANTHEM PRESS

Anthem Press
An imprint of Wimbledon Publishing Company
www.anthempress.com

This edition first published in UK and USA 2017
by ANTHEM PRESS
75–76 Blackfriars Road, London SE1 8HA, UK
or PO Box 9779, London SW19 7ZG, UK
and
244 Madison Ave #116, New York, NY 10016, USA

British Library Cataloguing-in-Publication Data
A catalogue record for this book is available from the British Library.

Library of Congress Cataloging-in-Publication Data
A catalog record for this book has been requested.

ISBN-13: 978-1-78308-644-3 (Hbk)
ISBN-10: 1-78308-644-0 (Hbk)

ISBN-13: 978-1-78308-645-0 (Pbk)
ISBN-10: 1-78308-645-9 (Pbk)

This title is also available as an e-book.

CONTENTS

Section 3.   PROSPECTS FOR/AFTER BREXIT

PREFACE

William Outhwaite

Less than six months after the United Kingdom referendum, sociologists and other social scientists are evaluating the implications both for the UK, or whatever remains of it, and, more importantly, for the European Union and for Europe and the world.

Some of these are already evident. The vote has revealed cleavages across the UK on a regional and class basis, paralleled, for example, in the support in France for the Front National. In the UK, we have seen the revival of a kind of class politics, in which working-class voters swing Right rather than Left, reinforcing the middle-class 'leave' vote in much of the richer south of England. The regional divisions are hard to explain: the most deprived areas of the UK, which have benefited substantially from EU development aid, were often those most hostile to membership in the EU.

In the rest of Europe, the vote has opened up as a serious prospect what was previously only a pipe dream of the political fringes: withdrawal from the EU itself. Although one can put this in the context of the Union's failure to attract the support of enough voters in Norway and Switzerland for membership, the shock effect is incomparably greater. The UK was always a semi-detached member state, with opt-outs from Schengen and the euro, but it still carried substantial weight in the formation of EU policy. Even if the vote had gone the other way, however, the UK had already trashed what remained of its reputation as a serious member of the Union. Although one of the immediate responses has been a rise in support for the EU across much of Europe, Brexit has massively strengthened the forces of (mostly right-wing) populist insurgent politics, adding withdrawal to the more local themes of migration and 'Islamization' that play out in different variations across Europe. In the UK, even before the vote, the campaign produced a wave of what, since it was the result of the government's decision to call a referendum, might reasonably be described as state-sponsored hate crime, which has so far cost the lives of a British Member of Parliament and a Polish resident.

This book aims to trace these implications, locating short-term political fluctuations in a broader historical and social context of the transformation of European and global society. It provides a forum for leading Eurosociologists (broadly defined), working inside and outside the UK itself, to rethink their analyses of the European project and its prospects as well as to reflect on the likely implications for what, as Timothy Garton Ash pointed out in a *Guardian* article, we may come to know as the former UK (FUK).

Ever since Theda Skocpol's call in the 1980s for 'bringing the state back in',[1] it has been conventional to distinguish between 'state-centred' and 'society-centred' explanations of social and political events. This book inevitably moves between both perspectives or emphases. The referendum can be explained in the short term as an attempt to fix an internal problem in the ruling Conservative Party and the challenge it faced from the right and from the poisonous racial politics that affect the UK and many other member states, and in the long term by at least half a century, if not many centuries, of an ambivalent relation to the rest of Europe. The result, similarly, was in one sense clear less than 24 hours after the polls had opened, although its legal validity remains uncertain as we go to press, and in another sense opens up an area of uncertainty that is likely to continue for at least two and probably more like twenty years.

It can be viewed in essentially three ways: as a much-needed warning to the EU to reform itself in one way or another (as Stefan Auer argues here), as a virus that threatens to weaken the Union's viability and perhaps to be the first domino to fall in its dissolution, or as a possible source of reinforcement of attachment to the EU, as Antje Wiener and Tim Oliver suggest, once the UK's or the FUK's fate outside becomes clearer and the dead weight of its long-standing resistance to integration is removed.

This book covers all these dimensions, focusing on the deep-seated social origins in the UK and the rest of Europe of an event that surprised almost everyone some time between 3:00 and 4:00 a.m. on 24 June 2016. As we go to press, its likely consequences range from a declaration that the process was legally flawed and requires a further ratification, which might or might not be forthcoming, to a post-Brexit future that could take a variety of forms and turn out more or less satisfactorily or disastrously for the UK and the rest of Europe.

Unlike the vote, which was evenly split, our view of Brexit is predominantly negative. A cynic might expect this of a cosmopolitan group of social scientists, many of us working in a country where a third of sociological research is currently funded by the EU. We hope, however, that this book will show the value of the sort of sober analysis that was marginalized, to a quite remarkable degree, in the debates before and after the referendum.

Having taken up Chris Rojek's suggestion to edit a book on Brexit, I am immensely grateful to the friends and colleagues who have come together here, after a mere six weeks instead of the more usual minimum of six months, despite other commitments and, in many cases, vicissitudes of health and relocation.

Note

1 Theda Skocpol, 'Bringing the State Back In', in *Bringing the State Back In*, edited by P. Evans (Cambridge: Cambridge University Press, 1985), 3–37.

Section 1

HOW DID IT HAPPEN?

Chapter One

THE INCREASING INEVITABILITY OF *THAT* REFERENDUM

Martin Westlake*

If the United Kingdom had responded positively to the 9 May 1950 Schuman declaration and if it had subsequently signed the Treaty of Paris establishing the European Coal and Steel Community (admittedly, two very big 'ifs'), there would surely have been no referendum. When, in May 1945, Winston Churchill, then prime minister, suggested that a referendum be held on whether to extend the life of the wartime coalition until Japan had been defeated, the deputy prime minister, Clement Attlee, refused, declaring, 'I could not consent to the introduction into our national life of a device so alien to all our traditions as the referendum which has only too often been the instrument of Nazism and Fascism' (quoted in Bogdanor, 1981, p. 35).

The same could surely have been claimed about the 25 March 1957 Treaty of Rome. Harold Macmillan had only taken over from Anthony Eden at the beginning of that year, but his Conservative government was still sitting on a 60-seat majority. The same, lastly, could surely also have been observed had the UK's 1961 application not been vetoed by President Charles de Gaulle. Following the October 1959 General Election, Macmillan had been returned with a 100-seat majority. Announcing the application to the Commons, Macmillan declared that 'no agreement will be entered into until it has been approved by the House' (1961). The subsequent vote was unambiguous: 313 votes to 4, with the Labour Opposition and some fifty Conservative Members of Parliament (MPs) abstaining. There was no mention of a referendum and no call for one. But that first 1961 move contained significant seeds of future complications.

First, the UK did not apply alone. The Danish and Norwegian economies were so closely tied to the UK's that they sent in their applications shortly after the UK's. Although never a European Free Trade Association (EFTA) member, Ireland's economy was so closely tied to the UK's that it anticipated the British application. When de Gaulle rejected the UK's application at the eleventh hour, the three other applicant countries withdrew their candidatures. A symbiotic relationship had been established – the four would always be seen as a bloc (de Gaulle later dismissively referred to the group as 'the British and their associates' (cited in George, 1994, p. 38)) – and all of them, with the sole exception of the UK, had constitutional provisions for the holding of referendums.

Second, *any* first application for membership of the European Economic Community (EEC) would have been significant. As a major economy and powerful country with a transatlantic tradition, the UK's application would have been additionally significant. But for it to bring three other candidate countries in its train would represent a major change. Third, as the July/August 1961 debate and vote in the House of Commons had demonstrated, the issue of the UK's relationship with the unfolding European integration process cut through both the main parties, as it has done ever since. This meant inevitably that any future referendum, were it to occur, would almost certainly have to be fought on a cross-party basis.

Lastly, the first application gave rise to a number of phenomena that would become increasingly familiar. A first was the organization of new groups seeking to mobilize public and parliamentary opinion against entry (Richardson, 2016). If the people had been irrelevant to the politicians' calculations to date, that would no longer be the case: 'It can [...] be safely said that it was with the application that the people came for the first time to be an influential factor in the United Kingdom's relationship to the Communities' (Milward, 2012, p. 341). A second phenomenon occurred on 22 November 1962 in the South Dorset by-election. A dissident anti–Common Market Conservative candidate, Sir Piers Debenham, denied the official Conservative candidate, Angus Maude, victory and gifted what had been a safe Conservative seat to the Labour candidate, Guy Barnett – a first example of what was to become a potent political force in the 1990s and again in the 2010s.

When the UK tabled a second application for membership (10 May 1967), the other three countries rapidly followed. These new applications were at first similarly vetoed by de Gaulle (27 November 1967). His successor, Georges Pompidou, had a change of heart, and a 1–2 December 1969 Summit of the Six agreed that negotiations should start. But when, in early 1972, those negotiations had been successfully concluded and the EEC stood on the cusp of its first enlargement, the French president announced he would hold a referendum on the enlargement package. Ostensibly, Pompidou felt the change to be of such momentous significance that the approval of the French people should be sought. However, 'it seemed like a political exercise for domestic consumption' (Berstein and Rioux, 2000, p. 66).

The referendum (23 April 1972), with 68 per cent of those voting in favour of enlargement, was duly followed by a referendum in Ireland (10 May), which approved the constitutional amendment necessary for the Republic to accede, with almost 84 per cent of those voting in favour. Next, on 25 September, Norway held a popular referendum in which, despite a large parliamentary majority in favour of joining, a 53.5 per cent majority voted to reject membership. Lastly, on 2 October 1972, the Danish people voted in favour of membership by a 63.3 per cent majority.

Meanwhile, in the UK, on 28 October 1971, after some six days and 300 hours of debate, the sovereign House of Commons voted in favour of accession, with 356 in favour and 244 against. Thirty-seven Conservative MPs voted against. Sixty-nine Labour MPs, led by Roy Jenkins, voted in favour. The official Labour Party line was to oppose entry 'on Tory terms'. Pro-accession Labour frontbenchers were instructed to remain silent during the debate – or toe the party line. In July, Edward Heath had rejected the need for a referendum, declaring that the House of Commons had the constitutional sovereignty to decide (Crowson, 2007, p. 38). But this position of insistence on parliamentary sovereignty as being sufficient was taken against a backdrop of apathetic, if not negative, public opinion.

In formal terms, no referendum was held in the UK in 1972 because of the doctrine of the absolute sovereignty of Parliament. But unlike in 1961, there *were* calls for one. Already, on 10 December 1969, a Conservative MP, Bruce Campbell, moved a bill arguing that the electors should have the right 'to decide by way of referendum whether Great Britain should enter the European Economic Community': 'The three major parties have all declared themselves to be in favour of this country joining the Common Market. It therefore follows that this question will never be an election issue and the people will have absolutely no chance of ever being able to express their views on it through the ballot box at a General Election' (Butler and Kitzinger, 1976, p. 10).

Fifty-five MPs voted in favour of the bill. Most notably, however, in April 1972, the anti-Market Conservative MPs Neil Marten and Enoch Powell tabled an amendment to the European Communities Bill calling for a consultative referendum on entry. Labour's Shadow Cabinet decided to support Marten's amendment. (Jenkins opposed the policy on principle and resigned as deputy party leader, and many Labour MPs abstained on the division.) Moreover, as has been seen, there were referendums elsewhere on precisely the same issue: in Ireland, Denmark and Norway, and 'even' in France.

This raises an interesting counterfactual question: what if the UK had joined alone, in isolation, and there had been no other referendum? There would, then, have been no possibility for the perception to arise that somehow the British people had been 'cheated' of their say. There would, in particular, have been no counterexamples of the Danish, Irish and Norwegian people having their say while the British allegedly could not. And there would have been no Norwegian counterexample of popular rejection of membership.

The absence of a written constitution did not help and, indeed, enabled those of that kind of a disposition to indulge in such arguments as that the subsequent 1975 referendum result could not be legitimate because the UK could not vote to stay in something that it had not, in constitutional terms, properly joined. In seeking to avoid such ambiguity, the 1997–2001 Blair administration would effectively entrench the principle of the referendum in British constitutional life.

The accession negotiations were tough, but from Heath's point of view there was no doubt that the prize was to be grasped. This determination was epitomized by his all-or-nothing, obstacle-clearing role in the 20 May 1971 Paris bilateral summit meeting with Pompidou (Margaret Thatcher Foundation, 2016). With this determined steer from above, the UK had acceded with a tacit acceptance among its negotiators that the entry terms it had been obliged to accept would have to be adjusted/renegotiated whenever that proved possible (Denman, 1997, p. 233 and pp. 243–244). Meanwhile, the Labour Party had remained badly split on the issue of membership, and now Harold Wilson, its wily managerial leader, was able to exploit both the manner of the UK's accession and the terms on which it had entered, to fashion election-winning party unity. The Labour Party's February 1974 General Election manifesto argued that 'a profound political mistake made by the Heath Government was to accept the terms of entry to the Common Market, and to take us in without the consent of the British people' (cited in Denman, 1997, p. 247).

The politicking and calculations that led to the holding of the UK's 5 June 1975 referendum are well known (see Butler and Kitzinger, 1976, pp. 12–20). But in the light of what has subsequently occurred, the importance of the 1975 referendum cannot be overestimated.

First, the referendum was the first-ever national plebiscite in British politics. The long-standing eschewal of direct democracy was no more. The *principle* that a referendum might be held had been acknowledged by Parliament, sovereign though it had always been and would always remain, through the Referendum Act 1975.

Second, no matter what the language used about the consultative nature of any referendum result, the potential for discordance between what a majority of MPs, on the one hand, and a majority of the people, on the other, believed had been irrevocably created. In 1975, those two majorities happened to concur. In 2016, they did not.

Third, more subliminally, because the first-ever referendum in the UK was a referendum about the UK's relationship with the European integration process, it created a sort of indelible link. Continued membership of the European Union (EU), it was implied, was an issue of such constitutional and political importance that it necessarily and quite logically could be addressed again by dint of a referendum.

Fourth, as one commentator has recently put it, 'the vast majority of modern national referendums are about undertaking a new project, whether joining the EU, approving a new constitution or constitutional amendments, becoming a republic or an independent state. In these cases, the referendums invited countries to take a step forward into a new future – one in which life would be better than it had been before' (Green, 2016). If such a presumption about referendums being perceived as opportunities to step forward were accepted, it would mean that any take-it-or-leave-it referendum about EU membership would imply that leaving might represent an improvement.

Fifth, the referendum device was not associated with accession per se but with the satisfactory nature of reform/renegotiation and subsequent continued membership. The UK had, for better or worse, already acceded to the EEC. Membership could thus be perceived as having been a fait accompli. The possible linkage of reform and a referendum, meanwhile, was a monster that would *not* raise its head with successful prime ministers enjoying substantive parliamentary majorities, but would inevitably haunt 'weak' prime ministers with small majorities.

Sixth, although there was a clear majority (67 per cent) in favour of remaining, the result was neither a strong one nor a particularly positive one: 'the verdict was not even necessarily a vote of confidence that things would be better in than out; it may have been no more than an expression of fear that things would be worse out than in' (Butler and Kitzinger, 1976, p. 280).

Lastly, the referendum and all that had preceded it had not only proven that 'Europe was now an issue for parliamentary rebellion' (Crowson, 2007, p. 43) but had legitimized it.

From 1979 until the mid-1980s, the UK's relations with the EEC were epitomized by Margaret Thatcher's combative attitude towards the EU and her determination to win the UK a proportionate budgetary rebate, culminating in the settlement reached at the June 1984 Fontainebleau European Council meeting. The subliminal impression given, once again, was of an unsatisfactory relationship arising out of unsatisfactory terms (unsatisfactorily renegotiated). Meanwhile, in its 1983 election manifesto, the Labour Party, under Michael Foot, pledged to begin negotiations to withdraw from the EU 'within the lifetime' of the following Parliament. (It was notably such policy stances that had led Jenkins (now a former European Commission President) and a number of other pro-EEC Labour MPs to break away, in 1981, and establish the Social Democratic Party.)

Thereafter, though Thatcher's combative attitude continued with the new French president of the European Commission, Jacques Delors, acting as sparring partner, it seemed that Thatcher's second administration might develop a more constructive role. After all, the 1986 Single European Act might not have been entirely to Thatcher's liking, but its core objective of creating a single market by 1992 was a project to which she and her government could not only enthusiastically sign up but also unashamedly champion. The Labour Party, too, under the reformist leadership of Neil Kinnock, was gradually converted to a pro-EU stance, not least through the creation of a flanking 'social Europe' that would lead to the 1989 signing of a social charter. But the latter was anathema to Thatcher. On 20 September 1988, she took advantage of a speech to the College of Europe to state, 'We have not successfully rolled back the frontiers of the state in Britain, only to see them re-imposed at a European level with a European super-state exercising a new dominance from Brussels' (Thatcher, 1988). Frictions steadily grew with her chancellor, Nigel Lawson, and foreign secretary, Geoffrey Howe, over policy towards Europe and particularly towards the European Exchange Rate Mechanism. Thatcher was increasingly sceptical about resurgent moves to create a European single currency. In protest at her interference, Lawson resigned on 27 October 1989, Howe on 1 November 1990, and by 22 November 1990, Thatcher was gone and, in retrospect, another subliminal message had been sent: 'Europe' had brought about the downfall of Margaret Thatcher – still a popular figure on the right and considered by many to have been the UK's greatest post-war prime minister after Churchill. More to the point, Euroscepticism now had a figurehead.

Although Europe had continued to be a source of division and friction within the two main political parties and between them, by the late 1980s membership was a given on both sides of the political divide. But by 1989, history was on the march. On 9 November 1989 the Berlin Wall fell, and it became apparent that Germany would unify and that Europe was about to undergo major geopolitical change. Momentum developed for the European project to respond through deeper political and economic integration. Space precludes a detailed account of the processes that led to the 7 February 1992 signing of the Maastricht Treaty (see, for example, Baun, 1996, and Dyson and Featherstone, 1999), which provided for both political and economic and monetary union (EMU). The Communities became a Union with citizens. Convergence criteria and a timetable were set for the EMU process. The Maastricht Treaty undeniably embodied a series of significant steps forward. The question was whether the UK would take all of those steps together with its fellow Member States. The pragmatic response of the new Conservative prime minister, John Major, was to stay on board as far as possible and to negotiate opt-outs, opt-ins and derogations where the UK could not take those steps. The most significant was the single currency. From the UK's point of view, there were two basic questions to be answered. Should it give its assent to the creation of a single currency? And, if so, should it be a part of it? The Labour Party's answer to both questions was 'yes' (as was that of the Liberal Democrats). For a long time, Labour had differentiated itself from the Conservatives by calling for ERM membership. But in 1990, Thatcher unexpectedly took sterling into the ERM. The party's leader concluded that differentiation could only be renewed through conditional support for membership of the currency union. Major's conclusion was, first, that he could not any more stand in the way of moves to a single currency (his proposals for a parallel currency had gained no traction) but should make sure that the envisaged EMU would be constructed on firm foundations, and, second, that the UK should adopt a wait-and-see attitude to membership for sterling, through an opt-out.

Major's positions were unacceptable to the Eurosceptics within his party, who believed that the answer to both questions should have been a resounding 'no'. At the 9 April 1992 General Election, Major's Conservative Party won a fourth consecutive victory but with a majority of just 21 seats. Major had successfully negotiated and signed the Maastricht Treaty. Now he had to steer its ratification through Parliament. Sterling's ignominious forced exit from the ERM on 16 September 1992 ('Black Wednesday') compounded a sense of outrage about the Treaty's plans for a single currency. A relatively small group of rebel backbenchers, combined with the behaviour of Eurosceptical ministers and Labour Party tactics designed to cause maximum discomfort for the government (primarily because of the opt-out from the Social Chapter) made the ratification process fraught, leading Major at one stage to call for a motion of confidence. One of the demands of the sceptics was for the Treaty to be put to a referendum (as it was in Italy, Ireland, France and Denmark – whose people voted twice 'until they got the right answer'). In an echo of Campbell's 1969 arguments (see above), they pointed to the fact that, since all of the major parties favoured ratification, the British people had been denied any choice in the matter. On 7 June 1993, during the Treaty ratification debate in the House of Lords, the Eurosceptics' figurehead, Thatcher, gave her voice to those calling for a referendum (1993, pp. 7–8).

Ultimately, the Maastricht Treaty was ratified and implemented. Major's government subsequently soldiered on until 1997. European issues seemed never to go away. Major, who had begun his premiership wishing to put the UK at the heart of Europe, became increasingly Eurosceptical in his pronouncements, but it was never enough for the Eurosceptics and the rebels, who were still determined to force a referendum.

It was in that context, in the run-up to the 1997 General Election, that the referendum Kraken was finally reawoken, as frankly admitted by Michael Heseltine in what he has recently described as being 'the worst judgement of my political career'. A lengthy discussion took place between Major and Chancellor Ken Clarke, with the prime minister pushing for the prospect of a referendum 'to achieve the semblance of party unity'. The discussion moved on to the single currency, and Heseltine suggested that, 'as we were not going to do other than keep open the option in the light of events at an unpredictable time, we could consider a referendum if, after the election, we decided to join. This was the formula we agreed and which John subsequently announced. The limitations of the commitment were swept aside by the media. The rest is history, as David Cameron followed much the same route in his bid for the Tory leadership' (Heseltine, 2016, pp. 19–20).

This was undoubtedly the turning point that would lead inexorably to the 23 June 2016 referendum. Once the Conservative Party had been returned to the Opposition benches, it rapidly accepted the idea of a referendum on the Constitutional Treaty and then the Lisbon Treaty. But its position could only morph in this way because the European integration process had been accelerated by the historical forces described above. The outcome of each intergovernmental conference was a fresh target at which the referendum camp could aim, whilst underlining the fact that the integration process was gathering speed and heading inexorably in a 'federalist' direction, and equally emphasizing the fact each time that the British people had not 'had their say'. In effect, the Maastricht Treaty's provisions on a single currency and in particular whether the UK should be in or out, became a proxy for the broader question of whether the UK should remain in, or leave, the Union itself. And when the prospects of sterling joining the single currency faded, one proxy was replaced by another (the Constitutional Treaty) and then another (the Lisbon Treaty).

Major's referendum commitment did not only open the floodgates for his own party. It was followed by an avalanche of referendum commitments from the other two mainstream parties. In the case of Tony Blair's Labour Party (uncertain, though this is now forgotten, of winning a sufficient majority to govern and assuming some sort of coalition arrangement with the Liberal Democrats would be necessary), there was a clear determination not to be outflanked tactically on the single currency issue, but its manifesto also promised referendums on a whole platform of constitutional reform issues (voting system, devolution in Scotland and Wales, London mayor, regional governments). Where referendums were felt to be constitutionally appropriate – one more, on the single currency, did not feel so out of place. In addition to a referendum commitment on the single currency, the Lib Dems generalized their promise to 'constitutional issues' and 'any transfer of power to European institutions'. The latter was the first incarnation of what would later become the 'referendum lock'.

By the 2001 General Election, the Conservatives had switched to a 'keep the pound' stance (and hence the negation of any need for a referendum), but had meanwhile borrowed the Liberal Democrats' 1997 'lock' concept, promising a referendum if 'any more of Parliament's rights and powers' were 'surrendered' to Brussels. With some of its reforms already implemented, the Labour Party now limited itself to two referendum promises – on the voting system and on the single currency. The Liberal Democrats promised both and made an additional referendum commitment for elected regional assemblies.

The Conservatives maintained their stance on the single currency for the 2005 General Election ('We will not join the euro') but promised referendums on the EU's Constitutional Treaty and on a Welsh Assembly. Labour added the EU Constitutional Treaty to its 2001 promises on the voting system and the single currency, whereas the Liberal Democrats limited themselves now to the single currency and the EU Constitutional Treaty. In 2001, the Conservatives further firmed up their commitment on the single currency. Now, they would 'Never join the euro'. But they not only revisited the referendum lock concept (promising a referendum on 'any proposed future treaty that transferred areas of power, or competences') but also promised a referendum on any use of a 'major' ratchet clause, as provided by the Lisbon Treaty. Since the Lisbon Treaty's ratchet provisions were pre-cisely designed to avoid heavy ratification procedures for minor Treaty changes, this promise would effectively prevent any Treaty change whatsoever. Labour added House of Lords reform to its existing commitments on the voting system and the single currency. The Liberal Democrats similarly promised a referendum on the single currency but now promised a referendum on a national constitution and an in/out referendum 'the next time a British government signs up for fundamental change in the relationship between the UK and the EU'.

By the 2015 General Election, the Conservatives had sought further to distinguish their position in negating the need to even contemplate referendums, promising 'No change to the voting system' and 'No to the euro'. But it took the final, fatal step in promising an in/out referendum on a negotiated 'new settlement for Britain in Europe' before the end of 2017. Labour, meanwhile, which had made a general promise to 'give more power to people', now joined the Conservatives in saying 'no to the euro', but added a commitment to an in/out referendum on any 'transfer of powers from Britain to the European Union'. The Liberal Democrats, in contrast, limited themselves solely to promising an in/out referendum on 'any Treaty change involving a material transfer of sovereignty'. In 1992, none of the three parties promised a referendum on any EU matter (or on anything else). By 2015, all of them were promising in/out referendums on EU membership. Major's 1997 promise on the single currency had acted as a sort of Sarajevo-like trigger.

During the same period, there was a proliferation of referenda elsewhere on EU matters: Ireland and Denmark voted on the Amsterdam Treaty; Ireland voted (twice) on the Nice Treaty; nine candidate countries held accession referendums in 2004; Denmark (2000) and Sweden (2003) rejected joining the single currency; Spain and Luxembourg approved the Constitutional Treaty, whilst France and the Netherlands rejected it, and further referenda were planned in six other Member States (including the UK); Ireland voted twice (again) on the Treaty of Lisbon; Croatia (2013) voted on accession; Ireland (2012) voted on the Fiscal Compact; Denmark (2014) voted on the Unified Patent Court; Greece voted (2015) on its bailout conditions; Denmark (2015) rejected opting in to the area of Justice and Home Affairs. The quantity not only made the holding of referen-dums on EU matters seem commonplace but also further highlighted the absence of a referendum in the UK. Moreover, some Member States had rejected Treaties – most significantly, France and the Netherlands rejected the Constitutional Treaty – which frus-trated those Eurosceptics who had wanted the UK to put a brake on the integration process. Lastly, a narrative grew about smaller countries being forced to reach 'the right answer'; the Danish people rejected the Maastricht Treaty – and had to vote again. Similarly, Ireland rejected the Nice and the Lisbon Treaties and had to vote again on each. The fact that substantive concessions and additional arrangements had been agreed each time was lost in the general impression created by Eurosceptics that the EU was a conspiracy against the publics it purported to serve.

As the inconsistency and changes on the referendum issue illustrate, the varying com-mitments entered into by the mainstream parties and their leaders were as much about tactics and party management as anything else. The contortions that party leaders had to go through in order to maintain some semblance of party unity or to win tactical electoral advantage led to situations that could be further exploited by Eurosceptics and the pro-referendum camp. Four examples illustrate this point.

During the 1997 General Election campaign, Major, confronted with a rebellion over the single currency, but wanting to keep his two frontbench pro-European 'big beasts' (Clarke and Heseltine) on board, declared, 'Whether you agree with me or disagree with me, like me or loathe me, don't bind my hands when I am negotiating on behalf of the British people.' This 'negotiate and then decide' stance 'did not persuade the Euro-sceptics and [...] was difficult to sell to the electorate' (Butler and Kavanagh, 1997, p. 106). In April 2004, in the run-up to the June European elections, Blair made a sudden U-turn on the draft Constitutional Treaty. Until then, the party line had been that the treaty was a cleaning-up exercise and that, despite its title, it did not justify a referendum. Now, suddenly, it did. When news leaked out, 'party strategists recognised the astuteness of the move. The referendum could not be held until at least autumn 2005, safely after the next General Election, and the Conservatives' position would enable Mr Blair to turn it into an "in or out of Europe" issue' (Butler and Westlake, 2005, p. 92). However, a senior Brussels official observed, 'It's a strategically brilliant move if you are concerned with British politics through 2005 but arguably strategically disastrous if you are concerned with Britain's long-term position in Europe' (White, *Guardian*, 20 April 2004).

The Constitutional Treaty was subsequently rejected by the French and Dutch electorates, but returned in a different format, after renegotiation, as the Lisbon Treaty, and placed Blair's successor, Gordon Brown, in an awkward position. On 5 March 2008, despite a rebellion by 29 of its own backbenchers, his government defeated a Conservative proposal to hold a referendum on the Treaty by 311 votes to 248. But Mr Brown 'sparked anger by refusing to give the British people a say on the deeply unpopular treaty claiming that it was unnecessary because it was "fundamentally different" from the constitution rejected by the French and Dutch three years earlier. [...] furious businesswoman Etta Cohen [...] said: "You have broken a major manifesto promise. Why should we believe a single word you say?"' It was, declared the same newspaper, 'one of the biggest acts of political betrayal in modern British history' (*Daily Mail*, 15 April 2010). As a way of somehow differentiating his position from that of outright support for the Lisbon Treaty, Brown travelled late to Lisbon and signed it alone. The media and the sceptics were not convinced.

The issue meanwhile split the Liberal Democrat party, whose leader, Nick Clegg, had ordered his MPs to abstain from the vote. In the event, a quarter of Lib Dem MPs defied his order and voted in favour of a referendum, with three frontbenchers resigning to do so. Clegg explained that he agreed with the government's stance on the Lisbon Treaty but instead wanted a referendum on Britain's EU membership (that is, an in/out referendum) to end ambiguities in the country's relationship with Europe. 'The prime minister once said that he would build a wider pro-European movement in Britain', which would not be achieved by blocking 'the in-out referendum that the British people really want' (https://www.euractiv.com/section/future-eu/news/uk-mps-reject-referendum-on-eu-treaty/).

For his part, then-Opposition leader Cameron declared that Brown's and Clegg's decisions meant that 'people feel cheated and cynical because promises made are promises being broken' (https://www.theguardian.com/uk/2007/dec/13/politics.world). Less than two years later, Cameron confirmed

> a complete U-turn on his 'cast iron guarantee' that a Tory government would hold a public vote on the controversial treaty; the party chief said the Czech Republic's decision to ratify the agreement meant he could 'no more hold a referendum on the treaty than [...] a referendum on the sun rising in the morning.' 'The Lisbon treaty has now been ratified by every one of the 27 member states of the European Union, and our campaign for a referendum on the Lisbon treaty is therefore over. Why?' he asked. 'Because it is no longer a treaty: it is being incorporated into the law of the European Union.' Cameron said he understood how much the people of Britain would resent the fact there could not be a referendum but he claimed the 'betrayal' was the Labour government's, 'backed and matched' by the Liberal Democrats. (*Guardian*, 4 November 2009)

Promising to ensure such a situation would never arise again, Cameron said that, if elected, he would change the law so that a referendum must be held before any further powers could be passed to the European Union:

> We will make sure that this never, ever happens again. Never should it be possible for the British government to transfer power without the consent of the British people. If we win the next election, we will amend the European Communities Act 1972 to prohibit, by law, the transfer of power to the EU without a referendum. And that will cover not just any future treaties like Lisbon, but any future attempt to take Britain into the euro. (*Guardian*, 4 November 2009)

The impression of these contortions, emphasized by political rhetoric, of promises not kept, was adeptly exploited by Nigel Farage in 2014: 'The fact that we haven't had a referendum on this has made people very angry because we keep being promised one, don't we? Dave (Cameron) even gave us a cast-iron guarantee that "If I become Prime Minister of Great Britain and Northern Ireland there will be a referendum on the Lisbon Treaty"; and then of course he let us down like a cheap pair of braces.' And, he added, 'So we are becoming cheesed off because time and again we are promised a referendum and it has not been delivered' (2014). The 2015 General Election enabled the UK Independence Party (UKIP) and Farage to segue off the back of this argument by pointing to the fact that, despite winning 12.7 per cent of the total vote, UKIP returned only one MP, whereas the Liberal Democrats returned eight MPs having won just 7.9 per cent of the total vote.

No account of the Brexit referendum saga would be complete without mention of the growing role played by the referendum parties. Alan Sked's Anti-Federalist League and, later, James Goldsmith's Referendum Party first generated media interest and the latter made some dents in a few marginal constituencies, but as part of its reformist programme Blair's first administration introduced proportional representation for the 1999 European elections. Following on from the 'denial' of a referendum on the Maastricht Treaty, the 1999 introduction of proportional representation (PR) for European elections, coinciding with a historic and record low for turnout in the UK (24 per cent – the record still stands), gave UKIP its first elected representation at the national level, and the return of Eurosceptic representatives in other Member States enabled the party to join a political group within the European Parliament and thus enjoy significant financial and other resources. As Farage happily admitted,

> Without the European elections, without getting three seats in 1999, without getting the resources that the European Parliament made available to us, without the letters 'MEP' after our names, UKIP would never have appeared on *Question Time*, or *Any Questions* or any of the major media programmes in this country. So *we* have always taken the European elections desperately seriously. (2014; emphasis in original)

UKIP's elected presence in one parliamentary forum raised a subliminal question. While critics of the party asked why UKIP was entitled to so much representation in the media when it had so little representation in the House of Commons, those more sympathetic to the party's arguments could equally reverse the question and ask why UKIP had so little representation in the House of Commons despite having sufficient representation in the European Parliament to merit appearing on such popular programmes.

The elected presence of the party enabled UKIP to force the mainstream parties together in their apparent sameness on the referendum issue and to outflank them by offering a simple and clear choice. It was this perceived threat to vulnerable Conservative backbenchers that forced both Major and later Cameron into referendum promises they would surely rather have avoided if they possibly could have done so.

The 2009 election of two British National Party (BNP) Members of the European Parliament (MEPs) enabled Farage to sanitize his party and his cause. Despite playing the immigration card to the hilt and in a way that would have been considered toxic in the recent past in British politics, Farage avoided any practical alliance with Marine Le Pen's Front National and was therefore able to distinguish himself from the 'Far Right' at home and abroad: 'I do not want the voice of Euroscepticism across Europe to be the voice that is led by Marine Le Pen or others far worse than her [...] I think it is really, really important that the Eurosceptic voice is seen to be something that actually believes and embodies liberal democracy' (2014).

Moreover, as UKIP's momentum grew, the party was increasingly able to use its binary message to turn the European elections into a proxy for the 'denied' referendum. As Farage put it in 2014, 'I think some people will choose to use these European elections, in the absence of a referendum, as their means of expressing the word "no"' (2014).

The pro-referendum camp was assisted by two further developments that effectively constitutionalized the use of referendums. The more important was the 2000 Political Parties, Elections and Referendums Act, part of the raft of the first Blair administration's constitutional reforms, which codified referendum campaigns and the conduct of referendums. The second was the European Union Act (2011), which institutionalized the referendum lock that Cameron had promised after his 'U-turn' embarrassment about the Lisbon Treaty. There was now no constitutional reason why the country should not hold a referendum on some matter deemed appropriate by Parliament.

One other issue tends to get overlooked in the referendum context: the euro crisis and its ramifications. In her November 2010 speech to the College of Europe, German chancellor Angela Merkel declared, 'We need a mechanism that can manage crises and that is anchored in the Treaty. That's why we have decided on a limited Treaty amendment which we intend to discuss in December.' In his 23 January 2013 Bloomberg speech, Cameron declared that

> At some stage in the next few years the EU will need to agree on Treaty change to make the changes needed for the long term future of the euro and to entrench the diverse, competitive, democratically accountable Europe that we seek. I believe the best way to do this will be in a new Treaty so I add my voice to those who are already calling for this. My strong preference is to enact these changes for the entire EU, not just for Britain. But if there is no appetite for a new Treaty for us all then of course Britain should be ready to address the changes we need in a negotiation with our European partners.

As we now know with the benefit of hindsight, Cameron was erroneously convinced that Treaty reform was considered both necessary and imminent. Since a destabilized eurozone was not in the British economy's interests, and since he had somehow to overcome the menace of being outflanked by UKIP, he hoped to make a virtue out of two necessities. But as Merkel pragmatically withdrew from a risky encounter with increasingly Eurosceptical public opinion, Cameron found himself marooned. In a bid to maintain party unity and electoral advantage, he painted himself further into the corner with his 2015 General Election manifesto promise of renegotiation followed by an in-out referendum by 2017, perhaps in the hope that a renewed coalition with the Liberal Democrats would prevent him from honouring such a commitment. In the event, his outright election victory meant that he had to honour his manifesto pledge. The present chapter deliberately overlooks the subsequent near-term issues: the renegotiation, the settlement, the timing of the campaign, the tactics. These have been the primary concern of commentators and pundits, but they seem all to have overlooked one stark truth: in the 2015 General Election, all three mainstream political parties offered the electorate an in/out referendum. By the end, all that divided them were the conditions and the timing.

To conclude, the principle of a referendum was first legitimized, then constitutionalized and, simultaneously, popularized. What was once a theoretical though radical option is now an accepted element in the constitutional toolbox: referenda are no longer rare nor exceptional. The use of the referendum is a growing phenomenon worldwide and not just limited to Western Europe nor, indeed, to the EU nor the UK (Qvortrop, 2014). And the referendum, rather than the general election, has increasingly become a primary vector for electorates to express preferences on European issues (Hobolt, 2009).

The 23 June 2016 referendum was not only 'about' Cameron's 2013 decision, nor was it only about the Conservatives and nor, ultimately, was it only about the UK. The UK's mainstream parties had been toying with the idea since before the UK even joined the EEC in 1973 and had increasingly played with it after 1993. Indeed, the most proximate triggers for the slide down to 2016 were the quantum leaps in the Maastricht Treaty (citizenship, the single currency, the Social Chapter) combined with slim parliamentary majorities and the rise of referendum parties – aided by the introduction of PR for

European elections and the constitutionalization of referenda. The increasing incidence of referenda of various sorts elsewhere in the EU further encouraged the idea that in the UK it could, or should, be 'only a matter of time'.

Indeed, only by taking an exceptionally short-term view can one argue that the 2016 referendum was a purely Conservative affair. Just 30 years after one great Labour leader (Attlee) had declared the idea anathema, another (Wilson) had made the promise a major plank of his electoral manifesto. Twenty-six years later, another (Blair) had enshrined the principle in the constitution (having already promised referenda on the single currency and the constitutional treaty). Just 13 years after that, and 39 years after Wilson's commitment, Ed Miliband had promised an in-out referendum in the event of any further transfer of sovereignty.

Perhaps it was this underlying sense of inexorability across the mainstream political divide that led Craig Oliver, Cameron's former communications director, to insist in an interview that it was 'naïve to suggest the government had not needed to call the referendum, adding: "You could either deal with it now or the reality is it would pop up again in a few months or a few years" ' (BBC, 2016).

Taking the longer view about the UK's relationship with the European integration process reveals a number of underlying trends, linking together events and developments over many years that collectively were leading, with increasing inexorability, to a second referendum on EU membership. If not, at first, inevitable, those trends became increasingly so. They were also, for anybody who cared to take that longer view, increasingly discernible. But generations of British politicians, condemned to live in the short-term environment of electoral cycles and pragmatic party management, were seemingly oblivious to them. 'Europe' was seen as something 'over there', an occasional and mostly irritating intrusion erupting into domestic politics, rather than a constant presence and process. The result was a disproportionate emphasis on reaction rather than action, on tactics rather than strategy and, perhaps, on international relations adventures rather than patient diplomacy closer to home. Not even Thatcher and Blair, despite long periods in office and large majorities, were able to develop and maintain a coherent EU policy. The probable truth is that the UK never managed to achieve escape velocity from the dynamics of the 1950–1970 period.

One last counterfactual question must remain tantalizingly unanswered: if the UK *had* held a referendum on the Constitutional Treaty and, as the polls suggested at the time, rejected it (as did the French and the Dutch), would that have been a more calamitous scenario than the UK voting to leave in 2016? Put another way, if the UK electorate had already rejected *something* about the EU, if it had put a metaphorical foot down and said, 'so far and no further', if it had managed 'at last' to have a say on something, would it still have felt sufficiently strongly to vote to leave the EU altogether?

Note

* The views expressed in this chapter are entirely personal. I am indebted to my good and long-standing friend and colleague Anthony Teasdale, not only for his comments, criticisms and suggestions of an earlier draft of this chapter but also for many conversations and discussions, over many years, on the vexed (for us) subject of why and how the UK seemed never able to achieve 'escape velocity' (see the concluding section).

Bibliography

Baun, Michael J. 1996. *An Imperfect Union: The Maastricht Treaty and the New Politics of European Integration*. Boulder, Colorado: Westview Books.

Berstein, Serge, and Jean-Pierre Rioux. 2000. *The Pompidou Years, 1969–1974*. Cambridge: Cambridge University Press.

Bogdanor, Vernon. 1981. *The People and the Party System: The Referendum and Electoral Reform in British Politics*. Cambridge: Cambridge University Press.

British Broadcasting Corporation (BBC). 2016. 'Nick Clegg: Michael Gove behind Queen Backs Brexit Story', 7 August. http://www.bbc.com/news/uk-politics-36986977.

Butler, David, and Dennis Kavanagh. 1997. *The British General Election of 1997*. Houndmills: Palgrave Macmillan.

Butler, David, and Uwe Kitzinger. 1976. *The 1975 Referendum*. London: Macmillan.

Butler, David, and Martin Westlake. 1995. *British Politics and European Elections 1994*. London: Macmillan.

———. 2000. *British Politics and European Elections 1999*. Houndmills: Palgrave Macmillan.

———. 2005. *British Politics and European Elections 2004*. Houndmills: Palgrave Macmillan.

Crowson, Nicholas (N.J.). 2007. *The Conservative Party and European Integration since 1945: At the Heart of Europe?*. Oxford: Routledge.

——— (N.J.). 2010. *Britain and Europe: A Political History since 1918*. Oxford: Routledge.

Daily Mail. 1973. http://www.dailymail.co.uk/wires/ap/article-3658942/Britain-joins-EU-1973.html.

Denman, Roy. 1997. *Missed Chances: Britain and Europe in the Twentieth Century*. London: Indigo.

Dyson, Kenneth, and Kevin Featherstone. 1999. *The Road to Maastricht: Negotiating Economic and Monetary Union*. Oxford: Oxford University Press.

Farage, Nigel. 2014. 'These European Elections Matter', lecture given at the London School of Economics, 23 January. London School of Economics and Political Science. http://www.lse.ac.uk/newsAndMedia/videoAndAudio/channels/publicLecturesAndEvents/player.aspx?id=2211.

George, Stephen. 1994. *An Awkward Partner: Britain in the European Community*. Oxford: Oxford University Press.

Green, Elliott. 2016. 'How Brexiteers Appealed to Voters' Nostalgia'. London School of Economics and Political Science (blog), 30 August. http://blogs.lse.ac.uk/politicsand-policy/how-brexiteers-appealed-to-voters-nostalgia/?utm_source=feedburner&utm_medium=email&utm_campaign=Feed%3A+BritishPoliticsAndPolicyAtLse+%28British+politics+and+policy+at+LSE%29.

Heseltine, Michael. 2016. Edward Heath Memorial Lecture 2016, Salisbury, 21 July (available here as filmed: Arundells. http://www.arundells.org/edward-heath-memorial-lecture-by-lord-heseltine/; and text here: https://view.publitas.com/british-influence/edward-heath-memorial-lecture-2016/page/1).

Hobolt, Sara B. 2009. *Europe in Question: Referendums on European Integration*. Oxford: Oxford University Press.

Legislation. 2000. Political Parties, Elections and Referendums Act 2000. Legislation.gov.uk. http://www.legislation.gov.uk/ukpga/2000/41/pdfs/ukpga_20000041_en.pdf.

Macmillan, Harold. 1961. 'Address Given by Harold Macmillan on the United Kingdom's Application for Members to the EC (31 July 1961)', Centre Virtuel de la Connaissance sur l'Europe. CVCE.eu.

MacShane, Denis. 2016. *Brexit: How Britain Will Leave Europe*. rev. ed. London: I. B. Tauris.

Margaret Thatcher Foundation. 2016. '"Condemned to Succeed": The Heath-Pompidou Summit Which Took Britain into the E.E.C., May 1971', 9 January. http://www.margaretthatcher.org/archive/heath-eec.asp.

Merkel, Angela. 2010. Speech at the Opening Ceremony of the 61st academic year of the College of Europe in Bruges, 2 November. Available in translation at http://www.bruessel.diplo.de/contentblob/2959854/Daten/.

Milward, Alan S. 2012. *The United Kingdom and the European Community*, vol. 1, *The Rise and Fall of a National Strategy 1945–1963*, pbk. ed. Oxford: Routledge.

Norton, Philip. 2010. 'The European Communities Act 1972', posted on 19 November on Nortonview (blog). https://nortonview.wordpress.com.

Qvortrup, Matt. 2014. *Referendums Around the World: The Continued Growth of Direct Democracy*. Houndmills: Palgrave Macmillan.

Richardson, David. 2016. 'Between Politics and the Public: The Anti-EEC Campaign in the 1960s'. Academia.edu. https://www.academia.edu/1698969/Between_politics_and_the_public_the_anti-EEC_campaign_in_the_1960s.

Spence, Alex. 2016. 'No Regrets: An Insider's Guide to Brexit Failure', *Politico*, 8 August. http://www.politico.eu/article/craig-oliver-david-cameron-no-regrets-an-insiders-guide-to-brexit-failure/.

Thatcher, Margaret. 1975. Excerpt from Hansard, House of Commons 11 March 1975 debate. Margaret Thatcher Foundation. http://www.margaretthatcher.org/document/102649.

———. 1988. 'Speech to the College of Europe ("The Bruges Speech")', 20 September. Margaret Thatcher Foundation. http://www.margaretthatcher.org/document/107332.

———. 1993. HLS (European Communities (Amendment) Bill) (speech), 7 June. Margaret Thatcher Foundation. http://www.margaretthatcher.org/document/108314.

Wall, Stephen. 2012. *The Official History of Britain and the European Community*, vol. 2, *From Rejection to Referendum, 1963–1975*. Oxford: Routledge.

Wallace, Helen. 2012. 'The UK: 40 Years of EU Membership', *Journal of Contemporary European Research* 8 (4): 531–546.

Westlake, Martin. 1997. 'Mad Cows and Englishmen – the Institutional Consequences of the BSE Crisis', *Journal of Common Market Studies, Annual Review of Activities 1996*, 35 (September): 11–36.

———. 2016. 'Chronicle of an Election Foretold: The Longer-Term Trends Leading to the "*Spitzenkandidaten*" Procedure and the Election of Jean-Claude Juncker as European Commission President'. European Institute at the London School of Economics and Political Science (LSE). *Europe in Question Discussion Paper Series (LEQS)*, Paper N° 102/January.

Chapter Two

VOX POPULI: NATIONALISM, GLOBALIZATION AND THE BALANCE OF POWER IN THE MAKING OF BREXIT

Jonathan Hearn

Today the term 'vox pop' most commonly refers to those snippets of opinion from people 'on the street' heard and seen on radio and television. We had many of these from those who would turn out to be part of the small majority for leave in the run-up to the Brexit referendum on 23 June 2016. Two main themes often repeated in these snippets were that people wanted to limit levels of immigration seen to be out of control, and that they wanted take back control over the laws by which they were governed. In both cases, behind fears of and resentments towards immigrants and European Union (EU) bureaucracy, lies a fundamental feeling of lack of control, of powerlessness. We need to understand this. The phrase *vox populi, vox Dei* (the voice of the people is the voice of God), or simply *vox plebis* (voice of the people) has a long history in English politics, serving the critiques of centralized power offered by medieval archbishops, Levellers and Whigs in turn (Maloy 2013: 124–126). David Hume famously claimed that 'it is […] on opinion only that government is founded' (1985: 32–33), by which he meant that centralized power can never ultimately force submission of a large mass of people. It relies either on active support or at least willing acquiescence. Either way, the point is that people are ruled through opinion, and opinions matter. The Brexit referendum gave a large portion of the British population that felt its opinions were disregarded, a single, highly constrained opportunity to express their views, and their resentment.

This chapter attempts to place the call for Brexit and what we know about those who voted for and against it in the context of concepts of nationalism, globalization and, most crucially, the evolving balance of power in society. The first two are necessary for framing this event, but the third gives us more analytic purchase on the general course of events. After considering Brexit from these three angles, I return to questions of public opinion and ideology, and their role in misrepresenting that general course of events and facilitating Brexit.

The Divide

Lord Ashcroft's polls provide a good initial portrait of the leavers and remainers and what tends to differentiate them (Ashcroft 2016). The younger you were, the more likely you were to vote remain. Higher education and professional and managerial employment were also markers of remain preference. Those identifying as Asian, black or Muslim were much more likely to vote remain. Those who supported the Labour Party, Liberal Democrats, Greens or the Scottish National Party (SNP) were also much more likely to choose remain. Conversely, leavers were more likely to be older, retired or otherwise out of employment. Those whose education ended at secondary school and who are at the lower end of the income scale in skilled, semi-skilled and unskilled manual occupations were much more likely to vote leave. Fifty-eight per cent of those identifying as Christian voted to leave. Conservative and UK Independence Party (UKIP) supporters made up the bulk of leave voters, 40 per cent and 25 per cent respectively.

In regard to reasons given for voting choices, the top two reasons given in Ashcroft's poll by the remainers, in order of priority, were that the risks were too great to 'things like the economy, jobs and prices', and that membership of the EU while being out of the euro and the Schengen area was 'the best of both worlds'. Leavers in contrast gave these first and second reasons: 'the principle that decisions about the UK should be taken in the UK', and that leaving offered 'the best chance for the UK to regain control over immigration and its own borders'.

Nationalism

Nationalism is clearly an aspect of these events, but if we are going to use this concept to make sense of events, we need to be clear about what we mean by it. Using it as a covering term for objectionable ethnic chauvinism will not do. I suggest we should think of nationalism as 'the making of combined claims, on behalf of a population, to *identity, jurisdiction* and *territory*' (Hearn 2006: 11; emphasis in original). By this definition, both sides of the Brexit debate were mobilizing nationalist ideas, but they disagreed about who we think we are and whether we have sufficient rule over ourselves, within the British territory in question. Far from being the antithesis of democracy, nationalism develops historically in the modern period as its concomitant. The wave of eighteenth- and nineteenth-century revolutions that promised variations on 'the rule of the people, by the people' created a world where the questions of who exactly the people are and what do they want, were permanently on the table, and routinely contested. The various institutions of democracy (parliaments, parties, elections, referenda) are rough-and-ready devices for steadily translating those questions and that contest into something manageable and relatively stable. Nationalism and democracy are joined at the hip. There are indeed a variety of answers that get posed to the fundamental questions of nationalism, some more 'ethnic' and some more 'civic', and any complex society is likely to have shifting mixtures of both of these in play (Yack 1999). The Brexit outcome reveals a certain polarization between these two types, particularly in England and Wales. But it is all nationalism on both sides nonetheless.

As the responses to the Ashcroft poll indicate, worries about the effects of immigration were an important, but secondary, aspect of what motivated leavers, a matter of much greater importance to a portion of the leave voters than the whole. Clearly there is an element of xenophobia, of nationalism as threatened British/English ethnic identity involved here. In some pre-referendum debates there was the mythical claim that immigrants are sponging benefits off the state, and some strains of plain old racism in the society were feeding into the leave argument. But such views were complexly intertwined with a more nuts and bolts economic argument, however questionable. That was that immigrants, despite their contributions to the economy through work and taxes, were displacing an indigenous working class from its rightful employment as well as access to residences and school places and so on. If true, this would be a very legitimate grievance. However, there is limited evidence that such displacement has been happening, and most research has suggested that the impact of EU migrants in this regard is negligible. But it appears that government and various pieces of research were more effective at countering the argument than actually correcting the perceptions, and it is the latter that ultimately matters in politics.

English voters were asked the 'Moreno question', that is, where they placed themselves on a scale: (1) English not British, (2) more English than British, (3) equally English and British, (4) more British than English and (5) British not English. There was a strong correspondence between voting to leave and a higher ratio of 'English' in one's identity. So here there is a connection between national identity and the leave vote, allowing that Englishness and Britishness are both kinds of national identity, albeit with different connotations. But that in itself does not get us very far. People did not give protecting Englishness, or for that matter Britishness, as an important reason for their vote. Across the board, both leavers and remainers were motivated by quality of life, the fate of the economy and the state of UK institutions such as its welfare system, the National Health Service (NHS) and legal autonomy. Voters on either side tended to interpret the implications of Brexit for these issues differently, and whatever national identity is, it seems to have been mediated by these concerns. It is noticeable, however, that remainers placed more emphasis on the state of the 'economy as a whole', inward investment and the UK's international standing, while leavers were more focused on those UK institutions and rights and quality of life in the UK in particular, along with immigration and border controls. Their general view of the world and its problems appears more nationally bounded by the UK, while the remainers seem to see their fortunes in a wider European and global frame.

It is widely believed, with some good reason, that the process of devolution to Wales and especially Scotland, has, over the last 15 years, had a stimulating effect on an English identity previously more submerged in Britishness. But the constituent nations of the UK do not move together on the Brexit issue. In Scotland, while the correlation was not as strong, those placing themselves at the Scottish end of a Scottish-British identity scale were more likely to vote to remain rather than to leave. And Scotland as a whole voted almost two to one to remain, in contrast to England and Wales. In Scotland, the normalization of devolution and independence arguments has involved connecting these to the idea of Europe, casting neo-liberal British government as an obstacle to developing a European social democratic normalcy in Scotland. These arguments tend to obscure the degree to which the EU is itself a kind of neo-liberal capitalist project, in which the overall direction of travel is away from the social democratic model. Be that as it may, in the context of British political rhetoric, the defence and promotion of Scottish interests has become largely aligned with the European project (with some exceptions such as the fishing industry). It remains to be seen whether Brexit will lead to the departure of Scotland from the UK, giving this cause an extra push and adding to the large 45 per cent minority that voted 'Yes' to independence in the 2014 referendum. The exasperation in Scotland with the present situation is palpable in some quarters, but so far polls show no discernable movement toward a pro-independence position in the population as a whole. This is not surprising given the complexity and murkiness of the situation. It is very difficult for people, whether politicians or punters, to contemplate the Scottish independence option again until the exact form of Brexit is on the table (for example, as a member of the European Economic Area or the European Free Trade Association, as part of a customs union or under general World Trade Organization rules). Moreover, setting aside the legal and constitutional complexities, the embattled state of the euro still makes rejoining Europe less attractive, and England is still Scotland's largest trading partner, with which one ideally one wants to share easy trade relations, if not a common government.

It has to be appreciated that Brexit, like devolution, mobilizes national identities not simply in terms of ethnicity and culture but also in terms of the adequacy of democratic government, of people's rule over themselves. Just as a generation of Scots tended to converge on the view that the 'radical' Conservative policies of the 1980s, weakly supported by Scottish votes, were undemocratic, and that devolution was a necessary response, a wider yet more hidden generation throughout Britain of leave voters has been moved by doubts about the democratic legitimacy of the EU. We can argue about whether these people have the right understanding of the problems that confront them, and the options available to them, but to deny the democratic impulse behind this nationalism is an act of wilful misrecognition.

Globalization

'Globalization' has also been invoked as one of the causes of the referendum result (see Runciman et al. 2016). Ashcroft's data tells us that leavers were more likely to see globalization as 'a force for ill' (69 per cent), and remainers were more likely to see it as 'a force for good' (62 per cent). Like nationalism, globalization has many dimensions, and what people mean by it is variable and often vague. It overlaps considerably with what is usually meant by the term 'neo-liberalism', the political and ideological project of rejuvenating capitalism by states giving greater scope to markets in the context of the slow weakening of American and West European economic hegemony established after World War II. It seems that in the Brexit vote globalization was associated not just with the economic processes of global capitalism but also with the political processes of European integration. While theories of globalization often treat world capitalism as the main driver, with states primarily in a reactive mode, in real-world politics most people look for the concrete agents of their troubles, and states and other large institutions are more visibly available to take the blame for people's woes. For all its democratic remoteness, the EU is much more identifiable than global capitalism. Similarly, cultural differences of language, religion, even dress, however minor in the larger scheme of things, are immediately sensible, in a way that transnational corporations, gross domestic products (GDPs) and trade imbalances are not.

Another aspect of the voting pattern is very relevant here. The remain vote was much stronger in large cities, especially those housing major universities. This corresponds with our observations at the outset about the age, educational, occupational and ethnic and religious profiles of the two sides. The highly educated and highly paid are concentrated in large, more ethnically diverse cities, paradigmatically, London. The highly educated and professional in particular are the denizens of what John W. Meyer (2010) calls 'world society', a global network of converging institutions and norms, in which institutions of higher education are central in creating new sectors of societies with increasingly transnational horizons. While plenty of scepticism and criticism of globalization can be found among people at the more privileged end of the population, nonetheless it is these same people who have benefited most and have the least to fear from the political economic changes of recent decades. Strikingly, leavers and remainers tended to diverge on two 'attitudes' questions. Leavers were much more likely than remainers to think that children will be worse off than their parents, while remainers were much more likely to think that 'life in Britain today is better than it was 30 years ago'. Fifty-eight per cent of the leavers think it is worse.

More generally, views on a set of social values suggest the divergence between these two positions. Majorities of remainers saw 'multiculturalism, social liberalism, feminism, the green movement, and immigration' as 'forces for good' in society, while even larger majorities of leavers saw these as 'forces for ill'. Interestingly, both sides were evenly split on whether 'capitalism' is a force for good or ill. A critical attitude towards capitalism is not clearly aligned with either side of the Brexit issue.

The Balance of Social Power

So the logics of nationalism and globalization go some way towards explaining why Brexit happened. However, to analyse the situation further, I think we need to turn to fundamental questions about the balance of power in society. The leave vote was a response to both perceived and very real deficits of power by a portion of the citizenry, and it is right to look more closely at that.

The polling data indicates two clear axes of polarization, around class and age. These need be distinguished. Those ensconced in the 'knowledge economy' and earning better-than-average incomes are more in favour of the European project, while those lower down the employment scale, who are more likely to work with their hands and who live on tighter month-to-month budgets, are more sceptical. The complex of the EU and the global economy have opened up horizons of opportunity for the former, not experienced or recognized by the latter. There are correlations between youth, being in higher education and being on track to join the more prosperous side of society. But I suspect there are also aspects of experience and the life course at play here. The young, especially those at university, are more likely to see their futures, however hopefully, somewhere in that more prosperous fold. The older are more likely to see their fortunes as largely set, less open and pliable. So however they combine in individual persons, there are views of life's opportunities and hazards that are distinctly shaped by class positions on the one hand and stages of life on the other. These are connected to relative senses of empowerment or powerlessness that are fundamental to the Brexit vote. And, of course, in all of this we must remember that we are only dealing in prevailing tendencies in these two populations (as we must), which are defined in this instance by a single referendum vote. Many people did not vote 'according' to their class or age position, and many are ambiguously placed by these criteria, and voted one way or the other nonetheless.

These different readings of the situation, and the merits and liabilities of the EU, rest on a very real long-term shift in the economy and class composition of British society. Deindustrialization has decomposed the industrial working class of the mid-twentieth century, leaving a much more fragmented occupational field of smaller manufacturing enterprises, highly mechanized industries with low labour inputs and a vast array of service-sector employment. Much of this is less stable and more precarious than it was in the past. A portion of the professional and managerial occupations have weathered this transformation, or even expanded under it (for example, universities), but the result is the polarized economy we have been discussing. Growth has been spatially concentrated in London and other major cities, often leaving smaller cities and towns to stagnate economically. Wealth has become conspicuously maldistributed, heavily concentrated in a small elite at the top, with those in the middle and below finding their incomes stagnating or declining. This trend has been papered over at various points through the artificial support of private consumption and of home ownership through easy credit and low interest rates.

One of the basic functions of a modern party system is to roughly reflect and express major cleavages in terms of class and economic interests. It is these that give parties shape and animating force in the formative periods of party systems. In Britain the emergence of the Conservative-Labour dualism out of the Liberal hegemony of the nineteenth century reflects the bedding-in of the industrial capitalist class structure. But the changes of the last few decades, whether we label them deindustrialization, globalization, neoliberalism, the decline of the Keynesian consensus or whatever, have restructured the economic field and class positions in it, such that the two major parties no longer map on in a coherent way. In effect the Conservatives and Labour have vied for the key support of the more successful 'upper half' and tried to bring in tow their constituencies from lower down the economic ladder, without really addressing the stagnating nature of their economic position. And thus these people have become more and more detached and alienated from the party system, sometimes expressing this through support for UKIP. Part of what sets Scotland apart is that the SNP has provided the main alternative to the existing party system, one that is pro-European, and as a focus of aspirations to improve society, the idea of Scottish independence occupies the same space that the idea of Brexit does for many elsewhere in the UK.

This disconnection of the parties is not a matter of sheer corruption and indifference on the part of UK politicians. The capitalist economy is maturing in its old heartlands in ways that pose intractable problems. Demand for labour is weaker and narrower, expectations for consumption push upwards, capacities for saving are limited and displaced onto speculative investment and the GDP growth of the post-war era may be permanently over (Galbraith 2014). Addressing these changes requires radically rethinking the economy and nature of capitalism in ways that have not really even been countenanced, ways that lie outside of the mainstream political discourse of the advanced capitalist world. Still, the effect is that the core party system takes a large portion of the electorate and its interests for granted, without really confronting the difficulties they face, thereby leading to the perception of elitism in the political class and to the attraction of more populist forms of protest politics.

Not only are the dominant parties out of tune with a large part of the electorate but also the Brexit process and its wider political economic context expose internal divisions. Paradoxically, despite the party being clearly divided on the Brexit issue, the Conservatives have managed to hold together, with merely a changing of the guard. It is unclear whether the Conservative leaders promoting Brexit – Boris Johnson and Michael Gove – really wanted to achieve this end or were using it as a method to mobilize factional support. Whatever the dynamics of internal party factions, it is significant that this split broadly corresponds to a split within the private commercial sector, between big businesses oriented to the global/European arena and smaller to medium-size businesses oriented more to national markets. The latter were also more favourable to leave. The Labour Party has also had its internal divisions on display of late. Here the divide is between an insurgent, more idealist, more youthful, and more left-leaning constituency that has clapped onto the renegade figure of Jeremy Corbyn, and the professionalized parliamentary party, more steeped in the harsh realities and compromises of democratic politics, but by that same measure, more emblematic of a detached London-centric elite. Despite their differences, both factions officially hold 'remain' positions, and neither was able to connect with the estranged leavers.

Political parties in democracies always confront a dilemma. Do they aim to keep the 'big players' happy and hope that their benefits will redound on those further down the social scale, or do they 'clip the wings' of the greater economic powers now and then, and respond more directly to popular pressures from below? Skilful democratic politics involves a judicious balancing of responses to these countervailing pressures. It seems to me that for many years the dominant strategy has been to prioritize the 'big players', especially the City of London, and hope that those not making out as well down below will either be content or too confused and divided to take any action. But something as simple as a two-choice referendum provides a brilliant mechanism for papering over underlying differences and prompting concerted action. As long as people agree that one answer will solve or at least address their problems, they can unite, despite highly varied interests and views of the world. Moreover, the post-2008 economic downturn provided an opportunity to make a political demonstration of sensitivity to this growing alienation, but it was not taken. Instead the main strategy has been to distribute the losses socially through austerity policies, allowing the continued overvaluation of property to inflate private assets and make do with a barely growing economy. The professions of banking and high finance could have been made an example of, but instead they got off relatively lightly, and no serious reform agenda was advanced. This may have tipped events towards the present outcome.

The actual distribution of power in the economy has become more polarized. Wealth has become highly concentrated at one end of society, and a series of industrial cities and regions, and their more localized economic elites, have lost ground to London. The role of the political parties as expressions of and correctives to power imbalances has weak-ened as the democratic political process has been largely captured by the more urban and affluent. This is an historical process, involving the evolution and maturation of capitalism and the institutionalization and stagnation of a party system that has become detached from the real contours of the society as a whole. It is fair to call the processes involved 'nationalism' and 'globalization', but fundamentally Brexit is a manifestation of the disequilibrium of power and a cry of protest against it.

Vox Populi

The people do not 'speak' directly from their structural situations. What they say and how they understand their situations is always mediated by ideological constructions, available analyses and explanations that they draw on to make sense of things. Here again the general public has been very poorly provisioned, with contending unrealistic utopianisms that gloss over the reality of matters. This includes various versions, both more leftward and rightward, of enthusiasm for the benefits of global capitalism, which fail to address its inevitable costs to those not lucky enough to be caught in its specific upward slipstreams. But the most severe failure in ideological provisioning has been pre-cisely to throw a veil over these more concrete issues of power balances, with an overly naturalized and law-like account of the economy and a failure to acknowledge the inter-dependencies of political and economic power.

We must broach the issue of ideology in relation to the economy and the balance of power. A whole generation, especially on the political right, has been weaned on a dubi-ous economic theory in which 'free' markets, as long as they are minimally 'interfered with' by law and regulation, will naturally lead to peace, prosperity and abundance. The underlying image is of a plethora of similar, equal economic actors set free to negotiate their respective interests to the benefit of all. Unfortunately this has little to do with how the real world works. And most of the big economic players, who enjoy degrees of, if not a monopoly over, strategic dominance in their arenas of action, know this. They tend to be realists, and know that their interests will best be met by positioning themselves within networks of markets, contracts, regulations and so forth that will serve their interests. This partly accounts for the varying views between small and big business in regard to the EU mentioned above. In fact, there are no 'natural laws' of markets and capitalism. All the law-like tendencies are the effects of various agents (from the average worker/consumer on up to global corporations) interacting within a set of artificial rules – cur-rencies, contracts, markets, pricing mechanisms and so on, all effectively enforced by law. All markets of any complexity, certainly those created by capitalism, generate a spectrum from small, to medium, to big players. These enter the market, an artificial game, with varying powers and capacities to press their own interests. Economies are a particular arena for this kind of power play among actors of varying powers. It cannot be otherwise. If economic power becomes too unbalanced, overconcentrated and dys-functional for the system, the only way to address this is through explicit politics, through changing the artificial laws of the economy to rebalance the distribution of economic power. It is very difficult to fathom what Nigel Farage, Johnson and Gove think about how economies work, but from much of what they have said publicly, it seems that they suffer from a naive faith in the natural capacities of unfettered markets to remedy matters. In fact, a UK outside of Europe will still have to operate within an arena of big to small players, which the big players will tend to dominate, manipulating markets to their needs. New sets of regulations will be required, to protect the interests of smaller players (businesses, workers); otherwise, they will find themselves enjoying simply a slight redistribution of the terms of their own economic domination, with no significant benefits from 'independence' from Europe.

The rise of the free market ideology is connected with the general political economic shift called 'neo-liberalism' and 'globalization'. This has often been presented as an eclipsing of the powers of states by the powers of major economic actors. But there are limits to this, precisely because these economic powers depend on states to generate the rule-governed system of markets that secure their interests and positions of advantage. The relationship between major political actors (states and other governing bodies) and major economic actors (corporations, banks and so forth) is one of complex symbiosis (Weber 2003). Since the post–World War II economic dominance of the United States and its sphere of influence began to slip, these states have given a lot of free rein to economic powers in order to re-establish capitalist strength. And the result has been stratospheric wealth accumulation for a small global elite, and relatively static middle and declining and insecure lower classes. It is not so much that states have been weakened as that they have strategically decided to privilege the interests of major economic players, giving them as much latitude for strategic economic action as possible, believing that this was essential for national interests. And the EU is one of the frameworks within which this power concession has been implemented. This is the larger context within which the leavers' alienation has been sown. As ever in politics, the problem that confronts us is not a pure issue of sovereignty and self-determination. It is one of the balance of power between contending social forces, which include states, economic firms and classes when they become politically mobilized. The leavers' strategy for rebalancing by taking the UK out of the EU is over-optimistic and ill-informed about underlying causes, but it is an impulse with a real basis, which needs to be recognized and taken seriously.

Not only does the party system no longer map well onto the political realities but neither do the predominantly available ideologies, or if one prefers, common-sense theories. For all its mythification of the class struggle, an older language of labour politics and conflict between capital and labour at least identified a real, basic power divide in society and related that to democratic politics. Feminism, the green movement and other lines of argument provide important critiques of society's power relations, but the fundamental role of the economy in the distribution of power (see Skidelsky and Craig 2016) has been obscured by the over-naturalization of the capitalist economy in public discourse and rather vague critiques, left and right, of globalization. The general public has been ideologically deprived of the means to analyse its situation and respond intelligently. Insecurities have been generated for a large portion of the population by a capitalism that is globalizing but also maturing beyond its heyday of growth in the core of it geographic development. These insecurities have been mischannelled into critiques of Europe and immigration that miss what should be their real target. Their real target should be the actual disposition of power in society. Without a robust public language for holding the powerful within British society to account – both its elites and the more fortunate half generally – is it any wonder that the EU is rendered as the main source of domination and object of critique?

Conclusion

Despite the effort to understand the leavers, this is not an argument for Brexit. There are good reasons to be sceptical and worried about the European project. The idea of a common currency zone without unified fiscal management has been shown to be disastrously misconceived. Key governing bodies are too remote and insufficiently democratically accountable. The guiding philosophy lacks a necessary critical perspective on capitalism and an understanding of the limits of its sustainability and that the economy may have to evolve into something rather different. But even with these profound problems, there are good reasons to stay. First, as has often been said, for better or worse, a state needs to be fully engaged in the relevant power arena to shape its own fate. Being next door to Europe makes it difficult to really be 'outside' of Europe. Our fates are bound together whether we like it or not. Second, although it might seem a distant concern to most people, the EU's role in the global balance of power matters. It matters that there are sizeable alternative paths for the evolution of capitalist and geopolitical power to those offered by the United States and China and their orbits of influence. Despite its serious problems, the EU, and Europe as a part of the world, have a contribution to make to the sober maturation of capitalism, one that can be better achieved if Britain adds its weight here.

I have focused on the British dynamic here, but comparison suggests that Brexit is a variation on a widespread theme of class restructuring and alienation, due to developments of global capitalism, resulting in movements of anti-immigration sentiments and calls to reclaim 'control' over national states. Marine Le Pen in France, Patriotic Europeans Against the Islamisation of the West (PEGIDA) in Germany and Donald Trump's Republican presidential candidacy in the United States all partake of the same trend. However, in other contexts current populist politics has a different cast. The movement in Brazil against endemic corruption in the economy and politics, targeted at President Dilma Rousseff and the governing Workers Party, while no doubt manipulated by the political right, seems to respond to popular frustration with a deep recession following a long boom period. The small population of Iceland deposed its government and prosecuted bankers in the wake of the 2008 economic meltdown (Boyes 2009) and is now again mobilized by a scandal triggered by recent revelations in the Panama Papers, where the corruption and nepotism of a small elite is under scrutiny. The case also bears historical comparison. Peaking in the 1890s, the agrarian populist movement in the United States that coalesced around the People's Party channelled resentments towards Eastern elites, big business (banks, railroads) and a corrupt party duopoly (Democrats and Republicans), also allying itself with an early labour movement. In a way similar to the current European crisis, and Brexit, this insurgent third-party movement expressed the sense of loss of power among rural farming communities, as a smaller-scale agrarian capitalism was being subordinated by the expanding power of industrial and financial capital (Maloy, 2013: 145–188). In this case as well, a period of economic boom, the Gilded Age of the 1870–1880s, was followed by a bust and depression in the 1890s, helping trigger events. And nativist and anti-Semitic strains in the movement reveal other striking parallels. So it may be we should think of Brexit as one current manifestation of recurrent major shifts in the structures of capitalism that in certain phases weaken the position of whole communities and their livelihoods, triggering resistance.

Are there any lessons to be learned from Brexit? None that is easy to apply. I have two tentative observations. Given that I have argued that the party system in the UK as a whole has disengaged from its social terrain, reforming the party system would seem to be important. Ultimately the logic of power means that major political conflicts will tend to generate alliances into two major blocs, a tendency that is built into the single constituency, first-past-the-post elections that produce two-party systems. But this duopoly also tends to mask more complex variation in power and interest in society, even if these may be revealed to a degree by insurgent third parties. Some system of proportional representation might allow the expression of divergent and conflicting interests and views to be more routinely evident in the political process, forcing a wider range of ongoing public debate and justification. This inevitably enables a higher profile for some ideologically objectionable groups, and governments formed under proportional representation (PR) alliances can be notoriously unstable. But the risks of obscuring social divisions under a party duopoly may be greater than the instabilities of a more diverse and divided party system. Secondly, it is notable that the leavers easily speak the language of elitism and its critique. However much this has been fed by figures like Farage, it has real roots in popular perceptions about a powerful social stratum, in Europe but also in the UK and London, that is disconnected from the wider population. However crude, it is part of a folk analysis of the state of society and politics. Meanwhile in the last 30 years or so, the concept of elites has tended to drop out of the social science vocabulary (Savage and Williams 2008), although the success of Thomas Piketty's *Capital in the Twenty-First Century* (2014) has helped bring it back in to some degree. But it has also tended to drop away from the mainstream political discourse of the major parties, leaving it to the various 'outsiders': UKIP, Occupy, the pro-Brexit campaign. For the leading party of the left to abandon the critique of elitism is curious, and perhaps says something about how its leadership and a crucial portion of its constituency is now based in the more fortunate, educated, professional, knowledge-economy-based part of the population. The shoe does not fit as well as it once did. The concentration of power in the hands of a few is in the nature of complex organization and society, and a healthy democracy requires a robust language critical of elitism, at the disposal of both the Left and the Right. In sum, a more realistic relationship between the contours of the party system, the public language of power analysis and critique and the actual divisions and conflicts within society is sorely needed. Even if they did not change the outcome, these might at least have made the political conflict and debate leading to Brexit more incisive and illuminating for the public as a whole.

References

Ashcroft, Lord (2016). 'How the United Kingdom Voted on Thursday ... and Why'. Lord Ashcroft Polls. http://lordashcroftpolls.com/2016/06/how-the-united-kingdom-voted-and-why/. Accessed 15 August 2016.

Boyes, R. (2009). *Meltdown Iceland: How the Global Financial Crisis Bankrupted an Entire Country.* London: Bloomsbury.

Galbraith, J. K. (2014). *The End of Normal.* New York: Simon and Schuster.

Hearn, J. (2006). *Rethinking Nationalism.* Basingstoke: Palgrave Macmillan.

Hume, D. (1985). 'Of the First Principles of Government'. In *Essays Moral, Political and Literary*, edited by E. F. Miller. Indianapolis: Liberty Fund, 32–36.

Maloy, J. S. (2013). *Democratic Statecraft: Political Realism and Popular Power.* Cambridge: Cambridge University Press.

Meyer, J. W. (2010). 'World Society, Institutional Theories, and the Actor', *Annual Review of Sociology* 36: 1–20.

Piketty, T. (2014). *Capital in the Twenty-First Century.* Cambridge, MA, and London: The Belknap Press of Harvard University Press.

Runciman, D. et al. (2016). 'Where Are We Now?', *London Review of Books*, 14 July, 8–14.

Savage, M. and K. Williams, eds. (2008). *Remembering Elites.* London: Wiley-Blackwell.

Skidelsky, R, and N. Craig, eds. (2016). *Who Runs the Economy? The Role of Power in Economics.* Basingstoke: Palgrave Macmillan.

Weber, M. (2003). *General Economic History.* Mineola, NY: Dover.

Yack, B. (1999). 'The Myth of the Civic Nation'. In *Theorizing Nationalism*, edited by R. Beiner. Albany, NY: SUNY Press.

Chapter Three

EXIT FROM THE PERSPECTIVE OF ENTRY

John Holmwood

The United Kingdom's relation to European cooperation has been uneasy since well before its entry into the European Economic Community (EEC) in 1973, and that unease has often been mutually felt. French president Charles De Gaulle famously vetoed the UK's application for membership in 1963, fearing that Britain's 'special relationship' with the United States would diminish the capacity for the member states to act independently as a group, and entry was again turned down in 1967. Since joining, the United Kingdom has promoted the idea of European union as primarily an economic project of trade while resisting wider political or social integration. Thus, the UK secured an opt-out from the social chapter of the Maastricht Treaty, which came into effect in 1993 and led to the redesignation of the EEC as the European Union (EU). This opt-out was extended to monetary union (with its implication of political integration), which was initiated at the same time, leading toward the creation of the eurozone and the European Central Bank on 1 January 1999.

If the UK's relation to other European countries since entry has been uncomfortable (George 1990), Europe has also been a source of internal division within the two main political parties. The Conservative prime minister Edward Heath had negotiated entry, but almost immediately faced opposition from within his own party. This was orchestrated, in part, by Enoch Powell, who exhorted a vote for Labour in the October 1974 election, an election Labour won by the narrowest of margins. Faced with divisions over Europe in his own party, the new prime minister, Harold Wilson, called a referendum in 1975, having made this an election pledge the previous October. This was won by a vote of 68 per cent in favour of continued membership following a campaign similar to that of 2016. Both main parties officially supported the remain option, albeit with significant figures within them arguing for exit. In 1975 there was also opposition from the trades union movement and key figures on the left of the Labour Party, such as Michael Foot and Tony Benn (connections with this group is one of the reasons why the current Labour leader, Jeremy Corbyn, was suspected of being lukewarm in his support for remaining). Opposition was also growing within the Conservative Party – and, of course, was to develop with the formation of the United Kingdom Independence Party (UKIP) in 1993, initially on the right-wing flank of the Conservative Party but more recently targeting Labour voters by focusing on immigration.

In what follows, I want to draw out the long-standing issues that formed the debate over Europe in the 1970s to show how they have continued to shape the debate over Brexit in 2016. My concern is not to validate these issues, but to suggest that the period of the UK's membership of the European Union (EU) has largely been one of wasted opportunities and sterile alternatives offered to the electorate. Indeed, the fact that the 2016 referendum produced an outcome the opposite of that of 1975, while providing no plausible alternative to membership, is, in itself, an indication of the unresolved problems of this period.

I shall suggest that these problems are largely associated with Britain's place in the world after the demise of empire. This includes the renegotiation of citizenship, as set out by Gurminder K. Bhambra in the present volume, but also a fundamental renegotiation of UK political economy from a system of imperial and commonwealth preferences to a system of free trade within Europe (by the 1960s, it was the UK's largest trading partner, and has been growing in importance since then). Both aspects are brought together not only in the recent referendum debate through ideas of controlling borders and immigration but also in the claim that trade with the commonwealth and other global partners can be more important than trade with the EU and be the basis of an alternative to the European single market (for discussion, see Peers 2015).

For some commentators on the left, the vote to leave the EU has been explained, at least in part, as a response to policies of neo-liberal globalization in which the ('white') working class has been left behind (for discussion, see Goodwin and Heath 2016). The flaw in this argument is that it fails to explain the emergence and dominance of neo-liberalism itself within British public policy. This largely occurs in tandem with the debate over the EU and, I shall argue, is itself to be explained by the politics of the United Kingdom after Empire. Indeed, an indication of the racialized politics of neo-liberalism is contained in the very idea of a working class that can be distinguished along racial lines as both 'left behind' and 'white' (this is a trope that is also evident in the United States in the Donald Trump election campaign, but which emerged earlier in the aftermath of the civil rights movement of the 1960s).

In the UK, these threads come together in the figure of Powell. The speech in 1974 in which he encouraged a vote for the Labour Party has strong echoes in the present: 'can [the electorate] now be prevented from taking back into their own hands the decision about their identity and their form of government which truly was theirs all along? I do not believe they can be prevented: for they are now, at a general election, provided with a clear, definite and practicable alternative, namely, a fundamental renegotiation directed to regain free access to world food markets and recover or retain the powers of Parliament' (Collings 1991: 458). Powell's reference to identity is significant. After all, the same Powell had delivered his infamous 'rivers of blood' speech in 1968 in which he warned of the threat to national identity that derived from the immigration of non-white British subjects to the UK. While immigration from the EEC was not an issue – although other EEC members were concerned about the movement of commonwealth citizens (Hansen 2000) – control of borders was, otherwise, a central concern for many. Nigel Farage's speeches for the UKIP campaign to leave the EU mirrored those of Powell, albeit with a new emphasis on EU migrants.

Convergence or Divergence?

Let me begin by first setting out expectations of sociologists and political commentators about the trajectory of UK public policy and political economy in the 1960s and 1970s. In retrospect, we can see the period as the coming to an end of the expansion and growth of the welfare state after what Thomas Piketty (2014) calls the post-war '*trente glorieuses*'. Widening income inequality returned across Europe in the 1980s led by the UK, such that having been more equal than the original six members of the EEC, by the 1990s, the UK was the most unequal (see the World Top Incomes Data Base).

Yet most commentators projected a continuing secular decline in inequality and institutionalized social rights of citizenship. If there was a concern expressed on the left, it was that membership of the Common Market might put a brake on such developments and undermine possibilities in the UK to achieve more significant reforms (see Anderson and Hall 1961; Barratt Brown 1961; Balogh 1962). But this was attributed to an 'external' constraint that the EEC might place upon the UK. The European project was widely regarded as a 'capitalist club' dominated by Christian Democratic parties (or their equivalent). As Perry Anderson and Stuart Hall put it, 'The Treaty of Rome, it is true, prescribes no common social character for the Community. But since integration must take off from the basis of the economic structures which at present characterize the Six, the common market will inevitably develop – even exaggerate – present trends' (1961: 7). Michael Barratt Brown, for his part, was concerned that free trade within the EEC constituted a form of protectionism for large cartels, describing the EEC as an entity where 'the motor-industry can over-expand while social services decay' (1961: 26).

By the time of the Maastricht Treaty, which, among other concerns, sought the protection of social services, the perspective had changed: the UK was understood to be driving neo-liberal policies of deregulation. While commentators in the UK now looked to the 'social chapter' as a means of redirecting social policy (for example, Hutton 1995), those from elsewhere in Europe saw the Treaty otherwise. Thus Wolfgang Streeck argued that the treaty tied integration to deregulation and that 'the Maastricht settlement was a decisive British victory over the federalist welfare state-building project' (1995: 404).

If the earlier position represented a form of 'functionalism' in its assumption of convergence of the UK on a dominant European model that (at that moment) seemed to have greater institutionalized inequalities than did the UK, the later argument continues with a different 'functionalist' theme. Now it is suggested that 'federal systems' have a systemic weakness against the assertion of the rights of states (see Streeck 1995). We can sidestep the paradox that the exercise of sovereignty is precisely what allows the UK to put a brake on wider developments, while the loss of sovereignty became the mantra of UK politics. What is significant is that the EEC is being compared with the United States as an exemplary case of weak federalism. Yet what is absent is the very context of 'race', which is the underlying issue in 'states' rights' in the United States.

Moreover, what explains the turn to neo-liberalism in both the UK and the United States?

Neo-liberalism and 'Race'

My argument here in relation to the United States is necessarily abbreviated, but is set out elsewhere (Holmwood 2016). The success of the civil rights movement in the 1960s gave rise to expectations that the US federal welfare regime would be desegregated and that social rights of citizenship would be extended to African Americans (Parsons 1965). Instead, rather than extend social rights in this way, neo-liberal public policy sought to remove social rights from everyone. This is associated with the Republican Party's 'Southern strategy' to detach white Southern votes from the Democratic Party (Fountain 2016). Ronald Reagan's Neshoba County Fair speech in 1980 (at the scene of a lynching of Mississippi freedom summer activists in 1964) articulated this strategy in the context of neo-liberalism: 'I believe in states' rights. I believe in people doing as much as they can for themselves at the community level and at the private level. And I believe that we've distorted the balance of our government today by giving powers that were never intended in the Constitution to be given to that federal establishment.' These words presage an attack on social rights of citizenship and the pathologizing of welfare dependency within neo-liberalism.

Paradoxically, the retrenchment of social rights more generally following desegregation in the United States has had the appearance of making 'class' more relevant in the explanation of the experience of African Americans than 'race' (Wilson 1978, 2015). This is because a significant proportion of white Americans have come to share a similar experience of disadvantage. However, what needs to be understood is that it is 'race' that explains the re-emergence of 'class', and not class that is the underlying explanation of 'race'. It is also the context in which the 'white' working class emerges as racially positioned by neo-liberalism as sharing material experiences with non-white citizens, but claiming 'whiteness' as a marker of difference and identity.

If the civil rights movement in the United States stands as a particular *postcolonial* moment (postcolonial because addressing the racialized consequences of 'settler capitalism' in the United States and its heritage of enslavement), I suggest that the end of Empire constitutes a similar moment for the United Kingdom in the 1960s. The British Empire had been based on a movement of populations to perform labour of different levels of skill and servitude (from bonded labour to colonial administration), a movement of 'subjects' who were hierarchically ordered on racial grounds. This ordering also extended to the perception of the different territories incorporated into Empire and their different trajectories of decolonization.

A process of decolonization was underway, dating back to independence for India and Pakistan after World War II and, earlier, the granting of special self-governing Dominion status for settler colonies such as Australia, New Zealand and Canada (South Africa was a more complex case). The 1960s saw independence movements in Africa, for example, Uganda and Kenya and Rhodesia/ Zimbabwe. The expulsion of South Africa from the commonwealth in 1961 and the declaration of independence by a white minority government in Rhodesia in 1965 had deep consequences within the UK body politic. Conservative politicians showed considerable sympathy for 'patrial' white settlers in South Africa and Rhodesia/ Zimbabwe, while the exodus of South Asian British subjects from Uganda and Kenya produced a crisis for immigration and citizenship policy in the UK. Notwithstanding that the immigration of white subjects from the commonwealth and from the rest of Europe far exceeded that of non-white citizens, it was precisely the idea of an immigrant-descended non-white population that Powell regarded as a threat to national identity. While the EEC constituted a threat to sovereignty, that sovereignty was understood to be necessary to protect white British national identity after Empire.

Of course issues of race and racism in the context of Empire were addressed at this time, not least by members of the Birmingham Centre for Contemporary Cultural Studies, such as Hall and his colleagues. Hall had also criticized membership of the EEC, but he did not connect the two. In fact, few sociologists addressed issues of welfare policy in the context of race and the politics of Empire and its aftermath. For example, by the time of Gøsta Esping-Andersen's (1991) landmark book on the three worlds of welfare capitalism, the UK was understood to be an example of a 'liberal welfare regime', distinct from the 'corporatist-statist regime' that was exemplified by the founding EEC members, while new members from Scandinavia represented a distinct 'social democratic' type. The latter two types were both regarded by Esping-Andersen as 'decommodifying' and, therefore, did not pose a problem for convergence, but the UK was now represented as distinct and potentially 'unintegrable', a status that seems to derives from Anglophone 'cultural' predispositions.[1] I suggest that a different understanding of the legacies of Empire will show that the UK is less of a special case, but part of a wider European problem.

Esping-Andersen does not address issues of Empire and race in the formation of welfare regimes, yet all the original members of the EEC were former colonial powers. One of the few sociologists to address issues of imperialism and decolonization as systemic aspects of Western nation states is David Strang (1992). He suggests that there is an 'inner incompatibility' between popular sovereignty and Empire. In other words, for him, the extension of democracy within the 'metropole' makes it hard to sustain domination in the relation between 'metropole' and 'dependency'. He traces this back to sympathy in the metropole for independence for the 13 colonies of the United States, suggesting that it is a continuing process. In part, it is presented as a growing understanding within the metropole that sovereignty should be extended to dependencies themselves, but it is also understood to derive from the 'export' of ideas of popular sovereignty which fuel movements for independence. What Strang misses is the complex process of identification and disavowal associated with the identities of those in the 'dependencies' and, in particular, patrial identification through patterns of 'white' settlement.

Strang applies the argument to the EEC, suggesting that 'decolonization brought the political economy of France and Britain closer to that of the Scandinavian, Alpine or Benelux countries' (1994: 293). In particular, he suggests that this convergence derives from increased domestic spending made possible by a reduction in the costs of sustaining Empire. Thus, he writes that, 'with massive de-colonization, Britain and France were reduced to second-rate powers and forced to turn inward. This inward turn may have facilitated the further expansion of metropolitan political, social, and especially welfare rights' (1994: 292). Yet the 'moment' of the 'expansion' of 'social rights', was also the moment of immigration, and this brought about a division in 'citizenship' between those who were attributed a patrial lineage in the metropole and those who were deemed to be 'immigrants'. There are echoes of this in David Goodhart's (2013) proposal that high rates of immigration undermine social democratic solidarities. However, this is to regard immigration as an exogenous factor and not connected back to the colonial formation of welfare states. The point is not that immigration has now begun to undermine solidarities, but that previous solidarities were formed on a racialized politics of colonial encounters. The turn to neo-liberalism in the UK represents a failure to extend social rights to non-white citizens in exactly the same way as occurred in the United States after the civil rights movement, and it is this that produces the narrative of a 'left behind' *white* working class.

Post-Imperial Political Economy

The neo-liberal turn in the UK in the 1970s was also occasioned by the particular economic problems that the UK was facing and which indicated a major problem of adjustment in its post-imperial political economy.[2] In the period before negotiating entry, what had appeared to British politicians as a problem of competition from EEC economies with lower wages and living standards, was by the 1960s reversed, with the UK performing much less well than the EEC members (perhaps especially Germany) and the gap in income per head narrowing (Lamfalussy 1963; Grant 1983). The UK was part of a system of commonwealth preferences marked by a monetary union based on sterling – the Sterling Area.

While this trading bloc seemed to have declining significance when compared with the rapidly expanding European market, British policy initially was to try to extend free trade arrangements through the Organization for European Economic Cooperation and the European Free Trade Association (EFTA). However, Alexandre Lamfalussy argued that the arrangements of the commonwealth were not conducive to export-led growth through capital-intensive manufacture. British exports were directed towards the slow-growing markets of the commonwealth (see also Jones, 1980), while the reciprocal cheap food policy and 'unprotected' British agriculture meant that, although the latter industry was uniquely efficient when compared with 'protected' European agriculture, the high volume of food imports put a strain on the British balance of payments.

The role of sterling as an international currency, however, committed the British government to protecting the currency with deflationary measures that undermined policies directed toward long-term investment (Strange 1971). In this context – and that of retrospective analyses of problems of economic integration of Greece within the eurozone – it is significant that the Commission of the European Communities offered a similar analysis in their 'opinion' on the (unsuccessful) British application for membership in 1967.[3]

These problems became yet more acute. As Lamfalussy argued would be the case, low productivity made it difficult to maintain the incomes policy necessary to shift resources toward investment, while trades union resistance to incomes policy encouraged the hostility from the left that undermined the two Labour governments between 1964 and 1970. In the short run, entry into the EEC could only exacerbate the situation, as imports were drawn in from competitive European manufacturers and higher European food prices put pressure on living standards and added further inflationary pressure on wages. On entering the EEC, the UK confronted a very different kind of economic order than that of the commonwealth bloc to which it had been tied. The EEC was a political economy characterized by high wages with highly productive and competitive industries, together with supported agriculture. In this context, what had been an earlier fear of competition from 'low wage' Europe became a possible advantage, that the UK could gain a competitive advantage from low wages. Neo-liberal economic policy (together with its various 'opt-outs', initially from labour rules, then from the 'social chapter') was born, notwithstanding that this had not been the basis of success within the EEC, while support for long-term investment in expanding industries had been.

Of course, a policy designed around the competitive advantage of low wages is quite consistent with the existence of sectors of the economy that do operate in terms of higher investment and productivity and a different 'wage bargain'. However, this helps create a polarization of earnings and the establishment of a 'domestic sector' of cheap leisure and household services consumed by more highly paid employees. In addition, it becomes necessary to organize social welfare policies accordingly. Benefits should be lower than wages for available jobs, and as wages in unskilled jobs fall, so, too, must benefits. In addition, unemployment became an instrument of social policy – a surrogate for an incomes policy – to control inflation and weaken trades unions as part of a deregulated labour market. Finally, with widening income inequality and increasing poverty, especially in households with children, circumstances favour a changing moral economy. Emphasis is placed on private responsibility and the disadvantaged are represented as responsible for their own fate; those who are *dependent* (as the new moral economy has it) become stigmatized in that dependency.

Back to the Future?

A paradox of the 1960s and the 1970s was the convergence of left-wing and right-wing criticisms of the EEC. If their aspirations were different, the failure of the Left to establish an alternative economic policy to that of neo-liberalism has ensured that anti-EEC feeling is appropriated through right-wing economic and social policies. Among critics at the time, only Tom Nairn (1972) warned of the potential consequence. He argued that left-wing criticisms of the EEC had some merit taken individually but that they all too easily transmuted into a petty nationalism and nostalgia for national greatness. This was especially so when the socialist rhetoric was removed to reveal what was being proposed as an alternative. The idea of an outward-looking Britain, champion of the developing world, was to be realized through the standard instruments of British policy, namely, the commonwealth and an expanded EFTA. The Left, Nairn believed, had become the defender of nation and sovereignty, and lacked a strategy *within* Europe.

Nairn (1977) also connected the argument to the post-imperial 'break up of Britain' and the rise of the Scottish National Party (SNP), which has, indeed, pursued a strategy within Europe. I do not have the space here to detail how the political divergence of the different nations of the UK is related to these issues (see Holmwood 2000). It is perhaps sufficient to indicate that the highly centralized nature of the British state derives from

Empire, while the process of devolution after 2000 has contributed to a constitutional crisis of representation. The collapse of the Labour Party in Scotland and its replacement by the SNP is part of a situation in which the Conservative Party now secures parliamentary majorities in national elections despite a declining proportion of the vote. In the absence of proportional representation, it is hard to see how an alternative can cohere. For all the recent talk of a progressive alliance, the Labour Party has, on all occasions, voted against proportional representation at Westminster, and it is difficult to see how it can be delivered against a Conservative Party that understands that the present electoral system is likely to provide it with its best opportunity for government.

The referendum provided the electorate with an opportunity to vote on a single issue, that of leaving or remaining within the EC. It is clear that for some of the population the question of leave was understood not to refer to leaving the EC as such, but was more about having non-white citizens and migrants from Europe leave the UK. For some on the left, this vote was also understood to be, in part, a response to the politics of austerity since the financial crisis of 2008. Those who argue that being working class has become a stigmatized identity (McKenzie 2016) are, perhaps, reflecting a reality of UK public debate. However, this is also overlaid by arguments about immigration that suggest that low wages are appropriate for migrant workers, but that 'British' workers need to be protected from the effects of competition. Yet it is precisely the policy of competition through low wages that draws in unskilled migrant workers, at the same time as it commits the UK to a low-productivity, low-investment economy.[4]

The real issue facing the UK remains that of how to achieve an inclusive political economy and transnational cooperation. It is tragic that the debate over Brexit remains framed in precisely the same terms as defined the debate at the moment of entry. These terms include the fantasy of a world of influence beyond Europe and a return to the commonwealth, which Paul Gilroy (2005) has aptly called a form of 'post-colonial melancholia'. It is a melancholia with real effects, one that reproduces hierarchies of worth that derive from Empire and colonialism and continue to serve the reproduction of inequality. There is a message from Brexit to the rest of Europe and it is that the failure to defend social rights for all gives rise to a situation where they are gradually removed from everybody.

Notes

1 The 'liberal welfare regime' is made up of the United States, Australia, New Zealand, Canada and the UK. It is striking that each country is a 'settler capitalist' country. This serves to constitute the agrarian interests that are so significant in their subsequent development as well as providing an explanation of a lower range in the distribution of wealth and inequality for much of the nineteenth century, as documented by Prasad (2012) and by Piketty (2014) alike. Of course, Britain is not a 'settler capitalist' country, but it is a country that settled and provided settlers, thereby creating interconnections with settler capitalist economies and shaping its own political economy through colonial encounters.

2 This section is derived from Holmwood (2000).

3 Britain's economic problems are described as, 'mainly structural in origin, and stem either from defects in the distribution of productive resources (inadequate and misdirected investment, numerous obstacles to the improvement of productivity, the pattern of employment, the tax

system) or from the economic, monetary and financial burdens inherited from the past, the second world war, and the country's international position in the postwar world' (Commission of the European Communities, 1967, p. 38).

4 The standard argument in economics is frequently invoked to suggest that an increased supply of labour must have the consequence of lowering its price. However, a study in the United States suggests a different effect, which is that states with higher minimum wages have lower inward migration of unskilled workers (Orrenius and Zavodny, 2008).

Bibliography

Anderson, Perry, and Stuart Hall (1961) 'The Politics of the Common Market', *New Left Review*, No. 7, July–Aug., 1–14.

Balogh, Thomas (1962) 'Post-War Britain and the Common Market', *New Left Review*, No. 16, July–Aug.

Barratt Brown, Michael (1961) 'Neutralism and the Common Market', *New Left Review*, No. 12, Nov.–Dec., 26–27.

Collings, Rex, ed. (1991) *Reflections of a Statesman: The Writings and Speeches of Enoch Powell*, London: Bellew, p. 458.

Commission of the European Communities (1967) *Opinion on the Application for Membership Received from the United Kingdom, Ireland, Denmark and Norway* (Brussels, 29 September).

Esping-Andersen, Gøsta (1990) *The Three Worlds of Welfare Capitalism*. Cambridge: Polity Press.

Fountain, Ben (2016) 'American Crossroads: Reagan, Trump and the Devil Down South'. *Guardian Newspaper*, 5 March. https://www.theguardian.com/us-news/2016/mar/05/trump-reagan-nixon-republican-party-racism.

George, Stephen (1990) *An Awkward Partner: Britain in the European Community*, Oxford: Clarendon Press.

Gilroy, Paul (2005) *Postcolonial Melancholia*. New York: Columbia University Press.

Goodhart, David (2013) *The British Dream: Successes and Failures of Post-War Immigration*. London: Atlantic Books.

Goodwin, Mathew, and Oliver Heath (2016) 'A Tale of Two Countries: Brexit and the "Left Behind" Thesis'. London School of Economics and Political Science (blog), 25 July. http://blogs.lse.ac.uk/politicsandpolicy/brexit-and-the-left-behind-thesis/.

Grant, Robert (1983) 'The Impact of EEC Membership upon UK Industrial Performance'. In *Britain and the EEC*, edited by R. Jenkins. London: Macmillan. 3(1): 87–110.

Hansen, Randall (2000) *Citizenship and Immigration in Post-War Britain: The Institutional Origins of a Multicultural Nation*. Oxford: OUP.

Holmwood, John (2000) 'Europe and the "Americanization" of British Social Policy', *European Societies* 2 (4): 453–82.

———— (2016) 'Moral Economy versus Political Economy: Provincializing Polanyi'. In *The Commonalities of Global Crises: Markets, Communities and Nostalgia*, edited by C. Karner and B. Weicht. London: Palgrave Macmillan.

Hutton, Will (1995) *The State We're In*. London: Jonathan Cape.

Jones, D. T. (1980) 'British Industrial Regeneration: The European Dimension'. In *Britain in Europe*, edited by W. Wallace. London: Heinemann.

Lamfalussy, Alexandre (1963) *The United Kingdom and the Six: An Essay on Economic Growth in Western Europe*. Homewood, IL: Richard D. Irwin.

McKenzie, Lisa (2016) 'Brexit: A Two-Fingered Salute from the Working Class', *Red Pepper*, August. http://www.redpepper.org.uk/brexit-a-two-fingered-salute-from-the-working-class/.

Nairn, Tom (1971) 'British Nationalism and the EEC', *New Left Review*, No. 69, Sept.–Oct., 3–28.

———— (1977) *The Break-Up of Britain: Crisis and Neo-Nationalism*. London: Verso.

Orrenius, Pia M. and Madeline Zavodny (2008) 'The Effect of Minimum Wages on Immigrants' Employment and Earnings', *Industrial and Labor Relations Review*, 61(4): 544–63.

Parsons, Talcott. 1965. 'Full Citizenship for the Negro American? A Sociological Problem', *Daedalus*, 94 (4): 1009–54.

Peers, Steve (2015) 'The Commonwealth and the EU: Let's Do (Trade with) Both'. London School of Economics and Political Science (blog), 10 December. http://blogs.lse.ac.uk/brexit/2015/12/10/the-commonwealth-and-the-eu-lets-do-trade-with-both/.

Piketty, Thomas. 2014. *Capital in the Twenty-First Century*. Cambridge, MA: Belknap Press.

Prasad, Monica. 2012. *The Land of Too Much: American Abundance and the Paradox of Poverty*. Boston: Harvard University Press.

Strang, David (1992) 'The Inner Incompatibility of Empire and Nation: Popular Sovereignty and Decolonization', *Sociological Perspectives* 35 (2): 367–84.

——— (1994) 'British and French Political Institutions and the Patterning of Decolonization'. In *The Comparative Political Economy of the Welfare State*, edited by T. Janowski and A. M. Hicks. Cambridge: Cambridge University Press.

Strange, Susan (1971) *Sterling and British Policy*. London: Oxford University Press.

Streeck, Wolfgang (1995) 'From Market Economy to State Building? Reflections on the Political Economy of European Social Policy'. In *European Social Policy: Between Fragmentation and Integration*, edited by S. Leibfried and P. Pierson. Washington, DC: Brookings Institution.

Wilson, William Julius (2015) 'New Perspectives on the Declining Significance of Race: a Rejoinder', *Ethnic & Racial Studies* 38 (8): 1278–84.

——— (1982) *The Declining Significance of Race: Blacks and Changing American Institutions*. Chicago: University of Chicago Press.

Chapter Four

BREXIT, SOVEREIGNTY AND THE END OF AN EVER CLOSER UNION

Stefan Auer

'Let's not beat around the bush', the German chancellor, Angela Merkel, said in response to the British decision to leave the European Union (EU), 'today marks a watershed for Europe' (Delcker 2016). For some six decades, and numerous setbacks notwithstanding, Europe's path has been unidirectional: towards an ever closer and ever wider union. No longer. A series of crises that have seriously tested Europe's unity – the eurozone crisis, the EU-Russia conflict over Ukraine, the refugee crisis – was followed in June 2016 by an event that will result in an EU that is smaller in its geographic scope and weaker both economically and politically.

Nevertheless, political earthquakes also create unique opportunities for conceptual clarity. Exceptional challenges show which structures and political constellations are viable and which are not.[1] Will there be an EU in five, or ten years from now that resembles what we have now? Will there be a UK in five, or ten years from now that resembles what we have today? I am less confident about the former than the latter, but both political entities face key challenges in the years to come, and in both cases they are centred around the contestation of sovereignty. In fact, Brexit both illuminates, and has been shaped by, competing understandings of sovereignty.

How Did We Get Here?

The UK has been rightly described as a reluctant member of the Union, with its antiquated political institutions and a strong attachment to parliamentary sovereignty, which sit uneasily with the continental project of a European federation in the making. Both the Conservative and the Labour Party have had an ambivalent relationship with Europe. It was thus primarily a party political gamble that the then British prime minister, David Cameron, took when he promised a referendum on the UK's EU membership.

Clearly, a referendum is a potent instrument of democratic control. It is also crude, because it can generate only simple results: 'yes', or 'no' are seldom satisfying answers in politics. What is more, resorting to the people as the highest arbiter of political conflicts is very much at odds with the distinctly British ideal of parliamentary sovereignty.[2] And yet, it is hard to challenge its legitimacy in a constitutional monarchy that like all Western democracies conceives of the people as the ultimate source of power. The slogan of the

Brexiters, 'taking back control', was thus primarily about democratic sovereignty (however odious that slogan might have seemed to many of its critics).

The referendum was to be preceded by a reform deal, which should have made the EU more palatable to the British electorate by reducing its federalist impetus. While Cameron failed to achieve significant reforms, he secured an important symbolic victory. In February 2016, the EU Council accepted the British demand to be excluded from the EU's founding ambition to forge 'an ever closer union'. This was too little too late both for the UK *and* the EU. Less controversially, it was too little for the UK: the concessions failed to prevent the British from voting out. But it was also too little, too late for Europe as a whole. The limits of European integration should have been acknowledged by the EU's leaders at the outbreak of Europe's sovereign debt crisis in 2010 at the latest. As I argue in this chapter, its outbreak marked the collapse of the unique European experiment with postnational democracy. It exposed the fallacy of the theoretical construct underpinning this project: the idea that the age of sovereign nation states is over, and that sovereignty can and ought to be shared.

I contend that the celebration of the EU as marking 'the emergence of the first truly postmodern international political form' (Ruggie 1993: 140) proved premature. Europe's attempt to 'reinvent itself beyond territoriality and outside of fixed frontiers' (Maier, in Zielonka 2002: 13) has backfired, exacerbating political fragmentation, instability and economic malaise. The 'unbundling of territoriality' (Ruggie 1993: 171) also reduced the EU's ability to respond to external challenges – whether it was Russia's imperialist ambitions towards its 'near abroad' (Auer 2015), or the influx of refugees from the Middle East. Europe's 'fuzzy borders' (Zielonka 2006: 7; 2014: 81) appear attractive in good times. In times of crisis, the calls for (some) control over borders appear irresistible. Whether we like it or not, the fear of uncontrolled migration from within and outside the EU played an important role in the UK referendum and remains a potent source of euroscepticism in continental Europe.

Sovereignty Obsolete?

Sovereignty is an elusive concept. Like its sibling, the state, it is impossible to define. In fact, for many scholars of European integration (particularly in Germany), both national sovereignty and the nation state have become obsolete. In an increasingly interdependent world, so the argument goes, any talk about sovereign power located at the nation-state level is misplaced. In an age of globalization, Saskia Sassen argued, 'sovereignty has been decentered and territory partly denationalized' (Sassen 1996: 29–30). The doyen of EU constitutionalism, Joseph Weiler, spoke for many when he remarked that 'to protect national sovereignty is passé' (Weiler 2001: 63).

Defending his postnational vision of European unity, Jürgen Habermas, for example, remains defiant. An experiment that hardly started cannot be declared to have failed, Habermas argued shortly after the Brexit, advocating a more social Europe that would address concerns of EU citizens, rather than just serving the interests of its technocratic elites (2016). In a similar vein, Ulrike Guérot seeks to build on the federalist ideals of the EU's founding fathers, such as the first European Commission president, Walter

Hallstein, who boldly stated that the ultimate aim of European integration was to overcome nation states. This, Guérot argues, cannot be achieved by nation states and their political representatives. What Europe needs instead is a new beginning, a European republic created by and for a truly European citizenry (Guérot 2016).

Drawing on the historical scholarship of Quentin Skinner, I challenge this view. The claim that sovereignty is outmoded is as fashionable as it is misguided. Ironically, the argument is not even all that novel. As Skinner (2010) convincingly demonstrated in his genealogy of the sovereign state, the prevalent conception of the state is seductively simple, but insufficient. A sovereign state is not to be equated simply with the government, or even the institutions of the state, neither can it be equated with the people. It is somehow related to both, but it is more than that too.

Consider Max Weber's classic definition, which postulates that 'a state is a human community that (successfully) claims the monopoly of the legitimate use of physical force within a given territory' (1946: 78). In common understanding, this reduces the state all too often to the coercive apparatus of the government. In fact, as Skinner noted, the 'terms state and government are in common parlance synonyms'.[3] With such a minimalist, empirical description of the state it is plausible to argue that EU member states have not lost their sovereignty, for no supranational agency in Brussels challenges their monopoly on the legitimate use of violence. In fact, such a conception of the state does not prevent us from conceptualizing the ideal of sovereignty shared, which underpins much of the legal, political and sociological theorizing about Europe.

From the perspective of international law, when a state volunteers to share sovereignty it does not abandon its independence, but proves its ability to act independently. As stated in the notable *Wimbledon* decision of 1923, 'the right of entering into international engagements is an attribute of State sovereignty' (cited in Koskenniemi 2010: 226). This reasoning reflects one of the foundational doctrines of the liberal international system, the idea of 'autolimitation' (Jellinek 1880).

Brexit can be seen as a paradigmatic example of the idea of autolimitation applied to the EU. When a state agrees to subordinate its sovereign powers to a higher authority through an international treaty, it retains the final say – it can always withdraw that assent. In this way, British parliamentary sovereignty was never compromised because the act of parliament that enabled the UK to enter the European Community (EC) could have been revoked. Yet, the idea that the EU represents more than just an international organization – that it is a new and unique political entity largely created by the bold decisions of the European Court of Justice – was based on a widely shared assumption that the integration process would be unidirectional. Like the one who-must-not-be-named 'for fear that it would actually emerge from the dark' (Koskenniemi 2010: 228), the possibility of a member state leaving was never seriously contemplated by EU scholars.[4] It was only recently, in the Treaty of Lisbon of 2009, that the right to withdraw from the Union was given legal form, and even then it was something of an afterthought. The EU has only ever expanded; that it would shrink seemed inconceivable. It is telling that more than six years after the outbreak of the eurozone crisis, there are still no legal provisions for leaving the single European currency, numerous speculations about Grexit notwithstanding.

Borderless Europe and Its Discontents

Whatever else it signifies, Brexit marks a serious setback to the ideal of borderless Europe, praised by EU enthusiasts as 'a conscious and successful attempt to go beyond the nation state' (Cooper 1996: 20). According to Robert Cooper, for example, European integration was meant to have given rise to 'a new form of statehood', heralding the emergence of a better, postmodern state system in which states 'are less absolute in their sovereignty and independence than before' (Cooper 1996: 7). In such a world, borders turn from nouns to verbs; they are seen as social constructs that are fluid, ever changing and contested. Thus, scholars working in critical border studies have advocated 'a move towards a more sociological treatment of borders as a set of contingent practices throughout societies' (Vaughan-Williams 2015: 6) and prefer talking about 'bordering practices' rather than borders. The very existence of the EU, on this account, has challenged old certainties about 'fixed and unquestioned political boundaries between states' (Agnew 2003: 2).

Indeed, from its early beginnings the project of European unity was about challenging borders. That is surely the practical meaning of the ideal of an 'ever closer union' spelled out in the Treaty of Rome of 1957. More recently, from the Schengen Treaty (signed in 1985, implemented in 1995) that sought to cement the ideal of freedom of movement for European citizens by abolishing internal borders between EC/EU member states, to the Maastricht Treaty of 1992 that further enhanced this project by creating conditions for a monetary union, Europe appeared to be moving towards this ideal. Up to mid-2015, the EU's internal borders continued to lose importance, yet all the while its external boundaries remained largely impenetrable. Its liberal, universalist ambitions notwithstanding, the European project remained (mostly) exclusive to Europeans. To be sure, Europe's borders continued to expand as the neighbours of yesteryear became fully fledged members, the collapse of communism in 1989 enabling the nations of Central and Eastern Europe to join in 2004, 2007 and 2013. And while the UK abstained from participation in the most ambitious aspect of a Europe without boundaries by opting out from the single European currency, it opened its borders to EU citizens from the new member states immediately after their accession in 2004 (with Sweden and Ireland as the only two other countries not seeking to impose temporary restrictions).

At any rate, freedom of movement for EU citizens is by now considered not just a major practical achievement of European integration but also as being indispensible for its self-understanding. Yet, whether and how it can be sustained is an open question. Brexit ought to serve as a catalyst for a debate that European elites need to have in order to maintain public support. Just as not all criticisms of Europe's federalist project are driven by a nativist backlash, not all political initiatives directed against an 'ever closer union' deserve to be labelled as populist. In fact, the idea that a political community needs to be bounded to sustain its democratic practices is not all that controversial, and it has a decent, liberal pedigree. No lesser figure than Immanuel Kant argued that a world federation would sooner or later resort to tyranny, making the ideal of a world government undesirable. Europe is not the world, but in September 2015, its largest member, Germany, came arguably closer to living up to the ideal of a world without borders than any other Western country in recent history.

Germany and Its Refugee Policies: Exceptional or Exceptionally Universal?

'If a just world had states, they would be states with open borders' (Carens 2015: 287). According to Joseph Carens, the EU has created such a world, if only internally so far. In fact, Carens believes that the EU practice of free movement for its citizens exposes the fallacy of the 'assumption that controlling borders is essential to sovereignty' (2015: 271):

> The fact that citizens of European Union states are largely free to move from one member state to another reveals starkly the ideological character of the claim that discretionary control over migration is necessary for sovereignty. No one can seriously doubt that the European states are still real states today with most of the components of state sovereignty. Indeed, every European state has a more effective actual sovereignty than most states elsewhere in the world. (Carens 2015: 272)

Though many aspects of Carens's reasoning appear morally compelling, such as his demands on all major Western states to be more welcoming towards refugees, his vision has serious practical limitations. In particular, Carens appears to discount the importance of community, which is necessary to produce the civic virtues that make democracy work. There is a large body of political philosophy making this argument, spanning the likes of Jean-Jacques Rousseau, John Stuart Mill and Hannah Arendt. Specifically, Carens takes issue with the more recent restatements by Michael Walzer (1983) and David Miller (2016). 'Bounded political communities that are able to sustain democracy and achieve a modicum of social justice', Miller argues, 'need closure to do this' (Miller 2016: 93). Intriguingly, though, even Carens acknowledges that sovereignty 'requires that states themselves be the ones to decide what their migration policies will be' (2015: 273), something that no EU member state can effectively do, as Cameron was to find out in 2015–2016 to his own peril.

In fact, just as Carens's long-awaited monograph on *The Ethics of Migration* appeared, a Europe without borders began to crumble. This was partly caused by a dramatic turn in German policy towards refugees, predominantly from the civil war in Syria, a turn that deserves to be discussed in more detail.

By her pragmatic temperament, Merkel is an unlikely advocate of Carens's radical prescriptions for a world without borders. She is an accidental cosmopolitan. In 2010, the German chancellor declared that the policies of multiculturalism 'had failed and had failed absolutely' (*Die Welt*, 17 October 2010). And as recently as in July 2015, Merkel argued in a television discussion with a group of high school students that Germany was in no position to accept all the refugees of this world. As Merkel sought to explain to a young refugee from Lebanon, who feared imminent repatriation,

> It can be really hard in politics. And when I see you here in front of me, you are incredibly sympathetic. But you also know that there are Palestinian refugee camps in Lebanon with many thousands of refugees, and if we were to tell them all: 'you can all come, and you can all come also from Africa, and you can all come.' This, we cannot manage. [Das, das können wir auch nicht schaffen.] So we face a real dilemma.[5]

This dilemma became more acute in September 2015 owing to a refugee crisis that unfolded in the Middle East and focused on Hungary. Tens of thousands of refugees found themselves stranded in Hungary, on their way to Germany (and other countries of Western Europe, such as Austria and Sweden). The Hungarian authorities appeared to be losing control – a situation exacerbated by the mixed signals that both the Hungarian government of Viktor Orbán and the refugees themselves were receiving from Germany. The official position of the German government was that all EU countries had to follow the provisions of the Dublin agreement, according to which refugees needed to be registered in their first country of arrival and were to be returned to that country. Yet, the director of Germany's Federal Agency for Migration and Refugees (BAMF) issued a tweet on August 25 confirming the suspension of the Dublin rules with respect to Syrian refugees in Germany. As a result, no refugees were willing to register in Hungary.[6] A few days later, many of them took the initiative in organizing a march to Germany that forced the hand of the Hungarian, Austrian and German governments. Having criticized the Hungarian government for inhumane treatment and for its attempt to resurrect borders, both the Austrian and German governments appeared to have no other option but to welcome the refugees. It was meant to be an exceptional measure in response to an exceptional humanitarian crisis, but it resulted in a radical turn in German migration policy that still divides both Germany and Europe. At the height of the crisis, thousands of refugees were arriving in Germany every day, totalling more than a million in less than a year. An investigative report about the events on 4 September 2015 published a year later in *Die Zeit*, a newspaper not known for sensationalism, was headed 'The Night in Which Germany Lost Control' (18 August 2016).

Merkel assumed a strong leadership position, mobilizing public support by a confident statement that attracted praise and scorn in equal measure: 'Wir schaffen es!' (negating her earlier, more cautious assertion to the young Palestinian refugee cited above). A swell of public support for the new policy earned Germans a great deal of admiration, but far less practical support, particularly when it came to sharing the burden across Europe. In fact, political leaders in Central Europe openly criticized what they perceived as Germany's 'moral imperialism'. By contrast, German media was overwhelmingly positive towards the new bold policy. However noble and generous the German response has been, it raises difficult questions about fairness identified by Walzer some time ago:

> Why be concerned only with men and women actually on our territory who ask to remain, and not with men and women oppressed in their own countries who ask to come in? Why mark off the lucky or the aggressive, who have somehow managed to make their way across our borders, from all the others? (Walzer 1983: 51)

'Once again', Walzer acknowledges, 'I don't have an adequate answer to these questions' (ibid.), only to make an observation that is directly relevant to the ethical dilemmas the German government found itself facing:

> We seem bound to grant asylum for two reasons: because its denial would require us to use force against helpless and desperate people, and because the numbers likely to be involved, except in unusual cases, are small and the people easily absorbed. (Walzer 1983: 51)

How small is small will always be a point of political contestation. A rich nation of 80 million may well have the capacity to absorb a million every year. But what if there are more people than that in urgent need of protection? Who and how is to determine a fair number? The German government, at any rate, refused to stipulate the upper limit all the while it worked intensively on a European solution to the crisis that consisted of two aspects: redistribution of refugees across the Schengen zone and better protection of the EU's outer borders. The former required EU-wide solidarity that was not present and the latter a determination to use force that no European and/or national authorities were willing to endorse. Out of this conundrum arose an uneasy alliance with Turkey, which, in exchange for significant financial assistance and a promise of expedited negotiations for EU entry, promised to better control its borders. In other words, the German-led EU subcontracted Turkey to do the unpleasant job of protecting its external frontiers. The policy significantly reduced the intake of refugees, but also complicated EU relations with Turkey.

These developments had a significant impact on the Brexit referendum. First, however insincere the EU promise to Turkey might have been regarding its prospects for full EU membership, it was difficult to disown by the UK government, which sought to reassure the British electorate. Cameron's statement that Turkey would not become an EU member 'in a hundred years' lacked credibility. Second, the perception that the UK had 'lost control' over its borders was exacerbated by the images of massive refugee movements in Hungary, Austria and Germany. To be sure, the UK was not directly impacted by this as it never signed up to the Schengen Treaty provisions, but this fact was easily lost on British citizens who felt betrayed by the earlier promise of their government to greatly reduce EU migration. This was easy to exploit by the leaders of the Brexit campaign, who (apart from Nigel Farage) argued not so much against migration as such, but rather in favour of the British state regaining its ability to control it. Contra Carens, by 2015–2016 at the latest, control of borders became very much associated with the question of state sovereignty in the UK and beyond.

In this respect Germany remained exceptional, following its *Sonderweg* [special path] based on the conviction that it was indeed impossible (and undesirable) to protect national borders in the twenty-first century. Wolfgang Streeck might have gone too far arguing that German open-border policies exemplify what he termed the 'Merkel system' (2016), but they undoubtedly reflect some peculiar features of German political culture. Particularly problematic is the elite consensus that denies the very existence of German national interest, and through so doing simply conflates German with European interests.[7] Streeck was adamant that the 'ever changing positions generated by the system Merkel', were not just baffling to many Germans but also had a negative impact on Germany's relations with its European partners, amounting as they were to a 'de-facto takeover of European and member state politics for the sake of German interests' (ibid.).

To be sure, the political challenges brought about by large-scale migration movements, particularly when it comes to finding adequate responses to refugees, are 'morally excruciating' (Miller 2016: 163); there are no simple solutions to the problem. And the German government is to be commended for having mobilized public support for a

humanitarian gesture that appears unprecedented in Europe's post–World War II history. Yet the costs are considerable too: as mentioned above, the policy proved divisive in
Germany and even more so across Europe. The key challenge for European societies will
be to maintain public support towards newcomers for decades to come. The experience
from countries of migration, such as Australia, show that there is a troubling relationship
between public acceptance of migration and the (perceived) porousness of the borders
(Hirst 2016). Electorates are more likely to support migration when they feel that their
government remains in control of the process. As Miller convincingly argued,

> what is needed is a clear policy on immigration that can be set out and defended publicly, with
> all the relevant data about how the policy is working also in the public domain. It should cover
> the overall numbers being accepted, how different categories of immigrants are treated, the
> criteria of selection being used, and what is expected of migrants by way of integration. This
> needs to be accompanied by strong border controls, and rapid assessment of the status of
> those who are admitted provisionally, as asylum seekers or as temporary protection measure.
> (Miller 2016: 160)

Its self-understanding as a post-sovereign, deterritorialized state par excellence notwithstanding, less than a year after opening its national borders, the German government
sought to implement policies that would very much follow from Miller's prescription. As
a 'good European', Germany found itself in an unenviable position: for any solutions to
work, it would have had to be European, yet a common position amongst 28 member
states was impossible to find. For example, Germany could only keep its borders open
while making the external EU borders less penetrable: a challenging task left to a motley
group of countries, such as Greece (in the Schengen area, but struggling owing to the
eurozone crisis), Bulgaria (the poorest EU member state and outside of the Schengen
area) and Turkey (which witnessed a turn towards authoritarian rule, after a failed coup
d'état against President Recep Erdogan in July 2016). While Germany was no longer
sovereign enough to control its borders, the EU as a political project in the making was
not yet sufficiently sovereign to rule over its territory. Another point of contention was the
idea of 'burden sharing'. An agreement to redistribute refugees across all EU Schengen
states was reached on paper against the vocal resistance of a handful of countries in
Central and Eastern Europe (the so-called Visegrad Four: The Czech Republic, Slovakia,
Poland and Hungary), but was never implemented. When faced with a crisis, the EU
member states simply failed to live up to the EU's normative ideal of supranational
governance, underpinning the EU's *demoicracy* (Nicolaïdis 2013), that is, a democracy of
democracies held together by a shared self-understanding as a community of fate.

Sovereignty Shared, Sovereignty Divisive: Whose Debt Is Sovereign?

At any rate, far from these exceptional challenges bringing Europeans closer together,
they are pulling them apart, exacerbating the EU's crisis of legitimacy. This would not
come as a surprise to observers suspicious of quasi-utopian projects driven by lofty normative ideals. As Hans Sluga reminds us, 'the precondition for the appeal to any norm is

a state of normality, but political conditions are only exceptionally normal' (2014: 22). In fact, dealing with numerous crises concurrently *is* Europe's new normal.

Which brings us back to the vexed issue of sovereignty. Following Carl Schmitt, to ask, 'Who is in charge of Europe?' is like asking, 'Who decides on the exception?', which is simply another way of asking, 'Who is sovereign?'.[8] If we are to accept Neil MacCormick's influential analysis of Europe's 'post-sovereignty', our inability to address such basic questions is a mark of progress as it speaks to the possibility of complex political entities, such as the EU, being governed in a way that is 'genuinely polycentric, without a single power centre that has ultimate authority for all purposes' (MacCormick 2010: 151). In a memorable image, MacCormick compared the pooling of sovereignty with virginity: 'something is lost without anyone else gaining it' (cited in Kalmo and Skinner 2010: 21). Yet, it might be wise not to rush with abandoning sovereignty. As long as we do not have a better system of democratic governance than the one that arose over the last few centuries alongside the rise of the democratic nation state, sovereignty as a concept and a living political project has a lot going for it. Burying it may well hasten the demise not just of the nation state but of democracy itself. That is the reason why Brexit can and should be seen as the possibility for a new beginning in the UK *and* in Europe.

No less controversial has been the German and the EU handling of the eurozone crisis, particularly in relation to its peripheries in the South. Though the eurozone did not play such a prominent role in the Brexit campaign, the EU's economic malaise certainly did, firstly, by increasing the push factor for intra-European migration, and secondly, and more importantly, by reminding the British electorate of the limitations of a post-sovereign and post-national Europe. Here too the key challenges are not just economic but also political: Who is in charge? Who decides what and in whose interest? These questions are particularly pertinent to the nations that found themselves at the receiving end of austerity policies. What is left of Greek sovereignty, for example?

Intriguingly, little has been written about the meaning of the 'sovereign' in the ongoing debates about the EU's sovereign debt crisis and its management. For Skinner, by contrast, the very possibility of a sovereign debt serves as a perfect illustration of the complex meaning of the term and its enduring importance. The idea of sovereign state remains indispensible, Skinner argues, so that we can 'make sense of the claim that some government actions have the effect of binding not merely the body of the people but their remote posterity' (Skinner 2010: 46). When a government decides to incur a public debt, Skinner asks, 'Who becomes the debtor?' (ibid.).

> We can hardly answer [...] that the debt must be owed by the sovereign body of the people. If the debt is sufficiently large, the people will lack the means to pay it. But nor does it make any better sense to suggest in commonsensical terms that the debt must be owed by the government that incurred it. If the government changes or falls, this will have no effect in cancelling the debt. (Skinner 2010: 46)

The only coherent solution to this puzzle, Skinner suggests, is to posit the idea of the state as a *persona ficta*, that is, the artificial and eternal 'person of the state', which is 'able to incur obligations that no government and no single generation of citizens could ever hope to discharge' (ibid.). In his reasoning, Skinner is following that very English early modern theorist of sovereignty, Thomas Hobbes, whose insights the EU was meant to have defied. Then for Hobbes, of course, sovereignty was meant to be indivisible. There is some sad irony to be found in the fact that the only aspect of Greek sovereignty that remains obdurately indivisible is its public debt.

Concluding Remarks: EU's Sovereignty Paradox

Which brings me to the 'EU's sovereignty paradox' (Scicluna and Auer 2016) that the UK may just manage to escape through Brexit. Both the refugee crisis and the euro-zone crisis, which were the backdrop to the British referendum, highlighted the paradox that no amount of rhetorical flourish about multilevel governance, *demoicracy* or Europe's experimental union can wish away: member states have ceded too much control to the supranational level to be able to set effective policies in important areas independently of each other and of the Union institutions. Yet, they retain enough initiative to resist compromise and thwart common solutions. As we have seen, the efforts of national and European leaders to deal with economic challenges and the unprecedented influx of migrants share certain features. These include the inability to agree on binding common policies, the unintended and unwanted elevation of Germany to the pre-eminent leader-ship position and a widespread populist backlash – particularly in those states in which a loss of sovereign control is most acutely perceived.

To be sure, sovereignty *could* move to a different level: from Greece *and* Germany to an EU that would be truly supranational. Consider the story of the United States of America.[9] There, the debt crisis in the late eighteenth century turned a confedera-tion into a federation, moving sovereignty away from the states to the centre. The debt was mutualized, making the United States truly united. The hopes for a similar process occurring in Europe have not been fulfilled. For there, unlike in the New World, the sen-timents of nationality have remained strong. If you destroy them, you destroy the very fundament on which democratic governance has been based for some time now. In order to endure, democracy requires a *demos*.

In the words of a former judge of the German constitutional court, 'Sovereignty's most important function today lies in protecting the democratic self-determination of a politically united society with regard to the order that best suits it' (Grimm 2015: 128). Brexit points to EU's limits in its relentless striving to reach 'a politically united society'. This simple insight had better be accepted not just in the UK but also in Europe at large. If the EU is 'far more than merely a case study', perceived as it is by its many propo-nents 'as the future in the present, a laboratory for trying out new forms of government' (Kalmo and Skinner 2010: 19), then its experiment with sovereignty shared should be seen as having failed. It has steadily eroded democracy in Europe and has not delivered the goods for its people. In response to Brexit, Europe's political elites should stop chasing Arcadia – the promised land of postnational 'democracy of democracies' – if they wish to regain popular support.

The vision of the United States of Europe resulted in political fragmentation at both the national and the European level, within and between member states. From France and Spain in the West to Slovakia and Hungary in the East, populist leaders benefited from Europe's disarray whether they positioned themselves on the right (Marine Le Pen, Viktor Orbán), or on the left (Pablo Iglesias, Robert Fico). The European federalist project has been losing legitimacy, giving rise to euroscepticism that has steadily made inroads into the mainstream of national and European politics. Shortly before Brexit, some realism appeared to be reaching even Brussels: 'I think that in the end too much Europe will kill Europe', opined the Commission president Jean-Claude Juncker in an interview with the German *Spiegel* magazine. The judgement of the former Polish dissident, prime minister and the current president of the EU Council, Donald Tusk, was more damning still: 'Europeans must depart from utopian dreams and move on to practical activities, such as for instance reinforcing the EU's external borders'.

Reclaiming strong external and (some) internal borders may well be necessary to revive the fabric of democratic societies in Europe. Accepting the EU's partial fragmentation would be preferable to the demise of the political communities that make democracy work. This is a challenge for the Western world as such. As Sluga reminds us, what we face today is 'the possibility of a world with no political community and with only weak individuals, committed to no common vision of the good and no shared search for such a good' (Sluga 2014: 4). It is the argument of this chapter, and the dictum of the British electorate resulting from the referendum, that national sovereignty will better serve the task of alleviating this danger than sovereignty fragmented.

Notes

1 As Carl Schmitt argued, normality (in politics and in life) is boring: 'Precisely a philosophy of concrete life must not withdraw from the exception and the extreme case, but must be interested in it to the highest degree. The exception can be more important to it than the rule, not because of a romantic irony for the paradox, but because the seriousness of an insight goes deeper that the clear generalizations inferred from what ordinarily repeats itself. The exception is more interesting than the rule. The rule proves nothing; the exception proves everything' (1985, p. 15).

2 When Lord Astor argued that 'the EU referendum is merely advisory; it has no legal standing to force an exit' (*Financial Times*, 6 June 2016), he was simply stating the obvious, but being Cameron's father-in-law, he caused something of a stir. For a scholarly account of 'the defence of Parliamentary sovereignty through the invocation of popular sovereignty' as laying foundation for contemporary English nationalism, see Wellings 2012. The arguments that Wellings advanced in relation to the 1975 referendum gained more relevance in 2016.

3 'Hobbes and the Person of the State', a lecture by Professor Quentin Skinner at UCD Dublin (University College Dublin), 18 November 2015, available: https://www.youtube.com/watch?v=NKD7uYnCubg. See also Skinner, 2010, p. 27.

4 Lord Voldemort from Harry Potter springs to mind, but other images from high culture would be applicable too. Koskenniemi refers to the medieval concept of absolute power that required no further justification: *potestas absoluta*.

5 See the transcript in *Die Welt*, 16 July 2015. A short segment from the interview had a disproportionate impact on public debate in Germany and beyond. Under the hashtags #merkelstreichelt and #primagemacht Merkel was ridiculed for being insensitive (see *Spiegel Online*, 16 July 2015), unfairly, I believe, as is evident from the entirety of the broadcast, rather than the unflattering segment that caused the twitter storm. In fact, we can cite Michael Walzer in Merkel's defence: 'if we offered a refuge to everyone in the world who could plausibly say that he needed

it, we might be overwhelmed. The call "Give me [...] your huddled masses yearning to breathe free" is generous and noble; actually to take in large numbers of refugees is often morally necessary; but the right to restrain the flow remains a feature of communal self-determination' (1983, p. 51).

6 'Until mid-August 2015', *The Guardian* reported on 25 August 2016, '150,000 refugees had been registered in Hungary. After BAMF's tweet, many refused to do so, reportedly holding up their smartphones displaying the message to police and border officers'. See also *Die Zeit*, 18 August 2016 and *Der Spiegel*, 24 August 2016, which writes about '14 days that changed German history'.

7 As Streeck put it, 'This position is linked with a moral claim for acceptance by all other Europeans, which can only provoke resistance that is further enhanced by the erratic nature of a "one-woman-show" that passes for German government policies, which are indebted to the internal and party-political struggle at least as exceptional as that of any other country' (2016).

8 Carl Schmitt's richly deserved bad reputation for appalling political judgments should not prevent us from accepting his key insight on sovereignty (which is as pithy as it is wise): 'Sovereign is he who decides on the exception' (1985, p. 5).

9 For Skinner, a paradigmatic example of the meaning of the state as democratic republic as opposed to a monarchy, it marks the emergence of popular sovereignty.

Bibliography

Agnew, John. 2003. *Geopolitics: Re-visioning World Politics*. London: Routledge.

Auer, Stefan. 2015. 'Carl Schmitt in the Kremlin: The Ukraine Crisis and the Return of Geopolitics', *International Affairs* 91 (5): 953–968.

Carens, Joseph H. 2015. *The Ethics of Immigration*. Oxford: Oxford University Press.

Cooper, Robert. 1996. *The Post-Modern State and the World Order*. London: Demos.

Delcker, Janosch. 2016. 'Angela Merkel: Brexit Is "Watershed for Europe"', *Politico*, 24 June, http://www.politico.eu/article/angela-merkel-brexit-is-watershed-for-europe-brexit-eu-referendum/.

Grimm, Dieter. 2015. *Sovereignty: The Origin and Future of a Political Concept*. New York: Columbia University Press.

Guérot, Ulrike. 2016. *Warum Europa eine Republik werden muss! Eine politische Utopie*. Bonn: J. H. W. Dietz.

Habermas, Jürgen. 2016. 'Die Spieler treten ab. Kerneuropa als Rettung: Ein Gespräch mit Jürgen Habermas über den Brexit und die EU-Krise', *Die Zeit*, 9 July, http://www.zeit.de/2016/29/eu-krise-brexit-juergen-habermas-kerneuropa-kritik.

Hirst, John. 2016. 'Europe Is Missing the Boat on Sensible Immigration Policy', *The Australian*, 8 January, http://www.theaustralian.com.au/opinion/europe-is-missing-the-boat-on-sensible-immigration-policy/news-story/e5cee469a222a4be3eb4038e1f1279da.

Jellinek, Georg. 1880. *Die rechtliche Natur der Staatenverträge*. Vienna: A. Hölder.

Kalmo, Hent, and Quentin Skinner. 2010. 'Introduction: A Concept in Fragments'. In *Sovereignty in Fragments: The Past, Present and Future of a Contested Concept*, edited by Hent Kalmo and Quentin Skinner, 1–25. Cambridge: Cambridge University Press.

Koskenniemi, Marti. 2010. 'Conclusion: Vocabularies of Sovereignty – Powers of a Paradox'. In *Sovereignty in Fragments: The Past, Present and Future of a Contested Concept*, edited by Hent Kalmo and Quentin Skinner, 222–242. Cambridge: Cambridge University Press.

MacCormick, Neil. 2010. 'Sovereignty and After'. In *Sovereignty in Fragments: The Past, Present and Future of a Contested Concept*, edited by Hent Kalmo and Quentin Skinner, 151–168. Cambridge: Cambridge University Press.

Maier, Charles S. 2002. 'Does Europe Need a Frontier? From Territorial to Redistributive Community'. In *Europe Unbound: Enlarging and Reshaping the Boundaries of the European Union*, edited by Jan Zielonka, 17–37. London: Routledge.

Miller, David. 2016. *Strangers in Our Midst: The Political Philosophy of Migration*. Oxford: Oxford University Press.

Nicolaïdis, Kalypso. 2013. 'European Demoicracy and Its Crisis'. *Journal of Common Market Studies* 51 (2): 351–369.

Ruggie, John Gerard. 1993. 'Territoriality and Beyond: Problematizing Modernity in International Relations'. *International Organization* 47 (1): 139–174.

Sassen, Saskia. 1996. *Losing Control? Sovereignty in an Age of Globalization*. New York: Columbia University Press.

Schmitt, Carl. 1985. *Political Theology: Four Chapters on the Concept of Sovereignty*. Chicago: University of Chicago Press.

Scicluna, Nicole, and Stefan Auer. 2016. 'From the Single European Act to EU's Sovereignty Paradox'. In *European Union Studies Association Asia Pacific Annual Conference 2016: 30 Years after the Single European Act*. Hong Kong: Hong Kong Baptist University, 29–30 June.

Skinner, Quentin. 2010. 'The Sovereign State: A Genealogy'. In *Sovereignty in Fragments: The Past, Present and Future of a Contested Concept*, edited by Hent Kalmo and Quentin Skinner, 26–46. Cambridge: Cambridge University Press.

Sluga, Hans. 2014. *Politics and the Search for the Common Good*. Cambridge: Cambridge University Press.

Streeck, Wolfgang. 2016. 'Merkels neue Kleider', *Frankfurter Allgemeine Zeitung*, 3 May, http://www. faz.net/aktuell/feuilleton/debatten/regierungsstil-merkels-neue-kleider-14212048.html.

Vaughan-Williams, Nick. 2015. *Europe's Border Crisis: Biopolitical Security and Beyond*. Oxford: Oxford University Press.

Walzer, Michael. 1983. *Spheres of Justice*. New York: Basic Books.

Weber, Max. 1946. 'Politics as Vocation'. *From Max Weber: Essays in Sociology*, edited by H. H. Gerth and C. Wright Mills, 77–128. Oxford: Oxford University Press.

Weiler, Joseph. 2001. 'Federalism without Constitutionalism: Europe's Sonderweg'. In *The Federal Vision: Legitimacy and Levels of Governance in the United States and the European Union*, edited by Kalypso Nicolaidis and Robert Howse, 54–70. Oxford: Oxford University Press.

Wellings, Ben. 2012. *English Nationalism and Euroscepticism: Losing the Peace*. London: Peter Lang.

Zielonka, Jan. 2006. *Europe as Empire: The Nature of the Enlarged European Union*. Oxford and New York: Oxford University Press.

———. 2014. *Is the EU doomed?* Cambridge: Polity.

Section 2

THE POLITICS OF BREXIT

Chapter Five

POPULISM, NATIONALISM AND BREXIT

Craig Calhoun

Brexit was a vote against London, globalization, and multiculturalism as much as a vote against Europe.[1] It was a vote against cosmopolitan elites who brought Britain into the European Union (EU), who benefited from the EU, and who were widely believed to look down on those who felt they did not. And of course it was a vote for the good old days, in complaint against a frustrating present.

The Brexit story is at once very British, especially English, and part of a troubling global pattern. Similar populist pushback against globalization is prominent on the European continent. It was a central theme of the Donald Trump campaign in the United States, where it was married to authoritarianism and open racism as well as a similar hostility to immigrants. Partially similar populism, nationalism, and indeed authoritarianism shape politics in Russia, India, and China. There is a tendency to discuss each in terms of national history, context, personalities, and cultural memes – but the explanations of each are partly international, not all idiosyncratically domestic.

There Will Always Be an England

In a sense, Brexit is misnamed: England voted to leave the EU. Technically, of course, the state that held the referendum and will now negotiate withdrawal was the United Kingdom of Great Britain and Northern Ireland. But Scotland and Northern Ireland voted to remain in Europe. It was England that decisively chose Brexit. Wales, lacking any significant independent economy, did stick with England against Europe but brought a tiny number of votes. In any case, England and Wales are not quite enough to make a Great Britain.

Curiously Brexit is an expression of English (more than British) nationalism. It came on the heels of a decades-long decline in British unity. Before the referendum, many proudly displayed the St. George's Cross – a symbol of England not Britain. Still, most supporters showed no desire for a breakup of Britain. Most seem to wish for Britain to be Great again, though their yearning for renewal of Great Britain presumes English dominance.

British nationalism, when it was ascendant, was anchored in the British Empire. The British nation was forged significantly overseas, in war and empire. These were backed up by trade and religion. But it was especially in empire that Britain was one nation (rather than an amalgam of four).[2] This could still be evoked as late as the 1982 Falklands War, and military service, including in that asymmetrical conflict, remained one of its touchstones. Scots played a proud role in the British Empire and its military. But the Empire is no more, and British identity has waned. Ironically, it is strongly expressed in relation to Europe because there the issue is precisely sovereignty and not cultural integration or shared history (which can as easily be a story of conquest and conflict as of unity).

The Brexit campaign married a claim to history and cultural cohesion that was particularly English to sovereignty vested in the four-nation United Kingdom. At a popular level, sovereignty suggests simply autonomy, the ability for the country to make its own decisions about its future, its relations with others, and who can cross its borders. For better or worse, in an intensively and increasingly interdependent world, that older notion of sovereignty is hard to operationalize.

With or without the EU, the UK is enmeshed in a welter of international treaties and obligations, trading relationships, and credit flows. The fault line between cultural definitions of a mainly English national whole and the legal unity of the UK is a further complication. But relying on a simplified and old-fashioned notion of sovereignty is unlikely to make either England or the United Kingdom great again. Addressing migration flows requires international cooperation. So does achieving security against terrorism and other forms of transnational conflict and crime. No country has perfect autonomy in addressing a global issue like climate change – or for that matter financial stability.[3] But stating the issue this way implies that most Brexit supporters were trying to find a solution to these global problems and making a mistake about what solving them would take. It may be more accurate to say voters were genuinely worried about a long list of global and national problems but expressing their discontent rather than choosing solutions. Voting for Brexit expressed unhappiness that the problems existed – and equally unhappiness at the web of interdependence limiting the autonomy of Britain as of other modern states. For some, clinging to the ideal of autonomy was simply defensive, the desire for a bulwark against a troubling, often nasty world. But it was not really an alternative plan for tackling the list of policy issues.

For most people, voting for Brexit was expressive more than instrumental action. A Brexit vote expressed frustration, rage, resentment, and insult – as well as hope that a vanishing way of life could be saved and a proud national identity celebrated. It was not a strategic effort to secure a particular political or economic outcome. Of course voters had ideas of varying clarity about what their votes might produce. But this is not an adequate account of their motivation, all the more since many did not expect for the "leave" vote to succeed. And though the frustrations and hopes underpinning votes for Brexit in the referendum are shaped by economic fortunes, they are not directly matters of economic strategy.

Economic concerns joined with other troubles to make Brexit voters unhappy with the status quo. While the campaign was not about economic policy, economic malaise helped turn the mood of the country sour. Leaders of the Brexit campaign encouraged the unhappiness with allegations that the UK gave far more to Europe than it received in return. Implicitly, the contention was that domestic problems inside Britain were caused or at least exacerbated by the EU. Was it hard to get your children into the school you wanted? Hard to get into social housing and harder still to buy a house? Were the queues getting longer at the doctor's office? Immigrants were seen as explanations for all these grievances. Lest anyone think the issues lay in domestic UK policy, or economy, or tax structure, the leaders of the Brexit campaign invented bogus claims like the notion that the UK sent £350M a week to the EU.[4] Brexit voters may have believed false claims about a number of specifics. But they were not wrong about everything. They were furious at elites for shaping the unattractive situations in which they found themselves, and, indeed, elite politicians and the businesspeople enriched by global finance (and far too many others) did do too little to create prosperity, opportunity, and security throughout Britain.

Obviously, many of the leaders of the Brexit campaign were themselves elites and elitists. Former London mayor Boris Johnson was born into wealth, educated at Eton and Oxford, and a very visible presence in the fancier reaches of London society. It is not as though he was a bus driver or shopkeeper from Sunderland. But the leaders of populist politics are seldom typical members of the populace for which they purport to speak. They are elites who articulate popular grievances and aspirations. And, of course, in this case as all, elite leaders had their own agendas quite distinct from the issues they promoted to the broader people. Perhaps above all, leaders like Johnson simply sought to advance their own prominence and careers. Certainly, they were strikingly devoid of clear plans for what to do after the referendum passed. Needless to say, there will be no £350M weekly saving handily available to stem deficits in the National Health Service or build public housing.

The England that most voted against membership of the EU is the England of vanished industry in the North, rural poverty in the Southwest, and people clinging to middle-class lifestyles in the suburbs of once-great cities that feel increasingly alien to them. Scotland has shuttered factories of its own, of course, but frustration at that fueled Scottish nationalism and was coupled with a desire to be more European. English nationalism was reinforced by resentment of Scottish nationalism. But whether on its own or claiming greatness under the banner of Britain, it grew and took on a populist character in reaction to real problems that seemed to have been brushed aside by many leaders in all major political parties.

Immigration was both a political issue and a social anxiety. The nastiest part of the campaign was the persistent fanning of anti-immigrant sentiment that extended into racism and open religious bias. This is something Brexit shares with populist and rightist politics on the European continent, in the United States, and in Australia. The open racism is startling after decades in which almost all public speech embraced virtues of liberal tolerance and often more active multiculturalism (whether in full sincerity or not). It no doubt reflects a sense of eroding racial and national privilege. But this is not simply free floating. It is shaped also by an economy that challenges the promise of upward mobility and makes downward mobility all too frequent. Racial and national scapegoating reflect not only cultures of entitlement but also a political economy of blocked opportunity and widespread insecurity.

Brexit was manifestly a vote against multiculturalism and for English nationalism.[5] A large part of the British population felt as though their country was slipping away from them. These were disproportionately white, older, and less educated voters – but they were not all wrong. Britain has changed enormously. Both Margaret Thatcher's Conservatives and New Labour presided over transformations of political economy and culture alike. These were partly due to factors like technological innovation that were not closely linked to the Brexit campaigns. But they also reflected globalization, immigration, international conflict, and perhaps, above all, economic transformation. And the Brexit vote made clear that the cosmopolitan elites who shaped the new Britain failed to generate a new narrative, a new national self-understanding to make sense of the changes and membership in the transformed country. Such a new narrative is needed not just to explain Britain's global and European engagements but also to create legitimacy in its changed domestic landscape. Changes in inequality, for example, both material and cultural, demand some legitimating narrative. What this could be is uncertain, but right now it does not exist. And this is not just an issue for egalitarians. It is an issue for a middle class that does not think it is getting its due and for a once-strong and unionized white working class that is not sure anyone actually speaks for it.

Arguably Brexit was a vote for some version of the past. Fully 75 percent of voters aged 18–24 opted for a future in Europe. Sixty-one percent of those over 65, along with a majority of all those over 45, voted against.[6] It will be important for leaders implementing Brexit to reach out to the young who did not want it – and who indeed worry that it will damage their future prospects.

The vote was grounded in nostalgia. This does not mean there are not good reasons to be dissatisfied with the EU, but rather, just that they played a secondary role in this referendum. The Brexit campaign was almost entirely negative and devoid of plans for an alternative future. It played on an old idea of sovereignty, old English ideas about the difference between the island nation and the mainland of Europe, alarm over immigrants, and claims that the UK was somehow subsidizing Europe. This was cynical for some careerist politicians but sincere for others and, I think, for almost all their followers. But those who will have to live longest with the consequences wanted a different choice.

Cosmopolitanism and Nationalism

Brexit is among other things a rejection of "Cool Britannia," the 1990s branding of a cosmopolitan, creative, and united Britain as a part of a happy vision of globalization. Consider as an example British Airways's rebranding as "a global, caring company, more modern, more open, more cosmopolitan, but proud to be based in Britain":

> What is vital to this new identity is its international feel. This is indicative of BA's desire to be a global player. Also, according to BA, it shows Britain's own multicultural mix. However, the emphasis is on presenting the positive aspects of different cultures and how British Airways truly supports its operations, including its many joint ventures, in different countries. All this leads to a positive image for the 60 per cent of BA customers who are not British.[7]

The message was not just for foreigners. As British Airways's branding consultants point out, "The United Kingdom is not keen on being seen as the country of outmoded traditions and old castles. The new surface shows a youthful, cosmopolitan Britain, confidently looking to the future."[8]

"New Labour" was in power, but hints of the Mod '60s and the once mighty Empire were not accidental. Public Relations firms and politicians sought to market national identity – and "cosmopolitan" was in part (if ironically) claimed as a part of British national identity.[9] London anchored the national brand. London was (and is) a global financial center, shopping center, cultural center, and center of advertising itself. It is multicultural, Anglophone, with a queen, traditional architecture, and four airports. In the 1990s, it had the Young British Artists and Geri Halliwell in a skimpy Union Jack dress. Cosmopolitans sought to claim this London-centered brand for Britain more generally. The queen's Golden Jubilee was a peak event. To be sure, BritPop faded. But while Conservatives under David Cameron sought to distance themselves from Labour in many ways, they largely maintained this orientation to the national brand. The slogans changed, but the marketing effort continued. It was carried over into the government's "Britain Is Great" campaign, joining the Department of Trade and Investment to promotion of tourism and education (and indeed, the presentation of British higher education as an export industry). It reached a second crescendo in 2012 with the queen's diamond jubilee and the London Olympics.

The Brexit campaign mobilized a different and less happy story of Britain. Perhaps most notably, it was unwilling to accept London as a stand-in for the country as a whole. The financial and cultural industries became foci of resentment rather than celebration.

Between golden and diamond jubilees, large sections of Britain's working class lost jobs, lost relative pay, or found only precarious employment. Large sections of the middle class found themselves in mortgaged housing with salaries barely keeping pace with inflation. Overall, there was indeed prosperity, but it was very unequally distributed. And it was easy to blame globalization. It was perhaps all the easier because globalization had a British face: London. For the unequal distribution was by geography as well as class.

Then came 9/11, the war in Iraq, Islamic terrorism homegrown in some of Britain's ghettoized urban neighborhoods, and financial crisis. Financial crisis was less a direct cause or focus of the Brexit campaign than a background condition. It shaped a national change of mood in which migration and anxieties over Islam and terrorism became much bigger issues. The ill effects of financial crisis were prolonged by the government's ideological insistence on a policy of austerity that lengthened Britain's recession, slowed recovery, and hurt most those most dependent on government support. Austerity forcefully promoted by the chancellor, George Osborne, did more than anything else to undermine the socially liberal side of Cameron's "One Nation Conservatism." And in this, finance seemed to demonstrate both the problems with globalization and the reasons existing elites could not be trusted.

Very quickly, a long-simmering renewal of nationalism was growing stronger. Scots nationalists were treated as a specific if troubling case. But nationalism grew among members of the white working class of England as well as an old country set and more modern Tories. It was largely a celebration of England, but when it was coupled to a claim for sovereignty outside the EU, it was labeled British. This would eventually culminate in Brexit.

The new nationalism is sometimes reactionary, but not because nationalism inevitably is. It is reactionary partly because elite liberals failed to show enough care for those who did not fully share in the economic boom and suffered under the financial austerity that was unwisely and ideologically chosen as an antidote. Many workers whose families had supported the Labour Party for generations thought that New Labour made it a party of privileged professionals. It is reactionary partly because illiberal leaders were prepared to manipulate both the symbols of old identities and the genuine stresses of contemporary situations to nurture anger at immigrants and suspicion of Europe. Nasty rhetoric from elite pro-Brexit campaigners gave permission to nasty assertions of racism, hostility to immigrants, and Islamophobia (sometimes wrapped in a St. George's Cross). It is reactionary largely because it is *precisely* a reaction to capitalist globalization that leaves many unemployed or in precarious work, and that makes it hard for many to have much confidence that their ways of life will flourish in their children's future.

Reactionary nationalism is not a good or particularly effective reaction to loss of jobs, competition for space in housing estates, or the unfamiliarity of immigrant neighbors. But it is naive of cosmopolitans not to expect a reaction and not to focus more on making national identity a positive framework for the incorporation of diverse groups and the deepening of democratic politics. It is naive of people who belong to an elite culture – in this case the culture of urban Oxbridge and London School of Economics and Political Science (LSE) graduates – to understand themselves as transcending belonging (just as it is naive to understand their positions as entirely the result of merit rather than privilege). It is naive not to expect that others who belong to different sorts of communities, who are invested in different sorts of identities, will seek to sustain them – whether these are white English workers or the descendants of immigrants from Pakistan. To offer the unemployed an ethical obligation to be cosmopolitan rather than an economic opportunity to work together with people of different backgrounds is not an effective approach to social integration.

Of course, there were many complaints about the EU as such. With its expensive bureaucracy, almost willful inefficiencies, and dysfunctional politics it has given more than a little justification to the frustration. Still, on the basis of almost all research and evidence, the UK was a net beneficiary of EU membership.[10] The Brexit campaign was one in which accuracy of evidence did not much matter. Politicians uttered outlandish claims, the media gleefully repeated them more often than it checked facts, and even after many were debunked, voters happily embraced those that fit their preconceptions. But the real point is not postevidentiary political campaigns – a bad thing, but not as novel as some think. The real point is the preconceptions.

The Brexit campaign was not driven by arguments about costs and benefits. It was driven by resentment and frustration and anger. It was emotional and expressive. And the grievances expressed had real foundations even if the EU was a partially misplaced target and no practical solutions were offered. In this the Brexit campaign was a close cousin to Trump's quest for the US presidency. Trump was in the UK as the referendum results came in and drew sustenance from the success of kindred forces. Both are part of a still wider populist surge that expresses frustration with radically intensified inequality, stagnant incomes, and declining economic security for middle- and working-class people in ostensibly prosperous countries. Populism expresses frustration equally with a version of globalization that has shifted power away from their countries and political elites who for perhaps 40 years told them there was no alternative. Not least, populism expresses anger with politicians who seemed not to have much time or attention for the complaints of those being bypassed by globalization. In the UK this includes members of the native working class who were once stalwart supporters of the Labour Party. In Scotland many voted Nationalist. In England they voted for Brexit. Very likely nationalism will not be able to solve their problems, but at least nationalist politicians pay attention to them.

Demagogues have steered this populism to the right in the UK, but like most populism, it does not come intrinsically from one side of the political spectrum or the other (and indeed reveals that the notion of a clear Left–Right distinction may be misleading). Unattractively, demagogues have played up the nativism and indeed racism that also inform populist nationalism. They have built on resentment of urban elites who prided themselves on their cosmopolitan sophistication and made clear they regarded their less cosmopolitan countrymen as backward. Those urban elites included most mainstream politicians, so it is not surprising they struggled to be credible in this campaign.

This is not a uniquely English set of frustrations and wishful thinking or political responses. Populism and nationalism are prominent around the world partly because since the 1970s inequality has grown sharply and the middle and working classes of once-prosperous countries have seen living standards stagnate and economic security disappear. At the same time, migration has increased globally – largely because of globalization itself as well as wars Western countries like the United States and the United Kingdom chose to fight in the Middle East. And the world quite simply looks scary. Nationalism flourishes precisely when people feel threatened by international forces. Populism flourishes when people feel betrayed by elites.

Britain was at the center of a 1990s global boom in talk of cosmopolitanism. This was a period of renewal in the cultural and financial life of British cities – especially London – with yuppies, art galleries, and startling improvement in restaurants. Reference to "cosmopolitan Britain" became standard speech – as in "cosmopolitan Britain has emerged as one of the world's most diverse and innovative food and drink markets."[11] These references evoked sophisticated, metropolitan culture versus the noncosmopolitan hinterlands, multicultural Britain versus monocultural English, Scottish, or Welsh national identity.

This was not only a matter of revaluing the different historically British national cultures but also of incorporating immigrants from former colonies, Eastern Europe, and elsewhere. Cool and cosmopolitan Britain was (ostensibly) postracial and enthusiastically diverse. Cosmopolitanism put the accent on black and brown faces at Cambridge and Oxford, in Parliament, and reading the television news – happy images only somewhat undercut by more concentrated and less happy black and brown faces in Brixton, Bradford, and other less thriving locales.

By this time, multiculturalism in Britain was becoming a label for two very different agendas and realities. On the one hand, it signaled a cosmopolitan vision of mixing: metropolitan life enriched by the presence of an ever-growing variety of ethnic restaurants. But on the other hand, it also denoted the targeting of government policy to specific cultural communities and a notion of cultural self-determination. Along with this, a serious housing shortage helped concentrate many immigrants and minorities in specific neighborhoods. Many cosmopolitans thought the latter sort of multiculturalism had gone too far.

Perhaps most of all, cosmopolitanism evoked a positive orientation toward European integration and engagement with the rest of the world. LSE (the London School of Economics and Political Science for those without this cosmopolitan knowledge) was a sort of academic headquarters for this, with a range of intellectual exchanges and conferences, new master's programs focusing on fields like human rights and nongovernmental organization (NGO) management, a clutch of international celebrity professors, and, not coincidentally, fee-paying students from all over the world. LSE became, in a sense, the first really European university.

Academic cosmopolitan theories focused on global governance and global justice, but popular cosmopolitanism was complicit in a "new Gilded Age." Supported by neoliberal policies and a financial bubble, the City of London grew as never before, and traders celebrated with magnums of astonishingly expensive expense-accounted wine. Britain was especially well placed to embrace this cosmopolitanism because English was increasingly the world language, because it had joined the EU without losing its special relationship with the United States, because it was a major financial center, and because its former Empire gave it unusually strong connections around the world.

Cosmopolitanism was embraced by prosperous urbanites. The ideological dominance of cosmopolitanism in the cities – again, especially London – obscured the extent to which the rest of England experienced the benefits of cultural diversity less, worried more about what seemed the refusal of some immigrant communities to assimilate, and mourned the passing of a certain comfortable Englishness. Even the cosmopolitans acknowledged losses: "It is a fine tradition, the great British 'cuppa'. But in an increasingly cosmopolitan London, it seems to be more and more difficult to get a decent cup of tea."[12] Coffee seemed to be the cosmopolitan drink, and urban Britons learned to appreciate £3 lattes.

These were the Tony Blair years. In praise after Blair stepped down as prime minister, *The Economist* said that "Mr Blair has helped make Britain a more tolerant, more cosmopolitan place."[13] When Blair's supporters wanted to criticize his eventual successor, they wrote (wrongly as it happens) that Gordon "Brown's thinking is neither cosmopolitan nor sophisticated, and he is a loner with few strong links to leading intellectual contemporaries."[14]

Blair supporter Tony Giddens argued that "the battleground of the twenty-first century will pit fundamentalism against cosmopolitan tolerance. In a globalising world, where information and images are routinely transmitted across the globe, we are all regularly in contact with others who think differently, and live differently, from ourselves. Cosmopolitans welcome and embrace this cultural complexity. Fundamentalists find it disturbing and dangerous. Whether in the areas of religion, ethnic identity, or nationalism, they take refuge in a renewed and purified tradition – and, quite often, violence."[15]

This was not simply a New Labour theme: a Liberal Democrat politician articulated in harsher terms much the same distinction Giddens had made:

Chauvinist: reactionary, isolationist, anti-European, anti-immigration, anti-asylum, thinks one party has all the answers, pro-hanging, anti-abortion, convinced 'prison works', little Englander, centralisation, nostalgic for a past world.

Cosmopolitan: outward-looking, internationalist, pro-European, pro-immigration, pro-asylum, pluralist, anti-hanging, pro-choice, believes in rehabilitation, multi-culturalist, devolutionary, anti-ID cards, anti-war, tolerant, progressive, forward-thinking.

Chauvinist and cosmopolitan: these, to me, are the big societal divides today.[16]

In other words: old versus new, traditional versus modern, bad versus good. But the claims to sophistication many cosmopolitans made for themselves could not help but communicate to others of more traditional tastes that the cosmopolitans considered them backward. This added insult to economic deprivation.

Cosmopolitanism in the discourse of the early twenty-first century was in many ways similar to talk of modernisation fifty years earlier. It embodied the same progressivist assumptions and often the same tendency to unreflexively identify the good with the new. It elided a personal attitude with a social process. To be modern was presented not just as a style but also an ethical virtue – with little attention to the material conditions that supported cosmopolitan modernity. There were two key differences: cosmopolitanism in the 1990s and the early twenty-first century had less of a plan for how the good qualities of life in the "advanced" countries (and dynamic cities) might spread to those less well-off. And where modernization theory opposed primordialism but praised national integration, recent cosmopolitans commonly showed only contempt for nationalists. They ceded the terrain of patriotism to those they called "chauvinists."[17]

The coalition government of 2010–2015 resumed aspects of neoliberal economic policy from which New Labour had partially backed away. But it too was enthusiastically cosmopolitan.[18] Both Cameron and Nick Clegg embraced the view that Britain's future was global, that Europe was a crucial condition of global greatness, and that London would lead the way. To be sure, there were dissidents among the Conservatives; indeed, it was to blunt their challenge that Cameron promised the Brexit referendum. It was a hasty promise. Whether a referendum was a good idea or not, little thought went into constitutional questions, whether a simple majority decision was appropriate, whether and when an act of parliament was required, or even, how to phrase the proposition put to voters: to leave was an action. To remain seemed passive.

The Conservative government from 2015 was always divided on Europe. In many ways, the intraparty divisions among the Conservatives gave the issue more traction nationally. They made taking sides seem an important career move for Tories who hoped for better jobs in future governments. Theresa May, the future prime minister, sided with the leave campaign but (perhaps cannily) expended no effort to advance it. As home minister she had been responsible for elevating the standing of immigration as an issue, publicizing it, and stating hard-to-reach goals for reducing net numbers. While Cameron led the campaign to stay in Britain, he did it in a narrow, instrumental way. He negotiated for a better deal, and he failed to articulate positive reasons why the EU was actually a good thing.

The Great Wen

Arguably, the EU was a scapegoat for English anger at London, the version of globalization it has helped lead and symbolize, and at the politicians who have championed cosmopolitanism at the expense of solidarity with significant parts of their own country.

London is home to 251 overseas banks and runs a financial services trade surplus of more than $100 billion.[19] London has generated the bulk of Britain's economic growth for more than a generation – and kept most of the proceeds. It is also home to Britain's remarkably centralized government. If business and community leaders in Britain's impoverished northeast or southwest want to innovate and invest to stimulate local economic growth, they have to work with the bureaucracy in the London borough of Westminster. Britain's great cultural institutions from the British Museum to the National Theatre are overwhelmingly concentrated in London. All of Britain's top five universities are in or within commuting range of London. Londoners now joke about seceding from England (thus confirming what people in the rest of the country always thought).

London has had a long love–hate affair with the rest of England. In the early nineteenth century, the great English populist William Cobbett called it the Great Wen, a cyst growing on the face of England. Speaking for the country against the city (and the City), Cobbett decried the rapid growth of London, the concentration of power and people, and its promotion of a system credit and debt that financed wars and the further enrichment of the already wealthy at the expense of ordinary, hardworking English people. He railed against immigrants, calling for renewal of the English sport of boxing as a bulwark against "cutters and stabbers and poisoners" from the Continent, "particularly the crying, canting, perfumiate, cut-throat Italians."[20]

London has long absorbed immigrants – from all around the UK as well as the European Continent and throughout the Empire. Immigrants totaled perhaps 40 percent of its population at the time of the referendum and were mainstays of the service and construction industries.[21] Relatively wealthy residents rely on them for service in restaurants and do not think of them as competitors. And London immigrants were less compartmentalized into quasi ghetto residential areas than in the great cities of the rest of the country. They were distributed across the class spectrum as well, with City of London bankers as emblematic as Uber drivers. This was not the pattern in most of England. The England of Brexit has had vastly more trouble than London in absorbing immigrants – largely because the economy offers fewer opportunities for immigrants and citizens alike. And this helps explain why immigration was so much less of an acute issue for Londoners.

Neither was London's economy typical of Britain's. With the surrounding southeast region, it dominates in UK economic growth. In the last few decades, finance has been ever more clearly in the lead than in the past. London has some of the world's most expensive real estate and richest residents (and absentee property owners). It has been one of the world's most global and cosmopolitan cities for centuries, and is currently home to nearly a million continental Europeans (out of perhaps 1.3 million in the UK as a whole).[22] It voted overwhelmingly to remain in the EU. The rest of England did not.

Though the English have long loved to disparage what they see as the centralization of French government, for most purposes power and functional administration are much more centralized in the UK. All manner of local projects can only move forward if they pass through Westminster gaining the support not just of politicians but also, perhaps even more importantly, of bureaucrats. Perhaps ironically, central government gained power in the Thatcher years and after, while local government was significantly dismantled. Manufacturing, mining, and other industries with stronger roots in various regions declined precipitously. And the finance industry flourished. London's primacy in Britain grew.

Opponents of Brexit campaigned in part by stressing negative consequences for the finance industry and the City of London. They were right that the potential for damage was large. And they were right that the prosperity of the financial sector had been basic to the overall prosperity of Britain, especially since the 1970s. But they greatly overestimated how much the rest of England would care – or would want finance to thrive. They did not really seem to think through whether "Brexit will be bad for banks" was a compelling pitch in most of Britain.

The first problem was simply that the "overall prosperity" of the London finance industry helped mask sharp regional and other differences. In the 1970s about a quarter of wealth had been held in financial instruments. By the time of the financial crisis and the Brexit vote this had risen to three-quarters. This "financialization" accompanied and indeed helped cause sharply rising inequality. Wealth was narrowly concentrated in geographic as well as class terms. The era of financialization was one of unremitting decline in British manufacturing, which had once been the source of more widely distributed prosperity. But financialization had bid up the price of real estate to previously unimagined levels. This was partly a ripple effect of purchases by the wealthy, both British and increasingly expatriate. But rising housing prices were equally produced by Britain's transition to a country of homeowners – based on mortgage loans.

In public opinion on the eve of Brexit, the finance industry suffered straightforward resentment. It was envied for its wealth, and there was more than a little suspicion that its gains were ill-gotten. Images of crass excess had circulated widely before the financial crisis. And in the crisis itself, bank failures spread suffering much more widely through the country than the preceding prosperity had done. Speculative trading was widely understood to be at the center of each. People might or might not recognize how much government fiscal policy favored the wealthy. Conservative success in the 2015 election suggests that the negative effects of voluntary austerity were not widely understood. But what was visible to everyone was that there was no recession in London commercial activity. Construction cranes, if anything, became a more prominent part of the London skyline in the five years before the referendum as the commercial real estate market boomed.

London is the world's single most important center of global finance. This leadership – and the income it brings – may now be at risk, assuming Britain does in fact leave the EU. This may well have adverse effects for the whole country and for many of those who supported Brexit. But it is not surprising that helping the finance industry was weak motivation during the campaign. Even more basically, Brexit voters distrusted arguments that leaving Europe would be bad for Britain's economy – something almost all mainstream economists suggested. This reflected partly the general distrust of experts that Michael Gove celebrated when economists challenged his (since disproved) assertions about the scale of British contributions to Europe. "People in this country have had enough of experts," he said.[23] The numbers Gove cited implied that he also thought the British people had had enough of facts. But he may have been right about experts. And economic experts in particular were in rather bad public repute since the financial crisis. Not only had most famously failed to anticipate it but also economists had joined business leaders and government officials in celebrating a particular version of so-called "neoliberal" globalization as though it were the only possible form economic prosperity could take. It was not only Thatcher who said "there is no alternative."

Frustration over Europe expressed anger over a situation much bigger than Europe. England could not vote to withdraw from London or neoliberalism or globalization. But the problems many wanted to fix were rooted in these at least as much as in the EU. Withdrawing from Europe was partly a stand-in. As often, appealing to populism and nationalism pointed to a specious or at least inadequate policy solution. Those who have benefited from globalization – the well educated and well-off, especially those linked to growing service industries in the southeast rather than old money in the Tory constituencies of middle England and the southwest – voted disproportionately to stay in Europe. But it is telling that there were not enough of them. Those with jobs mostly voted to remain in Europe. Those without jobs, or who were retired, voted heavily to leave. And so did many who worried about the future of their jobs or the prospects of their children.

The Damage Done

Intellectual and policy elites were in denial, but Brexit happened anyway. More precisely, the UK electorate voted, by a clear majority in a record turnout, to separate from the EU. This is not actually legally binding, which leaves EU supporters with a glimmer of hope that Parliament or the prime minister might balk at actually giving the notification required under the Treaty on European Union. In any case, withdrawing will take sustained negotiations. Flotillas of lawyers will be employed. Along with those financial speculators who bet correctly on the outcome, the lawyers will be among the few clear beneficiaries of Brexit.

The referendum did considerable damage independent of the potential consummation of Brexit itself and whatever actual institutional and market arrangements may be put in place in its wake. Much of this is down to the campaigns, which were not just poorly run but outright travesties on both sides. That the Brexit campaign was marked by the UK's first political murder in decades highlights the nastiness of the rhetoric used and the emotions aroused.[24] But more generally, it simply cannot be said that either the remain or leave campaigns rose to the challenge of educating and informing the British public.

The remain campaign relied heavily on trying to scare people into voting for the status quo. Indeed, it was foolish of the Cameron government to allow the seemingly passive term "remain" to define the potential future of the UK in Europe rather than asserting an active goal for building a better future. Hardly anyone in the remain camp presented an idealistic argument for a European future.[25] The leave campaign had its own trouble bringing disparate protagonists together. Mainstream Tory politicians were determined to marginalize Nigel Farage and the UK Independence Party (UKIP). The Labour leadership seemed half-hearted.

One result is that after Brexit, people are unsure what they voted for. To a quite remarkable degree the entire campaign failed to engage the question of exactly what would happen in the implementation of Brexit. This resulted in several days of chaotic and morbidly comic political theater topped by Gove's flamboyant betrayal of Johnson. Many citizens declared openly they had voted to leave but did not expect to win. Others revealed more surprising expectations, such as that trade with China would quickly replace lost trade with Europe, or the UK government would make up for the loss of EU funding for all important projects. Google reported that after the referendum, searches spiked dramatically for the question "what is the EU?", which one might have thought those who did not know would have asked earlier.[26]

Only after the referendum was there sustained discussion of basic questions like whether an act of parliament was needed to formally give notice to the EU under Article 50 of the Lisbon Treaty on European Union. Many people seemed to think actual withdrawal would be more or less immediate, but of course the referendum was not legally binding. Parliament could in principle have acted unilaterally to revoke the 1972 European Communities Act, but in reality the British relationship to Europe is too complicated and consequential for this. Years of negotiations will be required. This leaves open the possibility that Britain will never actually withdraw. However, not only would disregarding the referendum be politically difficult in Britain but also the other EU member states are not inclined to wait around for Britain to sort out its position. Their leaders have strong incentives to move on with Brexit quickly and turn their attention to reorganizing the EU itself. In any case, the issue is not just "exiting" but also developing new agreements on trade and a host of other matters. Britain may want out of the EU, but it does not want to cease all relations with Europe.

The leave vote triggered the collapse of the previous Conservative government, only a year after its resounding election. Its leaders seem to have done little or no planning on how to proceed in the event the leave vote won. Cameron, the prime minister who called the referendum – foolishly and it appears without deep thought – himself quickly resigned as prime minister. The Tories managed expeditiously to select May. She took an interesting gamble in naming pro-Brexit standard-bearer Johnson her foreign secretary. He will likely be erratic and prone to grandstanding, but not revolutionary. Putting him in charge of implementing Brexit (albeit in collaboration with others) follows a principle of "you made this mess, you clean it up" without actually compromising any policy on which the prime minister feels strongly. And it arguably buys the prime minister some distance from the specific negotiations. Johnson will need to negotiate a Brexit that works for Britain or be replaced. But May will not be able to delegate and escape responsibility for all the difficult decisions that have to be taken.

Brexit will almost certainly lead to the hegemony of a more emphatically right-wing Conservative Party. Cameron wanted to be a modernizer and a globalist, and in some ways he was. He combined his economic neoliberalism with social liberalism. He was good on gay rights, for example, though arguably this was just one more change that worried those nostalgic for an older Britain. He ran a poor campaign against Brexit and now will leave Parliament. The career prospects of other Tory moderates look dim. Those in ascendancy are from the harder right. They campaigned as populists (even those with inherited wealth and Eton/Oxford educations) and to their shame did not steer clear of racism and xenophobia. But they are likely to rule as a more conventional hard right. Their nationalism will blend with strong cultural conservatism – particularly, it is interesting to note, among those from less elite state school backgrounds. Tight visa regulations are likely to get tighter. The new prime minister was the old home secretary who tried to enforce immigration limits. Already, she has signaled that she may challenge the place of foreign students in UK higher education.

Still, the Conservative Party has options. It may try to balance the economic dominance of London by promoting home construction and industry elsewhere, which would not be a bad thing. It could build on the efforts launched under the previous government to support infrastructure projects intended to create jobs and long-term economic growth in the North. But because there were no clear plans, what will happen now or in the near and even middle-term future is a muddle.

On becoming prime minister, May offered an opaque slogan – "Brexit means Brexit" – in place of clear policy. Muddling through will very likely bring eventual separation of the UK from the EU, but this is not guaranteed, and many opponents of departure offer theories of how this outcome can be escaped. Still, there is now a secretary of state for exiting the European Union. The domestic stakes are at least as large as the external, since the United Kingdom itself could be dissolved.

As wags have started saying, on 23 June (or even in the early hours of the 24th), they went to sleep in Great Britain and woke up in Little England. The UK's new rulers will be almost as exclusively English as those who voted for Brexit. Scotland very clearly would rather remain part of the EU, and this may lead to another referendum on its separation from the UK. The current leadership in Scotland is wisely not rushing to this, but would like to know a bit more of what the UK will do. It is possible that Brexit will give impetus to Irish unification, but again it is too early to tell. Catholics were unsurprisingly more pro-EU than Protestants, partly because they recognized leaving Europe would mean more domination by England. But Protestant loyalists were split and were not solidly pro-Brexit. Few have fond memories of border checkpoints separating them from the South. And many see their future more closely aligned with the Europeans across the border than with the rather distant (and not always fondly regarded) English.

The Labour Party had already lost the majority it long enjoyed in Scotland to the Scottish National Party. Brexit reaffirmed its direct situation. Becoming an almost entirely English party would all but eliminate its chances to win national elections on its own. The Labour leadership faces strong challenges now, partly because it is seen as failing to mount any clear campaign on Brexit. Jeremy Corbyn and his colleagues have the advantage of hundreds of thousands of new members, but the disadvantage of almost complete estrangement from the Parliamentary Labour Party. The new members are mostly young people who are intuitively clear that the existing more "mainstream" elites lack a clear plan to change the neoliberal structure of globalization. Labour will try to reclaim the loyalty of the erstwhile working class (increasingly cast as a marginalized stratum of once unionized workers in geographically disadvantaged places).[27] But Labour is deeply split between, in effect, a London party – not just pro-EU but cosmopolitan, multicultural, and proimmigrant, and a party of the rest of the England (and Wales).

The Brexit campaign has both revealed and deepened a range of other divisions. One is between the English and the many immigrants and expatriates living and working (and paying taxes) in the country. These divisions overlap race and religion. "Muslim" and "Christian" matter as ethnic markers even for nonreligious people. Even before the referendum, British antiterrorist policy focused uncomfortably on Muslims. It will be important to build trust among those who feel they do not fit the image of England embraced by the leave campaign. It is telling that Sadiq Kahn, London's new Muslim mayor used the 2016 Pride parade as an occasion to emphasize tolerance and inclusion not only for gay residents but also for EU citizens.

But the question for the future is not just one of ethnicity, religion, or lifestyle. It is also one of political economy and global engagement. In the short run the economic impact of Brexit was felt mainly through an instant devaluation of the pound. Sterling lost 10 percent of its value – good for exports (including overseas students paying university fees) but a problem in other ways. Share markets rebounded from an initial fall. The more enduring implications will not be known until the terms of an actual separation from Europe are negotiated, assuming one does indeed take place. Will the UK have a Norway-like access to the unified market, albeit without a role in decision-making? This would minimize the economic impact.

Brexit supporters have suggested that any losses in European trade can be made up with increased global trade. This is true, but three challenges stand in the way. First, Brexit did not bring any new advantages for non-European trade. British industry was already trying to sell to China. Second, the EU was by far Britain's largest trading partner. It would take dramatic gains to make up for even moderate losses. And third, to the extent the Brexit vote revealed a streak of insularity and suspicion of globalization, this may make advancing in new markets harder. Better, it would seem, for Britain not to lose ground in Europe in the first place – but whether this will happen depends significantly on still very uncertain negotiations.

The Future of Europe? And the World?

Europe is not standing still. Guy Verhofstadt, the former Belgian prime minister appointed the European Parliament's lead negotiator on Brexit, is a strong EU federalist.[28] He will likely want simply to conclude negotiations with as little disruption to the EU as possible. Europe has other problems, and only modest incentives to be patient with Britain. And the UK must negotiate not only with the EU as such but with 27 different countries.

Disintegrative pressure is increasing within the EU. There are signs that several – including "core" countries like France, Italy, and the Netherlands – may hold referenda of their own. It is entirely possible Brexit will be remembered as an early step in the unraveling of the EU. Alternatively, there could be a "two-speed" Europe: a new (or renewed) core Europe could form, building on the Holy Roman and Hapsburg Empires, and the founding members of the EU. There might be a secondary status for other countries that wanted some trade advantages but without equally strong political ties – or without the demands of meeting all criteria for inclusion in the euro or fiscal union.

The EU has helped create its own problems. For a generation, its leaders have behaved almost as though their goal were to encourage populist revolt. In 2005 they brought a bloated basic law to referenda and were out of touch enough to be altogether startled at its defeat. All but impervious to reform efforts, the EU has built a cumbersome, insular, and easy-to-criticize bureaucracy. It has done better at opening capital markets than protecting labor (though in the era of neoliberalism and austerity, the EU has demanded more protection for workers than the UK government wanted to give). Still, the EU has succeeded not just in the mission of postwar reconstruction and preventing wars among European powers (inherited from the Coal and Steel Community and the European Economic Community). It has played an important role in providing Europeans with an impressively high standard of living and thriving cultural institutions.

The EU has also been important globally. It is among the strongest leaders in the struggle to address climate change. It is in the forefront of defending human rights. It is a primary supporter of humanitarian action – though its failures when refugee flows brought humanitarian issues close to home have brought that commitment into question.[29] But suffice it to say these are not the top issues for populist voters. And the EU has faltered in confronting two of the biggest crises of recent years. In the face of global financial crisis, it abandoned the idea of solidarity as its richer members sought to protect their national interests rather than help countries like Greece. This exacerbated structural problems. Notably, the eurozone linked economies at very different levels of development without the political integration or governance needed for cohesive action.

Member states found it hard to agree on common policies. The signal failure in this regard came with Europe's inability to develop a common immigration and refugee policy. This started with unwillingness to provide adequate support to Greece and Italy as they bore the brunt of new arrivals. It continued with a botched attempt to distribute refugees by national quotas (the UK was signally ungenerous). The failure continued to such a degree that some countries began to fortify internal European borders.

Brexit is likely to reinforce increasing nationalism in Europe. It will be even more difficult for the EU to address shared policy needs. And individual counties will more often reveal their own fears of globalization and cooperation, and sometimes their own racism and xenophobia. Populist movements are already challenging established political elites, parties, and governments across the Continent. It may seem paradoxical to see such an international trend in anti-internationalist politics, but it is not. The various populist and nationalist challenges respond to similar unsettling effects of globalization – more marked because the globalization proceeded on neoliberal grounds, minimally managed by nation-states.

Brexit is partly a symptom of the declining purchase of the great institutional structures put in place after World War II. These include not only the EU but also the welfare states for which the UK and Europe have been justly admired. National institutions have been slow to adapt to changing economic circumstances and other challenges. They need rebuilding. But it is a huge question whether European countries withdrawing from the EU – like the UK – will have the will and capacities to fully rebuild their institutions on their own. As the EU faces nationalist challenges, its difficulties are exacerbated by the growing weaknesses of national welfare states run on the bases of market logics rather than principles of solidarity.

These are all global issues. Global institutions like the United Nations, the World Bank, the International Monetary Fund are also creatures of the postwar era and in need of renewal – if not reimagining. They have been slow to adapt to finance-led globalization and the rise of non-Western countries. Rising powers outside the long-dominant Euro-American nexus are creating new institutions, like the Asian Infrastructure Investment Bank, often without full Western participation. Multilateral cooperation is weak at a time when it is more needed than ever to deal with climate change, security issues, crime (including financial crime), and migration.

Brexit is part of a populist–nationalist current that will make it harder to achieve effective policies and management of practical affairs in an interdependent world. The UK has remained a major contributor to effective global integration even while it declined as a global power. Europe has been key to building and leading existing global institutions. If internal problems and insularity mean either plays a smaller role, the world will suffer.

Nationalism is once again revealed to be a response to extranational challenges, not simply a product of national culture and traditions. It is a way of trying to secure some defense against anxiety-provoking globalization – not simply its opposite. Populism, like-wise, is less a positive political program than "an expression of anger, solidarity and some-times aspirations."[30] Yet populism is not an anomaly; rather, it is a recurrent response to problems with large-scale capitalism and centralized state power. Brexit offered few realistic solutions to the problems that frustrated those who voted for it. But that does not mean their grievances had no foundation.

Populism and nationalism are not inherently right or left wing. They are ideologi-cally labile and available to demagogues of right or left to steer. The Right steered Brexit and steers many similar movements around the world. There are obvious anal-ogies on the European continent (as well as a few Left-populist parties). The Trump campaign and the Tea Party movement before it fit a broadly similar pattern. In all these cases, frustrations with global economic trends are mixed with cultural and secu-rity concerns and a sense of not being taken seriously by national elites. In all these cases, too, mobilization has drawn on and released racial anger and ethnic resent-ments. If the decline of the British Empire is in the background of Brexit (and revers-ing it in the fantasies of surprisingly many backers), so the decline of US hegemony shapes Trump's effort to make American great again. And indeed, so frustration with the loss of Soviet power shapes Vladimir Putin's populist push to strengthen Russia. Analogies are less precise but not absent with Recep Erdogan's Turkey, Narendra Modi's India, and Jinping Xi's China. In every case, populism is a powerful aspect of elite attempts to mobilize mass support. Yet in every case, the masses are frustrated partly with the inability of previous elites to give them the respect and opportunities they desired.

Notes

1 This chapter is expanded from Calhoun, "Brexit Is a Mutiny against the Cosmopolitan Elite," *World Post*, June 27, 2016.

2 See Linda Colley, *Britons: Forging the Nation, 1707–1837* (New Haven, CT: Yale University Press, 1992).

3 On different models of sovereignty, see David Held, "Law of States, Law of Peoples: Three Models of Sovereignty," *Legal Theory* 8 (2): 2002, 1–44. Arguably sovereignty needs to be rethought, perhaps as the ability to wield effective influence in international decisions, not as a myth of autonomy.

4 For Gove's claim and its debunking, see http://www.theguardian.com/politics/reality-check/2016/may/23/does-the-eu-really-cost-the-uk-350m-a-week. (accessed September 17, 2016).

5 It has to be said that this is a bit more complicated than it appears. UK's Black and Minority Ethnic (BAME) citizens felt less kinship with continental Europe and were themselves less likely to take advantage of free movement with Europe. The Europeans who came to Britain were mostly white. Some BAME citizens of the UK having an easier time of migration. Some saw them as competition or a burden on poor communities. Some expressed the view that while they themselves had worked hard to succeed in Britain, other newcomers would contribute less than they received. Moreover, after the Conservative set out to limit overall immigration, the UK restricted access for people from its former colonies. Some British voters of South Asian ancestry thought restrictions on European migrants might actually lead to policies making it easier for them to bring family members. Not surprisingly, still, British citizens of immigrant backgrounds voted mostly to remain in the EU. See A. Kirk and D. Dunford, "EU Referendum: How the Results Compare to the UK's Educated, Old, and Immigrant Populations," *The Telegraph*. http://www.telegraph.co.uk/news/2016/06/24/eu-referendum-how-the-results-compare-to-the-uks-educated-old-an/ and N. Parveen, "Why Do Some Ethnic Minority Voters Want to Leave the EU?", *The Guardian*. http://www.theguardian.com/politics/2016/jun/01/british-asians-views-eu-referendum-figures-brexit (both accessed September 18, 2016).

6 See "How Brexit Vote Broke Down," *Politico*, June 25, 2016, http://www.politico.eu/article/graphics-how-the-uk-voted-eu-referendum-brexit-demographics-age-education-party-london-final-results/ (accessed September 18, 2016).

7 Bob Ayling (CEO, British Airways), in *British Airways News*, June 10, 1997; see also http://www.euran.com/BC/art&BritishAirways.htm (accessed April 7, 2007).

8 See http://www.jyanet.com/cap/0614fe1.htm (accessed January 15, 2007).

9 Advertising campaigns designed to brand nations have become common, in fact, situating countries in global communications and global markets. With their logos and slogans, nations are marketing themselves not just to tourists but also to investors and sometimes to their own citizens. Nearly every nation claims to be cosmopolitan but with distinctive arts and culture and delightful local scenery. See Melissa Aronczyk, "Nations, New and Improved: Branding National Identity," in *Practicing Culture*, ed. C. Calhoun and R. Sennett (Abingdon and Oxon: Routledge, 2007). The nation branding around the Olympics – whether in China, Greece, or very notably in London 2012 – always includes a reminder to citizens to feel good about themselves, and their government.

10 See the BBC's summary: http://news.bbc.co.uk/2/hi/europe/8036097.stm.

11 UK Ministry for Trade and Investment, online at http://www.investoverseas.org/United_Kingdom/UK_Sectors/Food_and_Drink.htm. Examples can readily be multiplied from almost any market imaginable: "With a more cosmopolitan Britain driven by 'lifestyle' and 'design' home and garden television programmes," (http://hiddenwires.co.uk/resourcesar-ticles2004/articles20040503-05.html). In Britain, as elsewhere, though, the years after 2001 marked a change. "Suddenly the celebration of postnational, cosmopolitan Britain has been eclipsed by the return of 'security and identity' issues," as David Goodhart put it in 2006, http://www.foreignpolicy.com/story/cms.php?story_id=3445.

12 http://www.npr.org/templates/story/story.php?storyId=10237248 (accessed December 27, 2007).

13 http://www.economist.com/opinion/displaystory.cfm?story_id=9149782 (accessed December 27, 2007). In fact, Blair was something of an ambivalent cosmopolitan with a strong communitarian side.

14 http://www.prospect-magazine.co.uk/article_details.php?id=9662 (accessed December 27, 2007).

15 Giddens, *Runaway World* (Cambridge: Polity).

16 Stephen Tall, from his blog, http://oxfordliberal.blogspot.com/2006/01/new-cosmopolitan-politics-smart-career.html (accessed December 21, 2007); Tall credited Robin Cook as his inspiration.

17 Gordon Brown made an attempt to develop a capacious understanding of Britishness and British values. "Liberty, tolerance, and fair play," he wrote in 2004, "these are the core values of Britishness," (http://www.theguardian.com/politics/2004/jul/08/britishidentity.economy; accessed September 17, 2016). Later he would speak of "British jobs for British people." Many self-declared cosmopolitans saw this as opening the door to the kind of nationalist discourse that would dominate in the Brexit campaign. In fact, throughout the New Labour years Brown was worried about a fatal opposition of urban, elite sophistication to the majority of Britain. In his 2004 speech, he specifically recognized the same set of issues that would bedevil his campaign in 2010 and remain current through the Brexit referendum: "our relationship with Europe, devolution and the constitution, asylum and immigration." The main addition to these was the financial crisis and the extension of suffering through George Osborne's austerity policy.

18 The coalition will be remembered for strides in recognition of diverse sexual identities and for important international policies, like William Hague's campaign against sexual violence in conflict.

19 https://www.thecityuk.com/news/thecityuk-uk-trade-surplus-in-financial-services-highest-ever/ (accessed September 18, 2016).

20 Not above inconsistency (like other populist leaders and politicians of more than a few stripes), Cobbett railed against immigrants not only in England but also when he was for a time an English immigrant to America. On Cobbett's diagnosis of the ills of finance and social change in the England of his day, and some parallels to the present, see Calhoun, "Beyond Left and Right: A Cobbett for Our Times," in *William Cobbett, Romanticism, and the Enlightenment*, ed. J. Grande and J. Stevenson, (London: Pickering and Chatto, 2015). The quoted passage comes from a letter to Windham cited in Adam Chill, *Boundaries of Britishness: Boxing, Minorities, and Identity in Late-Georgian Britain*, PhD diss., Boston College, 2007, p. 89. To his credit, Cobbett moderated his stance on immigration later in his life enough to rightly challenge those who would deny rights to the Irish and forget the role of the British Empire in producing both Irish poverty and migration. See Patty Seleski, "Identity, Immigration, and the State: Irish Immigrants and English Settlement in London, 1790–1840," in *Singular Continuities: Tradition, Nostalgia, and Identity in Modern British Culture*, ed. G. K. Behlmer and F. M. Leventhal, Stanford, CA: Stanford University Press, 2000.

21 S. Kohli, "London Has More People Than Ever – and 44% of Them Are Ethnic Minorities," *Quartz*, http://qz.com/337508/london-has-more-people-than-ever-and-44-are-ethnic-minorities/ (accessed September 19, 2016).

22 See K. de Freitas-Tamura, "'Brexit' Vote Worries European Up-and-Comers Lured to Britain," *New York Times*, May 15, 2016, http://www.nytimes.com/2016/05/16/world/europe/brexit-referendum-European-millennials-migrants.html?_r=1 (accessed September 18, 2016).

23 *Financial Times*, June 3, 2016, https://www.ft.com/content/3be49734-29cb-11e6-83e4-abc22d5d108c (accessed September 18, 2016).

24 Jo Cox, Labour Member of Parliament for Batley and Spen, was shot and stabbed to death outside a meeting in her constituency by a murderer who called out "Britain First!"

25 Gordon Brown did make an attempt in *Britain: Leading Not Leaving*. Deerpark Press, 2016, and a number of speeches and newspaper essays. See also the *Report* of the LSE Commission on the Future of Europe.

26 A. Selyuch, "After the Brexit Vote, Britain Asks Google: 'What Is the EU?'" *NPR*, June 24, 2016, http://www.npr.org/sections/alltechconsidered/2016/06/24/480949383/britains-google-searches-for-what-is-the-eu-spike-after-brexit-vote (accessed September 18, 2016).

27 A central theme for New Labour was reaching out beyond this older working class in the awareness that it could no longer deliver electron victories – and pursuing simply the protection of it could not deliver opportunities to future generations. But even if it was hard to see this older, once manufacturing-based working class as a dynamic force for the future, it remains a sizable block of citizens – and voters – and relatively concentrated in certain geographic regions.

28 Indeed, he has been dubbed Nigel Farage's "worst enemy," and Farage described him (in typical exaggeration) as "anti-British to the core," R. Smith, "Who Is Guy Verhofstadt?" *Express*, September 14, 2016, http://www.express.co.uk/news/politics/708996/Guy-Verhofstadt-Brexit-negotiator-Belgian-MEP-EU-Parliament-who-is-Farage-enemy (accessed September 18, 2016).

29 P. DeLargy, "Europe's Humanitarian Response to Refugee and Migrant Flows: Volunteerism Thrives As International System Falls Short," *Humanitarian Exchange*, 67, September 2016 (accessed September 18, 2016).

30 Calhoun, *The Roots of Radicalism* (Chicago: University of Chicago Press, 2012).

Chapter Six

A TALE OF TWO CONSTITUTIONS: WHOSE LEGITIMACY? WHOSE CRISIS?

Chris Thornhill

An Illness with a Cure

Two rather improbably connected lines of theoretical reflection on constitutional crises converged in debates attached to the referendum held in June 2016 that eventually, we assume, will lead to Britain's withdrawal from the European Union (EU). In fact, although surrounded on a day-to-day basis by a combination of slovenly self-interest and strategic deception, the Brexit referendum has a surprisingly high constitutional pedigree.

First, the decision by David Cameron to call a referendum on the UK's membership of the EU was shaped, at least rhetorically, by a broad sense, across the whole of Europe (and beyond), that the EU *lacked legitimacy*, and that it was not supported by a demos able to infuse its laws and institutions with popular authority and grounds for popular recognition. This view has been widely shouted at street level. Over many years prior to the Brexit campaign, however, it also provided good service for academic career building. Indeed, a minor industry had developed around the sceptical analysis of the legitimational foundations of the EU, and around the attempt to show how the EU might lay claim to resources of legitimacy more closely patterned on those of which, it is presumed, classical national states avail themselves.

It is not possible here to canvass all the opinions that feature in these debates. Broadly, however, critical analyses of the legitimational order of the EU follow two distinct lines of argument. On the one hand, many observers place a critical emphasis on the seeming opacity of the institutions involved in the European integration process. In particular, they criticize the committee structures and the judicial institutions that have contributed to the development of the European legal order.[1] On the latter point, many observers argue that the constitutional order of the EU has been created, in essence, by non-mandated judicial actors. For this outlook, the system of public law in the EU has been primarily created by the European Court of Justice (ECJ), acting *de facto* as a Constitutional Court in comity with national courts.[2] However, it is also suggested that the European Court of Human Rights (ECtHR) has had some hand in this process. The ECtHR enforces a distinct legal order, but the ECJ borrows and authorizes aspects of its jurisprudence through reference to the ECtHR,[3] and it uses the European Convention on Human Rights (ECHR) as a unifying normative parameter for scrutinizing transnational legislation and policy making.[4] For this critical perspective, the legal order of the EU is marked by a high level of political judicialization and a widespread displacement of political competence to judicial actors.[5] On this account, its reliance on courts of review as agents of transnational integration discloses the core lack of legitimacy that afflicts the EU. Tellingly, in fact, the construction of the EU polity has been described as a process of 'integration through rights', in which the ECJ and its doctrine of direct effect has played the most potent role in polity construction and constitutional formation.[6]

Alongside this, on the other hand, a large body of literature has evolved that attaches critical significance to the absence of an original constituent power in the EU, a fact that is reflected in the partly judicial foundations of the European legal order.[7] On one account, the EU is distinguished from other systems of public law because there is 'no scope for creation *ex nihilo* of a distinctive constituent power.[8] Other observers declare that in the EU constituent power and constituted power cannot be fully separated, such that the ECJ assumes the role of 'permanent *pouvoir constituant*'.[9] For the perspective set out in such critiques, broadly, a classical criterion of legitimacy needs to be applied to every order of public law, and, in the spirit of Jean-Jacques Rousseau, Emmanuel Sieyès and Immanuel Kant, all public orders are required to extract legitimacy either from a founding collective act of volition or from a founding collective procedure of rational consensus formation. As a result of such constituent acts, individual persons subject to the public authority of a given polity recognize themselves as constituent authors of the laws applied to them through society. This view is of course not unique to academic debate, and it is replicated in some notable rulings of national courts.[10]

As a result of these diagnoses, many cures have been prescribed for the lack of legitimacy of the European polity.

Many judicial practitioners, of course, have been willing to accept the judicial construction of the EU, and they have endeavoured to instil legitimacy in this system through a complex model of inter-judicial comity. In this analysis, national courts police the competence of the European courts by insisting that they act in accordance with rights prescribed in the ECHR, to which the EU is not actually a signatory, and in so doing they integrate the institutions of the EU within a shared normative-constitutional horizon.[11] The ECJ itself has encouraged this method, and it has actively incorporated ECHR norms in its own rulings in order to stabilize what might be called a *multijudicial constitutional system*, in which the European polity as a whole is held together by deference between courts, underpinned by an implied universal respect for human rights law.[12] In this method, judges and lawyers have effectively accepted judicialization as a viable mode of constitution making, but they have sought to control this by institutionalizing a Europe-wide commitment to the recognition of human rights law. Through this, a reciprocal auto-constituent relation between judicial actors has come into being: courts are allowed to constitute the legal order of the EU, as long as they are supervised by other courts, which extract their supervisory authority from human rights norms.[13]

Many academics, by contrast, have opted for a more overtly political solution to the problems induced to a lack of constituent power. Of course, some academics have simply advocated a more extensive use of democratic procedure in the EU.[14] Others, with variations, have devised the rather more cunning argument that the EU is in fact *already* founded in democratic sources of legitimacy: it is underpinned and internally legitimated by the constitutional–democratic traditions of the Member States, and, as it remains embedded within these traditions, it can claim to be sustained by a *two-level constituent power*.[15] The assumption that the EU has a foundation in a diffuse or multifocal source of popular sovereignty, from which norms established at national level are uploaded to the supranational level, is thus widely perceived as an answer to the implicit weakening of the EU through its lack of a constituent power.

Of course, the European Union Referendum Act passed by the Westminster parliament in London did not show extensive regard for such academic debates. However, there is no categorical bifurcation between the common claim in Westminster that its powers have been illegitimately and non-democratically usurped by Brussels and the academic anxiety about the lack of a constituent power in the EU. In fact, the two levels of debate often intersect.[16]

Second, the calling of a referendum was also informed by a less compact set of critical debates about the invariable legitimational weakness of parliamentary institutions, especially in the UK. This analysis of itself has a long prehistory. In the 1920s, for example, Carl Schmitt argued most pointedly that parliamentary democracy suffers from a crucial legitimational problem, which can only be resolved through the incorporation of a plebiscitary element in the parliamentary system.[17] In particular, Schmitt traced the legitimational weakness of parliamentary government to the fact that it is centred around *political parties*, for which mediation between sectors of their own memberships is usually more important than factual enactment of the will of the people.[18] Far from reflecting the will of the people, therefore, Schmitt argued that parliamentary systems invariably prevent this will from being formed; they are incapable of performing democratically authorized functions.[19] Like most contemporary theorists, in fact, Schmitt argued that only the original exercise of a constituent power can bring legitimacy to a political order.[20] In the UK context, however, the insistence on the holding of a referendum to address the relation between the UK and the EU can be observed as part of a wider set of analyses, which address the deep crisis, within the constitution of the UK, to which the classical supremacy of the Westminster parliament is currently exposed.

The connection between the referendum and the wider crisis of British parliamentarism contains a complex paradox. In recent years, a number of institutional developments have placed increasingly robust restrictions on the classical scope of parliamentary powers in the UK. These restrictions range from obdurate factual–institutional counterweights caused by devolution of powers to subnational parliaments, especially in Scotland, to the direct effect of EU law,[21] to the sharpened powers of the judiciary to exercise control of legislation, to the assimilation of the ECHR in judicial review, to the growth of proportionality (substantive review) in the UK courts.[22] As a result of these factors, clearly, the UK legislature can no longer perform legislative functions without encountering normative circumscription or institutional counterbalances, and the classical doctrine of parliamentary sovereignty has lost much of its plausibility. Indeed, it is clear that the UK is no longer a unitary parliamentary state, based in a clear hierarchy of public law, centred around the will of Parliament. Most notably, this weakening of Parliament has been expressed, judicially, in the (albeit oxymoronic, and enduringly contested) theory that normal parliamentary legislation is no longer the supreme expression of the popular will, and there are certain laws that require especially entrenched constitutional protection above the regular will of Parliament, as *constitutional statutes*, which can only be altered by clear and unambiguous wording of an act of parliament.[23]

In many ways, the growing use of referenda in the UK is an intense reflection of this deep lack of constitutional certainty. Both the weakening of Parliament and the attempts to explain the emergent constitution that now frames the functions of Parliament are clearly vital parts of the background to the referendum on EU membership.

At one level, for example, the idea that a referendum is required to bring authority to a constitutional arrangement clearly challenges the notion of constitutional statutes, and it reflects a wide concern with the erosion of the so-called *political* dimension to the UK constitution.[24] The doctrine of constitutional statutes originally surfaced as a theory for authorizing the judiciary to show particular attention in safeguarding laws with perceived higher-rank standing. Indeed, it was conceived as a model of de facto constitutionalization, in a polity with no formalized hierarchy of laws.[25] Self-evidently, this doctrine developed, in particular, as an express means of explaining the relative primacy of the European Communities Act (ECA) (1972) in relation to subsequent pieces of legislation.[26] At the same time, however, the argument for referenda as sources of higher-order legitimacy calls directly upon the principles that underpin the idea of constitutional statutes. Both positions share the claim that certain questions have such high constitutional importance that they are elevated above normal parliamentary procedure. The insistence that referenda can be deployed as a device for producing *higher legitimacy* is designed to cut though the penumbra that now surrounds the constitution, and to extract a hard nucleus of legitimacy that Parliament in its regular functions, it seems, cannot produce. Moreover, the enthusiasm for referenda shares with the doctrine of constitutional statutes the claim that the weightiest political questions can only be resolved by a higher articulation of the vox populi. Above all, the doctrine of constitutional statutes expressed a vague search for a constituent power, placed in the custody of the courts, and it fixed attention on EU membership as a question falling in the ambit of constituent agency, demanding authoritative entrenchment. Indeed, it projected an image of UK membership in the EU as a matter that can only be adequately addressed through the expression of higher law-giving will.

In this respect, the judicial doctrine of constitutional statutes and the populist craving for referenda are two consequences of the same constitutional crisis. In the referendum, in fact, the apprehension that created the doctrine of constitutional statutes was translated, implicitly, into a model for plebiscitary constitutionalism. In absence of a clearly identifiable higher law, the doctrine of constitutional statutes invited plebiscitary politics to stand in lieu of higher constitutional provisions. In any case, although advocates of the referendum were often heard to say that it meant a re-establishment of the sovereignty of British political institutions, the use of constitutional referenda to resolve questions of national policy reflects, most paradigmatically, the collapsing sovereignty of the British parliament. In no other recent development in British constitutional law is the marginalization of Parliament as clearly revealed as in the use of referenda.

The background to the EU referendum, both factual and discursive, lies, thus, in two overlapping diagnoses of constitutional crisis, one focused on the EU and one focused on the UK. Indeed, these two discourses are remarkably similar. Both react against a creeping process of constitutionalization, in which the factual source of authority (the author of higher law) is not immediately tangible or visible. Both react against the self-authorization of the judiciary as the holder of a de facto constituent power. In particular, both discourses circle around the claim that the polity that they analyse has lost connection with a popular will, and that the grounds on which the law demands obedience are unclear. In both cases, then, the activation of some originating mode of constituent power presented itself as a solution – in both cases, in a polity where the actual exercise of constituent power is very difficult to find.

The Cure or the Illness?

These lines of reflection on constitutional crisis in the EU and the UK are starkly polarized in their method, in their presuppositions and in their recommendations. Yet, they have clear similarities. Moreover, they make similar analytical mistakes, which ultimately undermine the sustainability of their claims.

For example, the claim amongst academic specialists in EU law, declaring that, in order to obtain adequate levels of legitimacy, the EU requires a recentration in constituent power, appears to repose on a twofold error.

One implication of this claim, clearly, is that the constitutions of classical European nation states, prior to the advent of the EU, brought legitimacy to their polities because they could demonstrate that they had been willed, factually or rationally, by some original constituent power. This purported general attribute of collectively founded constitutional states is then usually contrasted with the nascent constitutional order of the EU, whose constituent foundations lie primarily in the domain of judicial interaction. If we look closely at the factual origins of modern European democracies, however, it is difficult to see how and why the exercise of constituent power might be commonly defined as a recognized standard of political legitimacy. In the decades when the EU gradually began to take its contemporary shape, notably, the model of constitution making through constituent power was clearly losing prominence (in fact, it was never common, even in the era of revolutionary constitution making in Europe).[27] In the major examples of democratic state formation after 1945 (Federal Republic of Germany (FRG), Italy, Japan, Spain, Portugal), the exercise of raw constituent power only played a very marginal role, and the parameters of constitution making were largely defined either by international organizations or by international norm providers.[28] Paradoxically, in fact, in most processes of national constitution making in post-1945 Europe, judicial actors have played a key role. In many such processes, judicial bodies, located either at national or international level, have acted as de facto bearers of constituent power.[29] Ultimately, therefore, the legitimacy of the EU is widely questioned, not for its divergence from salient patterns of public law construction in national societies but for its reproduction of these patterns. Underlying much academic research on EU constitutional law we find a troubling conflation of historical fact and constitutional theory, and much critique of the EU is based in a rather wide-eyed willingness to take literally the normative claims of classical constitutional doctrine.

One further implication of the academic analysis of the legitimational problems of EU law is that it imputes a stable democratic constitutional tradition to the Member States of the EU, such that the embedded democratic normativity of these states remains, in effect, a live source of constituent power for the laws of the EU polity. If we look at the recent history of most Member States of the EU, however, it is very difficult indeed to imagine how their integration into the EU might be viewed as a process in which an already elaborated democratic culture was locked from below into a transnational constitutional order. In fact, it is unmistakably manifest that few Member States were formed as fully evolved democracies before their integration into the EU, whether this occurred through the Treaty of Rome or through subsequent accession. Older democracies that helped found the EEC or that joined later were hardly structured as consolidated democracies. In 1958, the FRG had not yet emerged as a secure democracy; it was widely and openly questioned in the FRG whether Konrad Adenauer's government could ever become fully democratic.[30] The French Fourth Republic was collapsing, and a Gaullist constitution was about to be implemented. Moreover, France, the UK and Belgium were involved in acrimonious processes of decolonization until the 1960s, and their democratic credentials were anything but reinforced by the events that accompanied this. Later, then, most states that joined the EEC after the Treaty of Rome were admitted after a process of recent democratic transition. In the majority of these transitions, the conversion to democracy was motivated, at least in part, by a desire amongst inner-societal liberal elites to join the EU and to satisfy threshold criteria for EU membership. In some more extreme cases, the demand for EU membership was the main plank of pretransitional pro-democracy movements. In Spain under Franco, famously, democratic reform was prescribed externally (by other Member States) as a precondition for EU membership.[31] In these societies, a democratic public–legal culture scarcely pre-existed the process of executive integration in the EU. In fact, executive integration in the EU was often *in itself* of constituent importance for the rise of a democratic legal–political culture in Member State societies.

Overall, the attempt to look for expressions of democratic popular sovereignty beneath the strata of legal and institutional formation that have grown around the EU displays a rather fateful lack of historical reading and realism. Certainly temporally, and probably causally, the EU and the general form of European democracy developed together: the Member States do not provide an originating constituent bedrock of democratic legal culture from which the EU can claim support.

In key respects, academic commentators on the constitution of the EU and its crisis, or crises, have fabricated inaccurate and ultimately damaging theoretical preconditions for their inquiries. Most obviously, in their quest for a constituent power to support the EU, they have measured the legitimacy of the EU against false criteria, and in so doing they contributed to an unfounded construction of the EU as wholly divergent from other constitutional models, or as a completely sui generis political entity. Far worse, however, they have falsified the basic institutional reality of modern European nation states, imagining that beneath the institutional complexity formed by interpenetration between the

EU and its Member States we can always find common democratic premises that will fertilize, stabilize and consolidate democratic legal–political order across Europe. The insistence on finding a common European people, or a common European constituent power, therefore, has led to a projection of democratic agency and democratic culture into historical spaces *where such agency and such culture never existed*. One danger in this is that it leads to an exaggeration of the democratic robustness of the states that have been integrated into the EU.[32] A further danger in this, in turn, is that it allows people to imagine that there can always be a return to an originating democratic power, and that, in each society, a national democratic subject, which (allegedly) pre-existed the EU, is still present and can be reactivated as an original democratic agent.

It is in this theoretically manufactured illusion of European democracy that theorists of European constitutionalism and advocates of national referenda in the UK now encounter each other. In fact, misinterpretations that reflect the historical fantasies of EU lawyers are clearly visible in debates about the constitutional form of the UK and its relation to the EU. Notably, in the referendum, members of British society were invited to imagine themselves as a sovereign democratic subject, reclaiming a lost democratic authority and expressing a new *higher law* both, at one and the same time, within their own constitution and in the constitution of the EU as a whole. The primary error underlying the debate about the referendum, however, was that its advocates imagined that it was possible for members of the British people to return to some original and pre-existing democratic form. Moreover, they imagined that, in this form, members of the British people could speak about a polity (the EU) in relation to which their own democratic substance was in some way *external*.

The UK, supposedly a long-standing democracy, obviously had some kind of democratic tradition before the rise of the EU. However, we should not be deluded in this regard, and a short history lesson is now needed to avert delusion.

Up to 1918, the elected chamber (House of Commons) of the UK parliament was elected by a franchise comprising circa 60 per cent of men and no women (so, about 30 per cent of the adult population).[33] Further, the UK only began regularly to conduct fully competitive elections after 1945, and the 1950 elections were the first elections held without plural voting. In fact, before 1945, the UK had only been governed for a very short period (1929–1931) by a government elected competitively and under conditions of universal suffrage, that is, by a government that, albeit still with certain caveats, we would be inclined by contemporary criteria to define as democratic.[34] In consequence, at the beginning of its integration in the EU in the early 1970s, the UK could not very plausibly present itself as an example of a historically consolidated political democracy, and its inhabitants could certainly not imagine that they possessed a structurally ingrained history of democratic self-determination. The UK had been a full democracy for about 25 years – not very long by the standards of more recent transitions.

Importantly, moreover, before the 1970s, the political system of the UK lacked many constitutional features that would today be taken as definitional prerequisites for a political order claiming to be based in democratic responsibility. For example, up to the 1970s, the basic principles of administrative accountability were defined in uncertain terms in the UK, and legal constraints that checked executive discretion were both very fragile and conceptually unclear.[35] A substantively defined body of public–legal norms to challenge public decision making only really began to emerge in the 1970s and 1980s.[36] In fact, this process has not yet ended. Notably, the intensification of governmental accountability that gathered pace after the 1970s was linked, in key respects, to the introduction of principles of European law into domestic public law. This process often occurred in attritional fashion, as the UK courts at times demonstratively refused to apply concepts of judicial scrutiny borrowed from European law.[37] Generally, however, the period 1973 to 1998, when the Human Rights Act hardened the statutory footing for these processes, witnessed a process of far-reaching constitutionalization, which significantly increased the constitutional protection offered to citizens. This occurred mainly through deepening interpenetration between domestic law and the ECHR. However, the assimilation of the UK into the legal order of the EU played an important role in this, and the process of institutional integration in the EU and the process of democratic-constitutional reinforcement coincided temporally.[38]

The democratic form of the UK polity, in sum, is not easily separable from a trajectory of norm production that is tied to European integration. Indeed, this form has been created in part through a tightening alignment between the UK and the EU. The concept of *interlegality* is commonly used to describe patterns of legal activism, intersectoral interaction and hybridization that are far more glamorous than the formation of a system of enforceable democratic accountability in the UK since the 1970s. But this term could certainly be used to describe the slow process of the UK's constitutional formation within the EU.[39]

On this basis, it is observable that the attempt to separate out a sovereign democratic people from the process of legal and institutional integration that has given rise to the EU is at once historically misguided and institutionally risk filled. For all the myths of a long tradition of British democracy, this applies to the UK as much as to any other Member State. Like other Member States, the UK contains a democratic people, whose legal form and legal subjectivity are intricately interlaced with the EU, and this people cannot be isolated, as an objective source of agency, from the EU itself. There can, therefore, be no return to a deep-lying democratic constituent power, standing prior to the given form of democracy. For this reason, it is no surprise that the activation of the sovereign demos in the UK in the buildup to the referendum did not look very democratic (it was quickened by a daily pulse of media lies, and it was punctuated by public and private xenophobic outbursts and, of course, a political assassination). Overall, the constitution of the EU and the constitution of the UK converge around a shared crisis. Both are gradually constructed constitutions. Both are plagued by the cure to their crisis – the image of an external sovereign democratic people.

The Dialectic of Transnational Democracy

It is always tempting to look for a democratic constituent power.[40] It was tempting to look for constituent power at the beginnings of democratic culture, and this concept provided a simplified point of attribution to unify the diffusely structured new nation states that emerged in France and the United States in the late eighteenth century. It is still tempting to look for it now. It is tempting to look for a national democratic people before or beneath the institutional forms that characterize transnational society. In the EU, as mentioned, it is tempting to imagine a starting position of national democracy, which either originally authorized the EU or which can revoke this authority.[41] However, the complex, interlinked, often unsatisfactory, and – above all – partial, institutions of democratic governance, centred on a complex mesh of representative and judicial organs, are all we have. Indeed, the fragile and imperfect reality of transnational democracy always risks being unstitched wherever we look for a simple democratic agent, positioned outside or before it, to elevate and intensify its legitimacy. If we wish to find a European constituent power, in fact, we need to look at the political experiments that followed the armistice in 1918, in which many European societies deliberately aligned their governmental order to a comprehensive theory of constituent mobilization.[42] These disastrous experiments in constituent politics were later replaced, in the longer wake of 1945, by more partial, filtered democracies, based in multiple normative sources, some national, some transnational, some participatory, some strictly institutionalized. *How can we think that a return to constituent power is the answer to any constitutional crisis that afflicts these democracies?*

Notes

1   For background, see Joseph H.H. Weiler, 'The Transformation of Europe'. *Yale Law Journal* 100 (1991): 2404–2483; Joseph H. H. Weiler, 'The Geology of International Law – Governance, Democracy and Legitimacy'. *Zeitschrift für ausländisches öffentliches Recht und Völkerrecht* (2004): 547–562; Alec Stone Sweet, *The Judicial Construction of Europe* (Oxford: Oxford University Press, 2004).
2   The status of the ECJ as a Constitutional Court is often disputed. See, for example, Martin Shapiro and Alec Stone, 'The New Constitutional Politics of Europe'. *Comparative Political Studies* 26 (4) (1994): 397–420; 411; Michel Rosenfeld, 'Comparing Constitutional Review by the European Court of Justice and the U.S. Supreme Court'. *International Journal of Constitutional Law* 4 (4) (2006): 618–651. However, its classification as a Constitutional Court began in the late 1970s and was generally established by the 1980s. See Klaus W. Weidmann, *Der Europäische Gerichtshof auf dem Weg zu einem europäischen Verfassungsgerichtshof* (Frankfurt am Main: Lang, 1985), p. 294. This view, although still not universal, is now common. See Bo Vesterdorf, 'A Constitutional Court for the EU?', *International Journal of Constitutional Law* 4 (4) (2006): 607–617. Note the recent description of the ECJ as a 'comprehensive Constitutional Court' in Lukas Bauer, *Der Europäische Gerichtshof als Verfassungsgericht?* (Baden-Baden: Nomos, 2008), p. 174.
3   On the partial comity between these courts, see Carl Lebeck, 'The European Court of Human Rights on the Relation between ECHR and EC-law: The Limits of Constitutionalisation of Public International Law'. *Zeitschrift für öffentliches Recht* 62 (2007): 195–236; Christian Walter, 'Die Europäische Menschenrechtskonvention als Konstitutionalisierungsprozeß'. *Max-Planck-Institut für ausländisches öffentliches Recht und Völkerrecht* 59 (1999): 962–983.
4   The at times weak or equivocating presumption in favour of rights in ECJ jurisprudence has been widely noted. See most notably Jason Coppel and Aidan O'Neill, 'The European Court of Justice: Taking Rights Seriously?', *Legal Studies* 12 (2) (1992): 227–245. Yet, it is arguable that human rights form something close to a *ius commune* underlying EU law. See Sionaidh Douglas-Scott (2011), 'Europe's Constitutional Mosaic: Human Rights in the European Legal Space – Utopia, Dystopia, Monotopia or Polytopia?', in *Europe's Constitutional Mosaic*, ed. Neil Walker, Jo Shaw and Stephen Tierney (Oxford: Hart, 2011), pp. 97–134; 129; Jean-Claude Piris, *The Constitution for Europe: A Legal Analysis* (Cambridge: Cambridge University Press, 2006), p. 64; Jan Hendrik Wiethoff, *Das konzeptuelle Verhältnis von EuGH und EGMR: Unter besonderer Berücksichtigung der aktuellen Verfassungsentwicklung der Europäischen Union* (Baden-Baden: Nomos, 2008), p. 37. Wiethoff (2008, p. 37).

5 Anne-Marie Burley and Walter Mattli, 'Europe before the Court: A Political Theory of Legal Integration', *International Organization* 47 (1) (1993): 41–76; 71; Michele Everson and Julia Eisner (2007) *The Making of a European Constitution: Judges and Law beyond Constitutive Power* (London: Routledge, 2007), p. 191.

6 This expression is used in Sionaidh Douglas-Scott, 'A Tale of Two Courts: Luxembourg, Strasbourg and the Growing European Human Rights Acquis', *Common Market Law Review* 43 (2006): 619–665; 630; Laurent Scheeck, 'Solving Europe's Binary Human Rights Puzzle: The Interaction between Supranational Courts as a Parameter of European Governance', *Questions de Recherche/Research in Question* 15 (2005): 3. Elsewhere, the EU is described as arising from a 'fundamental rights revolution': Mitchel de S.-O.-l'E. Lasser, *Judicial Transformations: The Rights Revolution in the Courts of Europe* (Oxford: Oxford University Press, 2009), p. 3.

7 For an early version of this claim, see Joseph Kaiser, 'Zur gegenwärtigen Differenzierung von Recht und Staat', *Österreichische Zeitschrift für öffentliches Recht* 10 (1960): 413–423.

8 Neil Walker, 'Post-Constituent Constitutionalism? The Case of the European Union', in *The Paradox of Constitutionalism: Constituent Power and Constitutional Form*, ed. Martin Loughlin and Neil Walker (Oxford: Oxford University Press, 2007), pp. 247–268 and 259.

9 Anne Peters, *Elemente einer Theorie der Verfassung Europas* (Berlin: Dunker und Humblot, 2001), p. 410. See also Christian Seiler, *Der souveräne Verfassungsstaat zwischen demokratischer Rückbindung und überstaatlicher Einbindung* (Tübingen: Mohr, 2005), p. 307.

10 See rulings in the Constitutional Court of the FRG, Solange I – *Internationale Handelsgesellschaft von Einfuhr- und Vorratsstelle für Getreide und Futtermittel*, decision of 29 May 1974, BVerfGE 37; 271 (1974); *Maastricht-Urteil*, decision of 12 October 1993, BVerfGE 89, 155 (1993).

11 See FRG, Constitutional Court, Solange II – *Wünsche Handelsgesellschaft*, decision of 22 October 1986, BVerfGE 73, 339 (1986).

12 This process began in the key early case of *Stauder v City of Ulm* (1969), in which the ECJ defined human rights as general principles of European law, implicitly promoting an incorporation of human rights norms in the Union Treaties. Subsequently, in *Internationale Handelsgesellschaft* (1970), the ECJ declared that rights were included in the corpus of constitutional principles common to the Member States, and the ECJ was authorized both to interpret these rights and to apply them as common law across the states in the union. See Andrew Williams, *EU Human Rights Policies: A Study in Irony* (Oxford: Oxford University Press, 2004), p. 145. It is widely agreed that through the cases described above, the ECJ 'fleshed out' an effective bill of rights to support its rulings: Henri de Waele, 'The Role of the European Court of Justice in the Integration Process: A Contemporary and Normative Assessment'. *Hanse Law Review* 3 (5) (2010): 3–26.

13 Chris Thornhill, 'The Formation of a European Constitution: An Approach from Historical-Political Sociology'. *International Journal of Law in Context* 8 (3) 2012: 354–393.

14 Hauke Brunkhorst, 'Europe in Crisis – an Evolutionary Genealogy' in *Law and the Formation of Modern Europe: Perspectives from the Historical Sociology of Law*, ed. Mikael Rask Madsen and Chris Thornhill (Cambridge: Cambridge University Press, 2014), pp. 308–348.

15 For variants on this argument, see Jürgen Habermas, 'Die Krise der Europäischen Union im Lichte einer Konstitutionalisierung des Völkerrechts – Ein Essay zur Verfassung Europas'. *Zeitschrift für ausländisches öffentliches Recht und Völkerrecht* 72 (2012): 1–44; 22–23; Ingolf Pernice, 'Multilevel Constitutionalism and the Treaty of Amsterdam: European Constitution-making Revisited?' *Common Market Law Review* 36 (1999): 703–749; Andreas Voßkuhle, 'Multilevel Cooperation of the European Constitutional Courts: *Der Europäische Verfassungsgerichtsverbund*'. *European Constitutional Law Review* 6 (2010): 175–198; John Erik Fossum and Augustín José Menéndez, *The Constitution's Gift: A Constitutional Theory for a Democratic Union* (Lanham: Rowman & Littlefield, 2011).

16 See Gisela Stuart's claims in Westminster in January 2008: 'Indeed, and that leads on to the referendum. When our then Prime Minister promised a referendum in 2004 on the new package of changes to the European Union, he did not do so for constitutional reasons; he did so because

it was the right thing to do. The second point about that is that this Labour Government, more than any other Government, have used referendums to settle certain questions – we used one in Scotland and Wales, and we even used one to decide whether Birmingham should have an elected mayor. The notion that using referendums undermines parliamentary democracy therefore does not sit easily with those on our Treasury Bench. Given that we had a promise about the use of a referendum, and given that one of the most fundamental problems in the European Union is a disengagement and a lack of democratic legitimacy, I cannot for the life of me understand why our side is reneging on its promise': http://www.publications.parliament.uk/pa/cm200708/cmhansrd/cm080121/debtext/80121-0015.htm#08012133000036.

17 Carl Schmitt, *Volksentscheid und Volksbegehren: Ein Beitrag zur Auslegung der Weimarer Verfassung und zur Lehre von der unmittelbaren Demokratie* (Berlin and Leipzig: Duncker und Humblot, 1927), p. 34.

18 Carl Schmitt, *Die geistesgeschichtliche Lage des heutigen Parlamentarismus* (Berlin: Duncker und Humblot, 1923), p. 11.

19 Ibid., pp. 19–20.

20 Carl Schmitt, *Verfassungslehre* (Berlin: Duncker und Humblot, 1928), p. 76.

21 This was triggered by the request for an ECJ preliminary ruling in *Factortame Ltd and others v Secretary of State for Transport* – (1989) 2 All ER 692.

22 On both last points, see *R v Secretary of State for the Home Department, ex parte Daly* – (2001) 3 All ER 433.

23 This doctrine was spelled out follows by Laws LJ: 'We should recognise a hierarchy of Acts of Parliament: as it were "ordinary" statutes and "constitutional" statutes. The two categories must be distinguished on a principled basis. In my opinion a constitutional statute is one which (a) conditions the legal relationship between citizen and State in some general, overarching manner, or (b) enlarges or diminishes the scope of what we would now regard as fundamental constitutional rights. (a) and (b) are of necessity closely related: it is difficult to think of an instance of (a) that is not also an instance of (b). The special status of constitutional statutes follows the special status of constitutional rights. Examples are the Magna Carta, the Bill of Rights 1689, the Act of Union, the Reform Acts which distributed and enlarged the franchise, the HRA, the Scotland Act 1998 and the Government of Wales Act 1998. The ECA clearly belongs in this family. It incorporated the whole corpus of substantive Community rights and obligations, and gave overriding domestic effect to the judicial and administrative machinery of Community law. It may be there has never been a statute having such profound effects on so many dimensions of our daily lives. The ECA is, by force of the common law, a constitutional statute': *Thorburn v Sunderland City Council and other appeals* – (2002) EWHC 195 Admin, 62.

24 This aspect of the debate links current controversies in UK public law to the Weimar context, shaped by Schmitt's ideas. Panu Minkkinen insists on a distinction between British political constitutionalism and what he terms Schmittian 'political constitutional theory': Panu Minkkinen, 'Political Constitutionalism versus Political Constitutional Theory: Law, Power, and Politics'. *International Journal of Constitutional Law* (2013) 11 (3): 585–610. Nonetheless, certain parallels remain.

25 Laws LJ argued further, 'This development of the common law regarding constitutional rights, and as I would say constitutional statutes, is highly beneficial. It gives us most of the benefits of a written constitution, in which fundamental rights are accorded special respect. But it preserves the sovereignty of the legislature and the flexibility of our uncodified constitution. It accepts the relation between legislative supremacy and fundamental rights is not fixed or brittle: rather the courts (in interpreting statutes, and now, applying the HRA) will pay more or less deference to the legislature, or other public decision-maker, according to the subject in hand': *Thorburn v Sunderland City Council and other appeals* – (2002) EWHC 195 Admin, 64.

26 See, accordingly, the repeated claim (Laws LJ): 'Nothing is plainer than that this benign development involves, as I have said, the recognition of the ECA as a constitutional statute': *Thorburn v Sunderland City Council and other appeals* – (2002) EWHC 195 Admin, 64.

27 See Chris Thornhill, 'The European Constitution – No Longer, Or Never, Sui Generis?', in *The Self-Constitutionalization of Europe*, ed. Jiri Priban (Abingdon: Routledge, 2016), pp. 13–36.

28 Constitutions in the FRG and Italy were subject to supervision by occupying forces, and both accorded high standing to international law. Constitutions in post-transitional Portugal and Spain also gave high authority to international law in order to assuage anxieties of external observers.

29 See, for example, the ruling of the Constitutional Court of the FRG, Lüth BVerfGE 7, 198; 1 BvR 400/51 (15 January 1958), which imprinted a rights-based constitutional order on the entire society of the FRG.

30 Ulrich Lohmar, *Innerparteiliche Demokratie: Eine Untersuchung der Verfassungswirklichkeit politischer Parteien in der Bundesrepublik Deutschland* (Stuttgart: Enke, 1963), p. 93; Heribert Knorr, *Der parlamentarische Entscheidungsprozeß während der Großen Koalition 1966 bis 1969: Struktur und Einfluß der Koalitonsfraktionen und ihr Verhältnis zur Reigerung der Großen Koalition* (Meisenheim am Glan: Hain, 1975), p. 19.

31 See Daniel C. Thomas, 'Constitutionalization through Enlargement: The Contested Origins of the EU's Democratic Identity', in *The Constitutionalization of the European Union* ed. Berthold Rittberger and Frank Schimmelfenig (Abingdon: Routledge, 2007), pp. 43–63; 58.

32 See the current examples of Hungary and Poland, which are keeping the UK good company.

33 See excellent analysis in Neal Blewett, 'The Franchise in the United Kingdom 1885–1918', *Past & Present* 32 (1965): 27–56.

34 Before the 1929 elections, most women in the UK could not vote. From 1931 until after World War II, occupancy of government office was not strictly correlated with voting outcomes.

35 In 1963, the following view could still be expressed in court (Reid LJ): 'We do not have a developed system of administrative law – perhaps because until fairly recently we did not need it. So it is not surprising that in dealing with new types of cases the courts have had to grope for solutions, and have found that old powers, rules and procedure are largely inapplicable to cases which they were never designed or intended to deal with': *Ridge v Baldwin and others* – (1963) 2 All ER 66. This was partly revised by the early 1970s. See the claim of Denning LJ that 'there have been important developments in the last 22 years which have transformed the situation. It may truly now be said that we have a developed system of administrative law. These developments have been most marked in the review of decisions of statutory bodies. Take first statutory bodies. [...]. The discretion of a statutory body is never unfettered. It is a discretion which is to be exercised according to law': *Breen v Amalgamated Engineering Union (now Amalgamated Engineering and Foundry Workers Union) and others* (1971) 1 All ER 1148.

36 See debates about this in *Bugdaycay v Secretary of State for the Home Department and related appeals* – (1987) 1 All ER 940.

37 In some cases, judges rejected the idea that stricter principles of judicial accountability 'recognised in the administrative law of several members of the European Economic Community' could be applied in the UK: *Brind and others v Secretary of State for the Home Department* – (1991) 1 All ER 720. Despite this, however, methods for ensuring heightened substantive control of public agencies had surely taken hold by the 1990s.

38 Diplock LJ linked the solidification of British administrative law to EU law in his famous arguments in the GCHQ case, stating that 'the possible adoption in the future of the principle of "proportionality" which is recognised in the administrative law of several of our fellow members of the European Economic Community' might contribute to the more robust constitutionalization of UK public law: *Council of Civil Service Unions and others v Minister for the Civil Service* – (1984) 3 All ER 935. Just as important as the growing application of proportionality as a principle for assessing executive discretion is the principle of legitimate expectations, which can also be ascribed to notions of legal certainty more common in European law than British public law. For a leading earlier case on this, see *R v Home Secretary, ex p Oloniluyi* (1989) Imm AR 135.

39 See Boaventura de Sousa Santos, *Toward a New Legal Common Sense*, 2nd ed. (Cambridge: Cambridge University Press, 2002), p. 437; Boaventura de Sousa Santos, 'The Heterogenous State and Legal Pluralism in Mozambique'. *Law & Society Review* 40 (1) (2006): 39–75; 70.

40 See Martin Loughlin, 'The Concept of Constituent Power'. *European Journal of Political Theory* 13 (2) (2013): 218–237.

41 See the paradigmatic expression of this in the *Maastricht-Urteil* of the German Constitutional Court, at note 10.

42 See Chris Thornhill, 'Fascism and European State Formation: The Crisis of Constituent Power', in *Law and the Formation of Modern Europe: Approaches from the Historical Sociology of Law*, ed. Mikael Rask Madsen and Chris Thornhill (Cambridge: Cambridge University Press, 2014), pp. 29–76.

Chapter Seven

LOCATING BREXIT IN THE PRAGMATICS OF RACE, CITIZENSHIP AND EMPIRE

Gurminder K. Bhambra

The UK referendum on continued membership of the European Union (EU), which produced a victory for the leave campaign, was less a debate on the pros and cons of membership than a proxy for discussions about race and migration, specifically, who belonged and had rights (or should have rights) and who did not (and should not). One of the key slogans of those arguing for exit from the EU was 'we want our country back'. The racialized discourses at work here were not only present explicitly in the politics of the event but they are also implicit in much social scientific analysis. Populist political claims are mirrored by an equivalent social scientific 'presentism' that elides proper historical context. In this chapter, I discuss the importance of understanding Brexit in the context of a historical sociological understanding that would enable us to make better sense of the politics of the present.

Race and Class in the Brexit Debates

The last few weeks of campaigning, prior to the UK's referendum on leaving the EU, were marked by an increasingly toxic discourse on citizenship and belonging and the rights that pertain as a consequence. This discourse provided at least part of the context for the brutal killing, before the vote, of a socialist and progressive Member of Parliament (MP), Jo Cox, and was followed by increasing racist and xenophobic attacks on migrants and minorities after the decision for Brexit (see Emejulu 2016). 'Put Britain first' was the call that resounded not only from Batley and Spen, where Jo Cox was murdered, but also, in various degrees of intensity, from up and down and across the country. It was also mobilized in media and social scientific accounts that sought to focus attention, in particular, on the plight of a *white (English) working class*. As Paul Mason (2016) asked in *The Guardian*, 'What happens when, instead of Poles, it is poor white English people herded into the polytunnels of Kent to pick strawberries for union-busting gangmasters?' The prioritization of 'poor white English people' over presumably, poor white Poles points to an analysis of class that is deeply racialized and ethnicized and one that marked many of the debates on Brexit.

Racializing the working class in the context of a populist discourse that seeks to 'take our country back' both plays into and reinforces problematic assumptions about who belongs, who has rights and whose quality of life should have priority in public policy. It also works with a misguided sense of who 'we' are and how 'we' came to be. The 'we' that was dominant within public debate on Brexit was a 'we' that was believed to be historically constituted in national terms, and it was this history of being located within the nation that was seen to determine who should or should not have rights. The most visceral attacks came in relation to a sense of that national community having been betrayed by a metropolitan elite that appeared to care more for the situation of 'non-British' others than it did for the 'legitimate' citizens of Britain. However, as I go on to argue, if we do not understand how we came to be politically constituted as a nation, as Britain, then our solutions to the manifest problems we are facing are likely to be profoundly misguided.

Since its very inception as a common political unit in 1707, Britain has not been an independent country but part of broader political entities, most significantly empire, then the Commonwealth and, from 1973, the EU. There has been no independent Britain, no 'island nation'. In fact, this period is rather marked by the creation of a racially stratified political formation that Britain led to its own advantage (O'Toole 2016; Bhambra 2016c). The rancour that marks the Brexit debate seems to stem more from the loss of this privileged position, based as it is on white elites and a working class offered the opportunity to see themselves as better than the darker subjects of empire – hierarchies of class and caste if you will, embodied in the hierarchies of race. Austerity has simply provided the fertile ground for its re-emergence and expression.

As I go on to argue, what it is to be British cannot be understood separately from empire or the imperial modes of governance that remained dominant well into the twentieth century. In the immediate post-war period, for example, Britain explicitly refused to consider itself as a nation and maintained empire and the Commonwealth as its key political imaginaries when thinking about what it meant to be British. While there is a much longer history that rests on the vicissitudes of empire and forms of imperial governance, the present chapter is concerned with a shorter history: one that sets the emergence of Britain, and what it is to be British, in the context of the decolonization of empire. Debates on British citizenship only emerged in the metropole in the 1940s, and it was not until 1981 that there was a legal statute specifying British citizenship as a category distinct from the earlier forms that had created a common citizenship status *across the populations of the UK and its colonies*. Disentangling a particular form of British citizenship from these earlier models was a protracted process and involved taking rights away from some citizens on the basis of race and colonial status (Karatani 2003).

Conceptualizations of Citizenship

In contrast to how citizenship is represented in many social scientific accounts – which relate its emergence and development to the modern nation-state – the political context for the emergence of British citizenship was empire. Rogers Brubaker (1989, 1990), for example, explicitly ties the concept of citizenship with membership of a nation state and operates with two ideal–typical constructions. One is France, which he presents as the originary modern nation state, where conceptions of nationhood and citizenship cohere around political unity rather than shared culture and continue to bear the mark of their origin in the 1789 revolution. The other is the idea of nation state as *ethnie* exemplified by the unification of Germany in 1871, where political unity is understood as derivative of ethnic and cultural unity. As he puts it, 'If the French conception of nationhood has been universalist, assimilationist, and state-centred, the German conception has been particularist, organic, and *Volk*-centred' (1989: 8). In each case, it is easy to elide empire in its relation to the construction of the national political community. In Germany's case, this is because the German empire was a relatively brief and ultimately failed project, defeated in the two World Wars (see Steinmetz 2007). In the case of France, empire is elided because of the apparent universalism of the republican claim undergirding conceptions of citizenship (see Stovall 2006; Rosanvallon 2013). Even where empire is mentioned, it is the nation state that is seen as the key determinant of citizenship, and empire is understood as a project of a preceding nation state.

Britain is presented by Brubaker (1989) as a case that falls somewhere between the two. The obstacle to the development of national feelings akin to those that emerged in France and Germany, he suggests, is the composite nature of the UK, which comprised England, Scotland, Wales and Ireland. In contrast, I argue that empire is central to the construction of the 'political community' in Britain and its related conceptions of citizenship.[1] Significantly, as is common with many writers on Britain, Brubaker only mentions empire at the point of it being left behind and does not comment on its role in constructing the very idea of Britain, nor of the deep consequences that it has had even after it has supposedly been left behind. For him, it was with the dismantling of its empire that Britain 'had to redefine itself as a nation-state, and to create for the first time a national citizenship' (1989: 10). While I would agree that this was the first time Britain developed an understanding of national citizenship, it did not do so by leaving empire behind but rather in negotiation with the changing relationships that were part of its dismantling. It was this that provided the dominant frame for thinking about citizenship within Britain until, at least, its entry into Europe in 1973 (and the idea of a special relationship with the Commonwealth also figured in arguments to leave the EU in the present).

The shift from empire and Commonwealth to the EU is significant in terms of other accounts of issues of British political community. It was during the decade that the British government was passing the Commonwealth Immigration Acts, which gradually took rights away from some citizens on the basis of race as will be discussed subsequently, that negotiations were also occurring about European membership. These negotiations were focused primarily on the free movement of capital, and, in Harold Wilson's own account of the negotiations, as Ann Dummett and Andrew Nicol (1990) point out, the movement of labour was only mentioned in passing and as a very minor concern. Indeed, where immigration was discussed, they state, it was only discussed in terms of Commonwealth immigration and not in terms of the movement of people throughout the European Community (EC). The key concern on the European side appeared to be how to limit the freedom of movement within Europe of British colonial and Commonwealth citizens. The domestic political imaginary, then, was entirely shaped by concerns with racialized others, even as the nation entered a larger political union that gave unlimited rights of movement to over 250 million people.

British Citizenship from Empire to Commonwealth

Given the complex and variegated nature of the British imperial state, even providing a brief history of the different types of citizenship at play at any particular time is not an easy task. In brief, up until 1948, when Britain enacted the British Nationality Act, the populations of Britain and its Dominions and colonies (both former and continuing) were understood as *British subjects*. After 1948, they were designated as *Commonwealth citizens* (Dummett 1994; Karatani 2003). People were not subjects of an authority specific to local territories but were all subjects of British Empire or (later) citizens of the Commonwealth (whether they were in Britain or elsewhere). The impetus for the British Nationality Act was not struggles internal to Britain but rather, a consequence of the political arguments and activities within Dominion countries and the moves for independence by India. From the early twentieth century onwards, the Dominions or, as they also came to be known, the Old Commonwealth (OCW) countries (Canada, Australia, New Zealand and South Africa) negotiated greater local autonomy and sovereignty from Britain (Karatani 2003). This was done primarily in relation to arguments for controlling movement into these territories by the darker subjects of Empire.

The unity of the Empire had been predicated, at least rhetorically, on free movement within the imperial polity of all subjects. The 'whites only' immigration policies instituted by Canada and Australia threatened this underlying principle. While these moves were initially resisted by the British government, by the 1930s an accommodation was reached that gave the Dominion countries greater autonomy over such matters, and by the late 1940s, they had established themselves as countries fully independent of Empire. In response to the move by these countries breaking away from formal subordination within the imperial polity, and India asserting its independence in 1947, Britain set out the British Nationality Act where British subjecthood was now termed Commonwealth citizenship, and this was itself categorized into four different subgroups. These were (1) citizens of the United Kingdom and colonies (CUKC), (2) citizens of independent Commonwealth countries, (3) British subjects without citizenship (BSWC), and (4) British protected persons (BPP) (Karatani 2003: 116).

At the very moment that the British government first sought to clarify what British citizenship meant, then, people in the colonies were formally stated to share citizenship with people in Britain, and populations of the former colonies and Dominions were also regarded as citizens of the Commonwealth. This meant that they continued to have rights to travel to, and to live in, Britain by virtue of remaining within the Commonwealth. Part of the explanation for this, as Randall Hansen argues, was the ideological commitment to the Old Commonwealth and, in particular, the fact that these countries 'were central to the United Kingdom's economic and foreign policy' (2000: 17). Further, as the debates over the subsequent decades illustrated, to institute immigration control would be to concede the end of the Commonwealth and the role and status of Britain as a world power, and many British officials were not ready to do this in the immediate post-war period (Hansen 2000). With increasing moves towards decolonization by the colonized countries, and the increased fears of 'coloured immigration' into Britain, the attachments to the Commonwealth loosened. These were only formally disentangled with Britain's

entry into the EC and the end also of the system of Commonwealth preferences in relation to trade in goods (Holmwood 2000).

Multicultural British Citizens and Citizenship

Nineteen forty-eight was not only the year of the British Nationality Act but also, as
James Hampshire (2005) points out, the year that the *Empire Windrush* entered the Thames
and close on 500 West Indians, holding British passports, disembarked at Tilbury Dock.
Although India and Pakistan had declared their independence from the British Empire,
Britain was still an imperial state with a number of colonies. More importantly, as discussed above, it continued to understand itself as presiding over a territory greater than
that of the island on which Westminster was based. This imperial territory was popu-
lated by British subjects, or now Commonwealth citizens, all of whom had the right to
travel and to live and work across its domains (subject, of course, to the racist immigration policies of local territories, for example, Canada and Australia). Given the realities of empire, the movement of people was not an unusual or unexpected occurrence.
Populations moved – indeed, many had been forcibly moved through enslavement and
systems of bonded labour – through the various circuits of empire throughout its history.
Indeed, the British, and more broadly the Europeans, had colonized much of the world
through processes of migration starting in the fifteenth century. By the nineteenth and
the early twentieth century such emigration was being encouraged by the British government 'through policies such as the Free Passage Scheme of 1919 and the 1922 Empire
Settlement Act' (Hampshire 2005: 8). What makes the *Windrush* significant is that it was
the darker citizens of empire who were exercising their rights to move freely and legally
as many of their paler compatriots had been doing throughout history, albeit without the
legal sanction of the territories they entered.

As Hampshire argues, this movement of people 'was a movement of citizens within
an imperial polity, rather than a movement of aliens to a sovereign territory' (2005: 10).
This rather mundane event – of Commonwealth citizens moving within the bounds
of the Commonwealth – has, subsequently, become foundational to mythologies of
the changing nature (or, more accurately, face) of Britain –mythologies that continue
to reverberate in the present and have taken on a renewed political vibrancy in light
of the debates regarding our continued EU membership. While the event of *Windrush*
is often cited as the inauguration of British multiculturalism, it could be argued, as the
British government itself argued, that the British Empire and later Commonwealth was,
in its very constitution, multiracial and culturally diverse (Karatani 2003). Given that
the polity under consideration was understood as a common space, through which all
subjects/citizens were free to move, then cultural diversity – in all its ethnolinguistic variety – was its common and unifying condition. This cultural diversity, however, was also
hierarchically organized around concurrent ideas of racial difference that would come to
determine the shape of British citizenship over the subsequent decades.[2] While Britain
had initially rejected an immigration policy based on racial designation, this was soon
to dominate the debates on population movement as the consolidated loss of empire left
behind it a small country unsure of itself or its place in a changing world.

Notwithstanding the easy association of citizenship with the nation state, then, British citizenship emerged in – and was configured by – the multiracial and ethnolinguistically plural context of empire and Commonwealth. The construction of darker citizens *as aliens* over the subsequent decades was to be based on a visceral understanding of difference predicated on race rather than in relation to any legal basis. Indeed, the cabinet seemed to have tied itself up in knots in the 1950s trying to resolve the conundrum of limiting migration from the New Commonwealth (NCW) countries without it appearing as if this was being done in a racially discriminatory way. As Hansen sets out, a draft bill on restricting the migration of British subjects was debated in 1955 that included sweeping powers for ministers 'to limit migration, impose conditions on entry, and deport British subjects resident in Britain' (Hansen 2000: 75). The interdepartmental committee assessing the feasibility of the bill suggested that there was a need for migration control but that this 'would be impossible to justify on purely economic grounds', as the committee had not found any 'evidence that immigrants were an undue burden on National Assistance' (Hansen 2000: 75). Some within the cabinet assumed that this bill would not apply to OCW citizens, and the colonial secretary, Alan Lennox-Boyd, 'made it clear that he would find the exclusive application of migration restrictions to colonial immigrants intolerable' (Hansen 2000: 77). Political divisions within the cabinet, and an overwhelming commitment to the Commonwealth in terms of how it secured Britain's position as a global power, meant that Britain, at least for now, maintained its open borders.

It was in the 1960s that migration control moved from being an issue associated with Britain's status in the world to a more regional and national issue. This was the period of negotiations of Britain's relationship to the newly formed EC and also of what came to be termed 'race riots' in major cities in Britain. The attacks on minority communities in Nottingham and London made the migration of those who looked different a domestic issue and ultimately brought about the racist immigration acts of that decade. While the government had sought informally to restrict the levels of coloured immigration through backroom deals with the colonies and NCW countries – in order to maintain the principle of 'the statutory right of all British subjects to enter and remain in the United Kingdom' (Hansen 2000: 95) – the numbers continued to increase, although it should also be stated that these numbers were far outweighed by Irish and other European migrants during this period. By the time of the 1961 census, for example, the foreign-born population of Britain was 5 per cent of the total population. Out of the top ten sending countries, eight were white and only two were darker nations. There were 683,000 people born in Ireland; 121,000 from Germany; 120,000 from Poland (to take just the top three white populations), and from the darker countries, there were 157,000 from India and 100,000 from Jamaica.[3] The constant concerns about 'coloured immigration' belie the fact that the total white foreign-born population, the majority of whom would have been migrants or aliens, was about ten times that of the 'coloured' population, the majority of whom would have been citizens.

The Commonwealth Immigration Acts (CIAs) of 1962 and 1968 were enacted precisely to restrict the freedom of movement of darker citizens and to enable those of the OCW continued access. The British government presented its concern over movement into the country by NCW citizens as an issue of numbers and the fact that they 'were entitled to claim all citizenship rights once inside the United Kingdom, and to be treated on an equal basis to those British who were born' there (Karatani 2003: 132). However, no similar concern was expressed about OCW citizens, about whom the same was true. Instead, the CIA 1962 was enacted on the premise of maintaining favourable relations with OCW countries and restricting the rights of NCW citizens by now grouping them as OCW *citizens* and NCW *immigrants*.

The institution of a common citizenship – citizens of the UK and the Colonies – in the British Nationality Act of 1948 meant that it 'could only be replaced through a complicated process that risked political instability within the dependent territories' (Hansen 2000: 104). As such, the most expedient solution was to retain that common citizenship but to discriminate among citizens in terms of their rights to enter and live within Britain. These restrictions, in the first act of 1962, were to be applied to any Commonwealth citizen who had not been born in the UK or who did not hold a Citizen of the UK and Colonies (CUKC) passport issued by the UK government (as opposed to the UK colonial office in the colonies or the Commonwealth countries). There was an Irish exemption from this act that was seen as problematic both by those who would have preferred exemption for the citizens of the Dominions instead of the 'disloyal Irish' and by those who were arguing that it was 'a racist act designed to exclude immigrants [citizens] of colour' (Hansen 2000: 118 and 117). In effect, this act brought into being two forms of citizenship – full and second-class citizenship – which were to have long-term implications for how issues of equality and justice would be dealt with in the UK.

Conclusion

The standard accounts of political citizenship align it with the contours of the nation state where non-citizens, 'aliens', are (or can be) admitted to citizenship (see Bauböck 1994). In the British context, however, the defining of British citizenship has been predicated on the basis of making citizens into immigrants on the basis of an explicit racial hierarchy (Karatani 2003). Indeed, as Hampshire has comprehensively demonstrated, 'the development of immigration controls in post-war Britain was governed by a racial demographic logic' (2005: 77). This points to the current British polity as deeply structured by race such that the state itself – and all associated concepts, such as citizenship – are racialized (see Shilliam 2016). As the debates on Brexit brought to the fore, most social scientific and media accounts of inequality in Britain erase race and the racialized histories that configure our present society and polity. As such, they can only offer 'white identity politics' when what is needed is a thoroughgoing address of inequality grounded in an understanding of the history of the broader British imperial polity.

Notes

1 I use the term 'political community' to indicate that it extends beyond the geographical territory currently associated with the nation state. In fact, empire is equally central to the emergence and development of understandings of citizenship in both Germany and France, though that is not my topic here. For a related discussion on France, see Bhambra, 2016a; and on Germany, see Bhambra, 2016b.

2 Similarly, the designation between the Old Commonwealth (the Dominions established on the basis of white settler colonization) and the New Commonwealth (the darker-skinned peoples over whom imperial rule was exerted) was itself a racial designation.
3 Home Office 2013. 'Immigration Patterns of Non-UK Born Populations in England and Wales in 2011' *Office for National Statistics* 17 December 2013, http://webarchive.nationalarchives.gov. uk/20160105160709/http://www.ons.gov.uk/ons/dcp171776_346219.pdfhttp://webarchive.nationalarchives.gov.uk/20160105160709/http://www.ons.gov.uk/ons/dcp171776_346219.pdf.

Bibliography

Bauböck, Rainer, ed. 1994. *From Aliens to Citizens: Redefining the Status of Immigrants in Europe.* Aldershot: Avebury.

Bhambra, Gurminder K. 2016a. 'Undoing the Epistemic Disavowal of the Haitian Revolution: A Contribution to Global Social Thought', *Journal of Intercultural Studies* 37 (1): 1–16.

Bhambra, Gurminder K. 2016b. 'Comparative Historical Sociology and the State: Problems of Method,' *Cultural Sociology*, 10 (3): 335–351.

Bhambra, Gurminder K. 2016c. '"Our Island Story": The Dangerous Politics of Belonging in Austere Times'. In *Austere Histories in European Societies: Social Exclusion and the Contest of Colonial,* ed. Stefan Jonsson and Julia Willen, 21–37. London: Routledge.

Brubaker, W. R. 1989. 'Introduction'. In *Immigration and the Politics of Citizenship in Europe and North America,* ed. W. R. Brubaker. Lanham, MD: University Press of America.

———. 1990. 'Immigration, Citizenship, and the Nation-State in France and Germany: A Comparative Historical Analysis', *International Sociology* 5 (4): 379–407.

Dummett, Ann 1994. 'The Acquisition of British Citizenship: From Imperial Traditions to National Definitions'. In *From Aliens to Citizens: Redefining the Status of Immigrants in Europe,* ed. Rainer Bauböck, Aldershot: Avebury.

Dummett, Ann, and Andrew Nicol. 1990. *Subjects, Citizens, Aliens, and Others: Nationality and Immigration Law.* London: Weidenfeld and Nicolson.

Emejulu, A. (2016) 'On the Hideous Whiteness of Brexit: Let Us Be Honest about Our Past and Our Present If We Truly Seek to Dismantle White. Supremacy'. Verso Books. Accessed 23 August 2016, www.versobooks.com/blogs/2733-on-the-hideous-whiteness-of-brexit-let-us-be-honest-about-our-past-and-our-present-if-we-truly-seek-to-dismantle-white-supremacy.

Hampshire, James. 2005. *Citizenship and Belonging: Immigration and the Politics of Demographic Governance in Postwar Britain.* Basingstoke: Palgrave.

Hansen, Randall. 2000. *Citizenship and Immigration in Post-War Britain: The Institutional Origins of a Multicultural Nation.* Oxford: Oxford University Press.

Holmwood, John. 2000. 'Europe and the "Americanization" of British Social Policy', *European Societies* 2 (4): 453–482.

Karatani, Rieko 2003. *Defining British Citizenship: Empire, Commonwealth and Modern Britain.* London: Frank Cass.

Mason, Paul 2016. 'The Global Order Is Dying: But It's an Illusion to Think Britain Can Survive without the EU,' *The Guardian,* 27 June. Accessed 23 August 2016. https://www.theguardian.com/commentisfree/2016/jun/27/global-order-britain-survive-eu-alternative-economic-model.

O'Toole, Fintan. 2016. 'Brexit Is Being Driven by English Nationalism: And It Will End in Self-Rule,' *The Guardian,* 19 June. Accessed: 23 August 2016. https://www.theguardian.com/commentisfree/2016/jun/18/england-eu-referendum-brexit.

Rosanvallon, Pierre. 2013. *Society of Equals.* Translated by Arthur Goldhammer. Cambridge, MA: Harvard University Press.

Shilliam, Robbie. 2016. 'Racism, Multiculturalism and Brexit', Robbie Shilliam Blog, July 2016. Accessed: 23 August, https://robbieshilliam.wordpress.com/2016/07/04/racism-multiculturalism-and-brexit/.

Steinmetz, G. 2007. *The Devil's Handwriting: Precoloniality and the German Colonial State in Qingdao, Samoa, and Southwest Africa*. Chicago: University of Chicago Press.

Stovall, Tyler 2006. 'Race and the Making of the Nation: Blacks in Modern France'. In *Diasporic Africa: A Reader*, edited by Michael A. Gomez. New York: New York University Press, 200–218.

Chapter Eight

GLOBALIZATION, NATIONALISM AND THE CHANGING AXES OF POLITICAL IDENTITY*

Colin Crouch

From the time of the French Revolution, mass politics has revolved around two core conflicts: that between preferences for more or less economic inequality, and that between conservative, authoritarian values and liberal ones. The main divisions among political parties in most countries fit into this frame, but we have become accustomed to seeing the former, raising issues of redistributive taxation, the welfare state and the role of trade unions as the senior partner. In Western Europe, if not in the United States, this has become even more the case as organized religion, the main historical carrier of social conservatism, has declined in importance.

This situation is challenged by the growing prominence of a chain of partly associated, partly quite independent, forces: economic globalization, immigration, refugees and the assertion of Islamic identities, which includes terrorism as its extreme. Together these reassert the old struggle between authoritarian conservatism and liberalism. Many people feel that everything familiar to them is being threatened, that they are being confronted with decisions, cultural artefacts and the presence among them of persons, all coming from outside their familiar and trusted sphere. They seek security by trying to exclude the forces and people that are doing this to them. Most affected are those whose own working lives give them little control in any case, and who are accustomed to the security that comes from the enforcement of rules that exclude troubling diversity. This response takes various forms. Many Russians become both highly nationalistic and also stress their homophobia. Many people in the Islamic world assert their religion (which is here far more important than nationality as a symbol of a preglobalized past) and impose strict dress codes on women. Many Americans not only become fearful of Mexican immigrants and Islamic terrorists but also become agitated about abortion. A more general social conservatism, most powerfully embodied in deep-rooted feelings around sexuality, mixes with xenophobia to produce new social supports for the traditional, not the neo-liberal, Right.

Europe, especially Western Europe, has been a partial exception. The final great battles of the 1970s in Catholic lands over contraception, divorce and finally abortion petered out, the churches, the main bearers of European social conservatism, became weak and in many cases often liberal in their social attitudes. There are today few supports for general authoritarian conservatism, and matters have narrowed down more closely to immigration and the following chain: the European Union (EU) is a supernational force that suppresses traditional national identities. In particular, it brings immigrants with unfamiliar cultures and languages; it is difficult to distinguish immigrants from refugees, who come in alarming numbers from even more unfamiliar cultures; and since these refugees are Muslims, they are likely to include terrorists who will try to kill us.

Against these beliefs and fears stands a liberal, inclusionary mindset that sees in globalization and multiculturalism a series of opportunities for a richer life, more varied cultural experiences and perhaps new possibilities for individual advancement.

A Brief History of Political Identity

To put this confrontation into context, we need to understand how it happened in the first place that ordinary people in the late nineteenth and early twentieth centuries, whose daily lives were very remote from big political issues, ever came to have political identities. It occurred as they found that aspects of their social identities, which they understood very well, were engaged in struggles over inclusion and exclusion in voting and other political rights. Depending on one's social position, one's identity was implicated in either demands to be included or demands to exclude others. Class and property ownership, religion and occasionally ethnicity (in Europe normally with reference to Jews, in the United States African American people) were the key identities around which these struggles revolved. By the end of World War II and after considerable bloodshed, the concept of universal adult citizenship had become accepted in almost all advanced economies. Spain and Portugal remained outside the consensus until the mid-1970s. Greece flitted in and out. In Central and Eastern Europe a very backhanded kind of universalism dominated, where universal inclusion came to mean universal exclusion except for a small communist party elite, but in general in the West, politics became peaceful and more or less democratic.

Once universal citizenship was achieved, those identities forged in struggles to achieve or prevent citizenship began to lose their raison d'être, but so deeply rooted were they that paradoxically they became the basis of democratic electoral politics. Over time they could do this not as direct memory but only as memories of parents' and grandparents' experiences. These necessarily faded, and in any case many people moved away from the social locations of their parents and grandparents. Democracy therefore began to depend for its vigour on forces that its very achievement had weakened. Their decline was reinforced by three major changes. First came the rise of the post-industrial economy and the creation of many occupations that have no resonance with the struggles of the past, and whose practitioners cannot easily relate their occupational identities to political allegiance at all. Class declined as a reliable source of political identity. Second, (in Europe but not the United States) religious adherence declined, and along with it both the power of the identity struggles surrounding it and general conflicts over authoritarianism versus liberalism. Finally, the use of ethnicity or nationality as identity resources in partisan struggles had been rendered horrifying to most politicians and ordinary people, partly as a result of the two World Wars and their demonstration of the destructive force of nationalism, and partly through knowledge of the Holocaust and the passions that had lain behind it. A nationalistic fringe continued in some countries, and the separate issue of racial entitlements to citizenship continued to flourish in the United States until the 1960s, but in general this became a no-go area in political conflict.

We should not puzzle at declining voting turnout and even more strongly declining identification with political parties once we appreciate that a strong interest in politics by the mass of citizens who have no chance of being politically effective needs social supports, and that those bequeathed to us by the struggles of the past have declined in salience. There has now been such a general loosening of ties between parties and voters that it has increasingly seemed inappropriate to include a discussion of voting behaviour within a discussion of identities. Does voting for a party, even repeated voting for it, necessarily imply an 'identity' with it any more than frequent purchase of a brand of soap implies an identity with the firm making the soap? Certainly, election campaigns increasingly resemble advertising campaigns for products, suggesting that parties do indeed consider that they bond with voters no differently from the way producers of goods bond with customers.

But this may now be changing, as economic globalization and its broader consequences start to reproduce social identities with powerful political potential. Central is revived national consciousness. While the great majority of politicians had for decades abjured using national identity in party conflict, there was no reason for them not to use it as a non-conflictual rallying call, since after all their role is to care for the nation. As a result national sentiment has been left lying around in popular consciousness, available for other purposes if occasion arose. Globalization, immigration, refugees and terrorism provide such occasions. Meanwhile, memories of the appalling consequences of the political use of nationalism in the first half of the twentieth century are fading. Nation is strengthening as a political force, while class and religion (unless the latter becomes implicated in conflict around Islam and therefore absorbed into nationalism) are declining.

The turnaround can be seen most clearly in parts of Central Europe. The political implications of class identities had been stood on their head under state socialism, and national identity remains the only strong link that people can feel to their polity. This helps explain the puzzle of the Czech Republic, which has suddenly become the most Europhobic country in Europe after the UK. The country has benefited more than any other from the EU, which has provided its modern infrastructure, a safe framework for the divorce from Slovakia, an easy channel for the German and other investment that has equipped an advanced economy and a base for trading with the rest of the world that the infant country would otherwise have had to create from scratch. Then the EU asked for some payback, putting pressure on the Czechs to help bear the burden of Middle Eastern refugees arriving on the coasts of Greece and Italy. Czechs – whose nationalism historically never hurt anyone but has been a badge of resistance against various forms of foreign domination – suddenly became responsive to the wave of anti-foreigner feeling sweeping through Europe.

One major, unexpected result of these developments is that the old predominant conflict axis around inequality and redistribution is itself becoming interpreted through nationalism rather than through class politics. The new nationalist movements nearly always include the global financial elite in their attacks. Many observers were surprised when there were relatively few mass expressions of anger after the 2008 financial crisis. We can now understand why. For ordinary non-political people to take any kind of action, including voting, against powerful forces they need some confidence-boosting assurance that they are part of something wider, something rooted in a strong social identity. Given the decline of class, only national identity has been available to give them that assurance. All contemporary xenophobic movements, from Donald Trump in the United States and Marine Le Pen in France to Geert Wilders in the Netherlands and Norbert Hofer in Austria, link their attacks on immigrants and refugees to those on the national elites implicated in the financial crisis. In turn, some protest movement that began as non-xenophobic opponents of elites, like il Movimento Cinque Stelle in Italy, find that they can get more traction if they include resentment at refugees in their rhetoric. Groups like the UK Independence Party in the UK or Alternative für Deutschland, which started life as critics of the EU, have found success by responding to fears around immigrants and Muslims. The challenge to powerful elites is hereby made safe, because it is enfolded in attacks on the weaker symbols of globalization. One might be frightened to kick a strong man, but one might kick what one believes to be his dog.

In a recent *Guardian* article, Martin Jacques claimed that the successful Brexit campaign and various other instances of widespread support for populist movements around the Western world constituted the return of class politics in general and a political reassertion of the working class in particular.[1] This was wistful thinking. Outside Greece, Spain and possibly Scotland, the new populism is precisely *not* articulating itself as class movements but as nationalistic, anti-immigrant, anti-refugee – quite apart from the fact that a majority of Brexit voters were comfortably off Conservative voters in southern England.

The Social Supports of Multiculturalism

Is nationalism therefore set to trump all other political forces, as its deeply rooted emotions come up against little more than voting behaviour of the soap-buying kind? Are persons holding liberal opinions anything more than randomly scattered individuals? Joseph Stalin invented the term 'rootless cosmopolitans' to stigmatize Jews, but the general idea that cosmopolitanism or a positive approach to multiculturalism implies rootlessness or normlessness is widespread. Some recent research suggests otherwise, providing evidence that liberal attitudes are associated with particular social locations.

The starting point is the work of a Swiss sociologist, Daniel Oesch.[2] He became dissatisfied with the idea of an undifferentiated middle class used in so much academic as well as popular discussion, given that the category was coming to mean the broad majority of occupational positions in the advanced economies. He proposed that social and political attitudes were formed not just by the positions people occupied in organizational hierarchies (class) but also by the kinds of work tasks on which they were engaged. He distinguished three of these: technical (for example, manufacturing), administrative (for example, banks, public bureaucracies), interpersonal (for example, public services). If these categories were combined with hierarchical position, he found that one could account for differences in, say, voting behaviour among those occupying middle-class positions.

Oesch's idea was applied to issues of direct relevance to us here by two German political scientists working in the United States, Herbert Kitschelt and Philipp Rehm.[3] Gathering data from all Western member states of the EU, they examined typical differences in attitudes among people working in different hierarchical positions and on Oesch's different types of tasks along the three dimensions that I have used here: inequality and redistribution; the role of authority versus liberty; and immigration. The first of these relates to the inequality axis, the other two to the authoritarian versus liberalism axis. Unsurprisingly, they found that people at the upper and middle levels of hierarchies in all types of task held less egalitarian views than those in lower positions, though senior and middle-ranking persons in interpersonal services were considerably less inegalitarian than the others. Those at higher and middle levels in all work tasks had liberal attitudes on both general authoritarianism and immigration, though there were differences. The most liberal were professionals in interpersonal services, then those engaged in technical tasks and least so those in administration. Those at the lowest levels of hierarchies held illiberal views on both dimensions, and egalitarian views on the third dimension. These findings held true after controlling for whether people worked in the private or public sectors, or whether they were male or female.

Without more detailed research it is difficult to know to what extent people with certain social attributes are drawn towards working at particular tasks, or working at particular types of tasks leads people to develop the attitudes in question. From the finer details of Oesch's and Kitschelt and Rehm's work it emerges that the more people have discretion in their work tasks and work directly, face to face, with other human persons, the more liberal and inclusive they are, while the more their own work follows rules and routines in impersonal contexts, the more they support authoritarianism and exclusion. There does not seem to be any important difference between attitudes to immigrants and those on general issues of authority. For example, people who believe that immigration should be restricted are also likely to believe that school discipline should be tougher. This finding is supported by the analysis of social attitudes of Brexit and Trump supporters made by Eric Kaufmann[4]. He found that both sets of voters were considerably more likely than their compatriots to believe that it was more important that a child be 'well mannered' than 'considerate'.

It seems clear that attitudes on issues of authority and liberty are not just personal whims but socially rooted. The Brexit referendum similarly revealed sociological regularities. Young, particularly female, well-educated people living in large cities were more likely to vote to remain in the EU. Older, mainly male persons in both declining industrial cities and prosperous provincial areas not much touched by the new economy tended to vote to leave. The politics of this question is more complex in the British case than elsewhere. Whereas the Brexit campaign played on fears of foreigners and implicitly encouraged isolationist tendencies, the purpose of the ministers involved in negotiating the UK's future economic place in the world seems to be to expose the country to intensified global competitive pressure. How they will eventually reconcile that with their mass supporters is a very interesting question, but beyond our concerns here. Most important is to recognize that openness to multiculturalism and internationalism have become deeply felt, socially grounded beliefs among those parts of contemporary populations whose work and other aspects of social location lead them to reject exclusion and value inclusiveness. This determined cosmopolitanism might be based on a positive appreciation of being enriched by engagement with other cultures or on a desire to be free of constraints on individual freedom. In either case, it is necessary to note that the revival of exclusionary nationalism is not the only popular development in contemporary politics. A major cleavage is opening between two sets of deeply held attitudes.

Long-Term Implications

These changes will have long-term and unpredictable consequences for all main political forces in advanced societies. The biggest challenge is to the alliance of neo-liberals and conservatives, currently the world's dominant political formation, expressing the inegalitarian end of the inequality and redistribution axis. Hegemonic as the economic ideology of an international elite, neo-liberalism is rarely a powerful force in democratic party politics. When it appears virtually alone in a party's identity, that party is usually very small (as with the German Free Democrats). More normally it appears within conservative parties, as with the UK Conservatives or US Republicans. But classic European democratic conservatism is weakening alongside its former religious supports. Its parties then face a strong temptation to rediscover the nationalism that is part of their heritage and become part of the new xenophobia. They can do this either in coalitions or deals with far-right parties (as in Scandinavia) or through shifts within the party (as with British Conservatives). But this threatens the heart of the neo-liberal project, which is globalizing and highly cosmopolitan. So far the tension has been even more severe in the United States, where the Christian Right is far stronger than in most of Europe. The Republican Party is being torn apart between the neo-liberals who have dominated it for years through their billionaire backers and the protectionist nationalism represented by Trump. Neo-liberalism and conservatism are allies when the main conflict axis is that around inequality and redistribution. If that is gradually replaced by one that sets liberalism and a nationalist conservatism against each other, they stand at opposite poles.

Moderate conservatives do not necessarily follow the nationalist path. Using their central position in most political systems, they can achieve simultaneous accommodations with the two main rival forms of liberalism, neo-liberalism and social democracy. One sees this most clearly in German Christian Democracy – in the country where the nationalist option is seen as most dangerous. It was also there in the currently defeated Cameron–Osborne wing of British Conservatism.

Neo-liberals also have the option of shifting to the left by making compromises on the inequality axis, if that axis is being dwarfed by that over conservatism–liberalism. There are certainly precedents. Tony Blair's New Labour, Gerhard Schroeder's Neue Mitte SPD and Bill Clinton's New Democrats have all been examples, as are today Matteo Renzi's Democratici. These may seem uncomfortable antecedents, but arguably the largest social change in recent times, the move towards gender equality, has been a shared neo-liberal/social-democratic, anti-conservative project. When, following the financial crisis, the Organization for Economic Cooperation and Development (OECD) and the International Monetary Fund (IMF) began to resile from their earlier neo-liberal policy stances, they were motivated mainly by the risks being posed by growing US inequality in terms of mass consumption.[5] In the wake of the Brexit vote, some global investment advisers went further and began to worry whether growing inequality was not nourishing xenophobic resentment against globalization. How far are neo-liberals willing to accept redistribution and strong welfare states in order to safeguard their other achievements?

Social democrats have their own crises. As the manual working class declines in size, they reluctantly face the reality that they will never again be the assured representatives of the biggest fraction of society. Instead they fight for their share of that large middle mass of the post-industrial world. Thanks to Oesch's analysis, we can see that this mass is no longer just the conservative bourgeoisie of the past but also includes, particularly among those engaged in interpersonal work tasks, the new constituency of the Left, though where voting systems give them the chance, they often prefer environmentalist and other non-social democratic forms of the Left. These people are primarily liberal, though also favourable to redistribution, and there is growing tension between them and the old working class as the conservatism–liberalism axis grows in importance. Can social democrats reassert the priority of the inequality axis to hold their coalition together?

David Goodhart,[6] Wolfgang Streeck[7] and some other observers have pointed out that the social democratic welfare state was an essentially national institution, rooted in people's sense of shared membership in a national community. The idea is expressed most clearly in the Swedish idea of the welfare state as *folkshemmet*, the place where people can feel at home. These meanings could be stretched to include small numbers of immigrants, but to how many? Is the US aversion to a strong welfare state a reflection of its cultural heterogeneity? Thinking on these lines leads some to seek a national social democracy, which requires severe limitations on immigration, a rejection of liberalism and, in the case of European countries, withdrawal from the EU.

Political clocks cannot be put back. The great welfare states developed under the aegis of a benign form of national identity that was not directed against outsiders. The most advanced welfare states developed in open trading nations – Scandinavia, Germany, the Netherlands, the UK. That world cannot be recaptured. To assert the limitation of social citizenship to 'real' nationals now can no longer be the *folkshem* of a people who just happen to be ethnically homogenous, but becomes symbolized by the demand of the Front National that rights be limited to *français de la souche* (best translated broadly as 'true born French'), requiring active exclusion of those deemed to be outsiders. Non-aggressive nationalism is still possible in places like Scotland or Greece, where resentment against external domination does not require the victimization of immigrants and refugees. Elsewhere it has become very difficult to sustain.

Also, free trade is now nested in a regime with global rules, not a series of national decisions to choose how much free trade they want to accept. In this context the EU constitutes an opportunity to extend social policy alongside free trade, expressing the pooled sovereignty of its members, rather than the loss of sovereignty implied by the pure free trade of the World Trade Organization.

But is the direction of pooled sovereignty towards the construction of transnational social policy possible with the current politics of the EU? Today's European tragedy has two components. First, Europeans are being asked to absorb large numbers of dispossessed people from the other side of the Mediterranean. Second, the EU is coping with both this and the free movement of labour from Central Europe at a moment when EU policy makers and the European Court of Justice have experienced an extreme neo-liberal turn, rendering it unwilling to provide the social policy support that these large movements of people require. The first was not Europe's fault; the second it is fully within the power of its policy makers and jurists to change. This is again dependent on some rethinking by European neo-liberals, which the withdrawal of the UK might make easier.

No political family can look forward to a comfortable future. The outcomes of these tensions and their explosive consequences for the main contemporary political currents will be very varied. A particularly important variable is the balance between the electoral (democratic) component of political systems and that which concerns lobbying, the role of big money and bargaining power of global corporations. The latter is probably more important in shaping our politics, though since it is largely invisible, we can say least about it. It is the arena within which neo-liberalism mainly operates as a political force. Ironically, it is likely to be here that alliances between neo-liberals and social democrats are forged. It may be easier for neo-liberalism to soften in this non-democratic but dominant part of political life, because change involves rational calculation by small numbers of self-interested individuals and corporations, not the deep feelings of large numbers of people. One can already see the framework for this elite compromise in the changing approaches of the OECD and IMF. As international organizations, these can never share in the new xenophobia. Since the late 1970s they have helped forge the neo-liberal hegemony and have been major protagonists of an open global trading system, but their recent fears about the impact of growing US inequality on mass consumption, and the role of big money in political lobbying marks a major shift. The OECD has also started to change its earlier hostility to the work of trade unions and collective bargaining. This could be the start of a new neo-liberal/social democratic historic compromise.

In the electoral sphere much depends on the relative sizes of Oesch's different fractions of the middle class, on party structures and voting systems. The tensions within both conservative and social democratic parties as the relative importance of the two great axes of conflict changes can be most fruitfully released in systems where new parties can form and then make various alliances. Electoral systems of the British and in particular US kind force everything to remain within existing parties, sometimes contorting them out of all meaning. Within all this complexity, generational change and economic restructuring seem to favour the growth of various kinds of liberalism, while every new horror emerging from the Middle East strengthens xenophobic nationalism.

Notes

* This article was first published in autumn 2016 in *Juncture*, the journal of politics and ideas of the Institute of Public Policy and Research (IPPR).

1 M. Jacques. 2016. 'The Death of Neoliberalism and the Crisis in Western Politics', *The Guardian*, 21 August.

2 D. Oesch. 2006. *Redrawing the Class Map*. Basingstoke: Palgrave Macmillan.

3 H. Kitschelt and P. Rehm. 2014. 'Occupations as a Site of Political Preference Formation', *Comparative Political Studies* 47 (12): 1670–1706.

4 Kaufmann, E. 'Trump and Brexit: Why it's again NOT the economy, stupid', http://blogs.lse.ac.uk/politicsandpolicy/trump-and-brexit-why-its-again-not-the-economy-stupid/, November 2016.]

5 See, in particular, Organization for Economic Cooperation and Development (OECD). 2011. *Divided We Stand*. Paris: OECD.

6 D. Goodhart. 2013. *The British Dream: Successes and Failures of Post-War Immigration*. London: Atlantic.

7 W. Streeck. 2015. 'The Rise of the European Consolidation State', *MPIfG Discussion Paper 15/1*. Cologne: Max Planck Institute for the Study of Societies.

Chapter Nine

A DIVIDED NATION IN A DIVIDED EUROPE: EMERGING CLEAVAGES AND THE CRISIS OF EUROPEAN INTEGRATION

Gerard Delanty

Introduction

The startling result of the referendum of June 23, 2016, at first defies explanation. How could a relatively prosperous country with a fairly stable state system act against its economic and political interests? Do people willfully act against their interests? Do they even know what their interests are? The Brexit phenomenon has been widely viewed as the biggest crisis for the UK since 1945. In bringing the country to the brink of a crisis of governability and marking a new milestone in the history of the post–World War II project of European integration, it has also brought about a new political context, in which the populist anti-immigration Right has made large gains, and a climate of considerable political uncertainty as well as economic decline. The circumstances by which the referendum was set up are of course the primary causal factors in accounting for Brexit, as are the failure in political leadership in allowing a referendum to take place on a complex issue that referenda are ill-equipped to deal with. Brexit is also an interesting sociological case study of major societal change and institutional transition.

The aim of the present chapter is to explore the sociological ramifications of the referendum, which I argue is hugely significant. The fact that the outcome with a narrow majority of approximately 1.2 million could easily have gone the other way—that is, if just over 640,000 had voted remain—does not detract from that the fact that 17.4 million voted leave (51.9 percent). In fact, the narrow split—51.9 percent against 48.1 percent—has served to enhance the magnitude of Brexit, which if implemented will entail major change and impose the will of one-half of the population on the other. Referenda, unlike elections, are not just cases of simple majorities determining outcomes. There are many reasons why this is the case, and it is not the aim of this chapter to examine the constitutional questions that Brexit raises (see the chapters by Chris Thornhill and Antje Wiener in this volume), but one point must be noted: election outcomes are reversible at the next election. Referenda generally are not reversible, however, and in the case of Brexit a more or less irreversible systemic course of action will ensue that will almost certainly set the historical clock back by several decades. Societies may undergo societal learning, but they are also prone to regressions.

Had the result gone the other way, which obviously could easily have happened, or if the government faces either a successful legal challenge or Parliament does not ratify the outcome, for the purpose of this chapter the referendum outcome is still sociologically interesting. The figures for leave are sufficiently large to be accounted for and in the context of a situation in which extreme right-wing politics and an increase in hate crimes are on the rise, it is all the more significant and, I argue in this chapter, an expression of a new kind of cleavage. The thesis of this chapter is that Brexit is an expression of new societal cleavages that in the case of the UK have been amplified by a number of factors that are of a more British-specific nature and which have a lot to do with the singularity of English nationalism. The new cleavages, which are European wide, reflect a new division in national societies across cultural, social, and political lines between what might be referred to as nationals and cosmopolitans, that is, those who are nation centered and those who are not. Brexit, made in the UK, is not British: the Brexit phenomenon from a sociological perspective is an expression of societal trends that are not specifically the outcome of British exceptionality, even if the UK is a particularly striking example of emerging social divisions and patterns.

The first section discusses the theme of divided societies and possible explanations for Brexit. The second examines old and new cleavages. The third section discussed new contradictions of capitalism and democracy and reflects on the implications of Brexit for European integration.

Explaining Brexit: Divided Societies

One explanation frequently given for Brexit is that it is an expression of anti-austerity politics and that in voting leave many people were voting against the official position of the government. There is clearly some basis to this view that the masses rebelled against the elites, but I argue that it is not sufficient to account for the magnitude of the leave vote and for the dynamics of change. Obviously in a referendum there is only a yes/no option and in many such instances there is an antigovernment protest vote, which when unpacked will reveal a broad coalition of often contrary political positions. There can be no doubt that the leave vote included a resounding "no" to the political mainstream and to the official position of the government. Indeed anecdotal evidence suggests many people voted leave secure in the knowledge that the remain voters were more numerous. Notwithstanding such paradoxes that result when people attempt to reconcile self-interest with adherence to a principle, there can be little doubt that protest against austerity politics was not the main causal factor. Indeed, much of the leave campaign was fought on the claim that all political ills come from the undemocratic and bureaucratic European Union (EU). The political debate gave almost no consideration to the fact that austerity politics derives from the neoliberal policies of the government of the UK. The UK is not Greece and not in thrall to something like the neoliberal regime of the Troika. The UK may be Germany's largest trading partner, but it is not ruled by Berlin. In any case, the government is more or less intact, despite a shift in the cadres at the top. There is no sign of a change in domestic policies, aside from Scotland. The Conservative Party has been much strengthened and has apparently overcome its major internal split. The

UK Independence Party (UKIP) in achieving its purpose has lost its raison d'être, and the main opposition party has imploded. It is difficult to see in all of this a revolt of the less well off against the elites.

A second possible explanation is a more historical one and worth considering. This is the argument of British exceptionality, namely the view that Britain was never really European and that its island mentality and history has always led it into a position of conflict with Europe. The leave campaign made much of this account of Britain's relation with a despotic Europe. I believe this is wrong and that on the contrary Britain has always had a strong and positive relationship with Europe. This can be illustrated by Winston Churchill's "majestic circles" in which Britain is located: the Commonwealth, the Atlantic alliance, and Europe. In the Churchillian vision, the UK is firmly part of Europe. Its history and culture are European, and its Euroskepticism is also European. English nationalism is, of course, a potent force and was never fully challenged by the European currents (see Kumar, 2010, 2015). British political modernity was shaped by an axis that cuts across some of the main political traditions, an insular nationalist one and a liberal European one. As I argue below, the outcome of the referendum has in fact confirmed the strong European character of Britain as well as bolstered the inward-looking nationalist current. The anti-EU current, I argue, is to be largely explained by factors other than deep-seated nationalism, but when infused with right-wing English nationalism gave particular potency to the drive for Brexit. In this context I would discount the specificity of British factors as the most sociologically salient, for instance, the fact that the main center-right party has a significant minority of Members of Parliament (MPs) sympathetic to the anti-Europe and antimigration UKIP, or the cultural ethos of superiority displayed by elements of the British political elite, the remnants of imperial nostalgia, or the power of the right-wing tabloid press. The historical failure of the British state to develop a viable model of federalism to solve its regional divides should also not be excluded. While the specificity of British political culture may indeed account for the balance tipping in favor of the vote to leave, it does not account for the phenomenon more generally.

Another line of argument is that Brexit is a reversal of the usual logic of choices driven by interests. Instead, it would appear that identity overruled interest. How else can it be explained that in those parts of England and Wales that most depended on EU subsidies the leave vote was significantly higher? Clearly economic interests were not factors, and the remain campaign, in concentrating on economic advantage, did not help its cause. But does this mean that instead people voted leave for reasons of identity? While it is difficult to see how economic interests could have led people to vote leave, it is also not apparent that leave identities were sufficiently strong or coherent. As mentioned, the leave vote was a very broad spectrum of positions that was not underpinned by a strong identity. Right-wing elements in the Conservative Party and left-wing elements in the Labour Party could both embrace the same cause that defined the political ambitions of UKIP. So I do not see identity as a primary force, except in one case: the leave vote in Northern Ireland was mostly due to the Unionist voting population, for whom their primary identity is the unity of the UK.[1]

There are clearly complex questions on how people understand their interests and how they perceive external threats, such as the view that the EU is tending toward a suprastate and that Turkey will join the Union, leading to an influx of migrants into the UK. Unpacking objective fact and subjective perception in a situation in which perceptions rapidly become facts is not easy. The general trend until now is that there is widespread public support for the EU so long as the EU appears to serve national interests (Bruter, 2005). It would appear that public perceptions of the EU have changed and that such changes are not necessarily due to a change in the nature of European integration as such. The extent to which such external changes might be a contributory factor will be considered in the third section of this chapter. The presumption for now will be that such developments are marginal in explaining Brexit.

A sociologically more plausible explanation for Brexit is that it is an expression of divided societies. A pronounced current in many parts of the world is toward the internal fragmentation of the nation into two worlds, those who are benefiting from globalization and those who are not. Depending on where in the world one looks, these differences will be small or very great. The United States is one of the most vivid examples of a deeply divided nation. The Donald Trump presidency is a clear demonstration of how deep the divisions lie. Ideological positions between Republicans and Democrats are so far apart that they amount to major cultural visions of the nation and world (see, for example, Campbell, 2016). In the past year a deep political divide has arisen in Brazil around the indictment of the president and the seizure of power by right-wing politicians seeking to escape corruption charges. Turkey, especially since the 2016 attempted coup, is also a graphic example of deep cultural and political divisions. Similar tendencies are evident in Russia, where the nationalist trend is stronger than the cosmopolitan countercurrent. All such divisions are underpinned by forces that have their roots in the democratic process. Democracy, rather than being only an integrative force, can also be a means of division if not of societal polarization. Europe is not immune to these developments, which oscillate from division to polarization. I argue that Brexit is an expression of this phenomenon and that, while having British characteristics, it is a European-wide phenomenon that fits into a wider global pattern.

In Europe the nation-state has for the most part been the basis of European integration and, with its capacity to offer relative solidarity and cohesion since 1945, it has provided the EU with the basic structures for its project of integration. The early decades of European integration had little to do with democracy, but once issues of democratization were opened up, it was inevitable that they would also entail a questioning of the very notion of European integration. This situation coupled with new divisions brought about by capitalism has led to multiple contradictions at the core of national and European levels of governance, even to the point that there may now be a new crisis of governability (Delanty, 2016). The result is that national culture and the national state have become severely fractured. Nowhere was this more vividly expressed than in the calamitous Brexit referendum.

Emerging Cleavages

The old cleavages in post-1945 Western European societies were defined by Right and Left, and generally underpinned by class politics. They thus took the form of capital versus labor. Since the 1980s, as the older industrial economies gave way to increasingly postindustrial ones, new cleavages emerged, adding to the existing ones and in part transforming them. These new cleavages have often been referred to as the new politics of class and reflected cultural issues rather than the older ones of labor versus capital (Eder, 1996). The rise of environmentalism and feminism were two major social movements that led to a change in the political cultures of late twentieth-century Europe around so-called postmaterial values. Many of these developments have been associated with the political values of the university-educated middle class and the new values of individuated life styles. This emerged at a time of major change in capitalism with the rise of neoliberalism and technocratic governance, on the one side, and on the other the declining power of older cultural traditions, for example, religion, and more generally cultural authoritarianism that rested on patriarchy and religion. In this context a new cleavage took shape, which did not replace the older class one but added a new level of political contestation around cultural politics. It can be described as a cleavage between radical cultural pluralism and neoliberal techno-conservatism (see O'Mahony, 2014).

Since around 2001, with 9/11 as a symbolic marker, a new range of cleavages arose and which were associated with the emergence of security agendas and the rise of the populist right and xenophobic nationalism. This led to a much more complicated mosaic of cultural and political divisions in European societies, with the old political parties in many cases challenged by new right-wing parties and no longer able to rely on the traditions sources of authority, religions, patriarchy, and deference to the upper class. The progressive cultural left was also challenged. Since the worldwide financial crisis and subsequent lurch to low-growth economies after 2008, pro and contra EU became an additional level of political contestation, and for the first time the very rationale of European integration was called into question. To put it simply, at the present time there are three main cleavages that structure the political–cultural field of Europe and shape the public sphere: there is, first, the still strong capital versus labor cleavage that still resolves around left versus right issues; second, there is the cleavage of radical cultural pluralism versus neoliberal techno-conservatism; and third, there is is the emerging cleavage of cosmopolitanism versus nationalism. The first two reflect the social critique and the cultural critique of capitalism and are largely to be contextualized within national settings (see Boltanski and Thévenot, 2006). The third cleavage, which is the main focus of this chapter, is driven, on the one side, by populist reaction to globalization and to radical cultural pluralism but also draws on right and left currents. On the other side is the diminishing influence of the national culture on many people whose habitus is increasingly more plural, if not hybrid, and whose lifeworld has been transformed by antiauthoritarian and postmaterial values. This value divergence is now very great and underpinned by different kinds of work.

It was against this background of multiple levels of division in a rapidly changing political environment that has also witnessed an increase in terrorist attacks in European cities, that the referendum of June 23, 2016, took place. It became clear only close to the end that it was a referendum not only on Britain in the EU but also about many other things. It also marked the point at which a new cleavage began to crystallize. This emerging cleavage could be described as one between the locals or nationals and cosmopolitans, between nation-centeredness and cosmopolitan pluralism. One the one side, there are those whose lifeworld is defined by the national state and the traditional markers of class. On the other side, there are those whose lifeworld has been significantly shaped by wider horizons than those of the national culture and who, while having class positions, do not identify with class as such or with class-based lifestyles. This second group will not only have been considerably Europeanized in terms of their lifestyle and habitus but will also be pro-European and highly mobile and urban (see Favell, 2008). Until now this cultural difference did not amount to a division as such and was overshadowed by the other cleavages. Moreover, as noted, attitudes toward the EU and more generally the spread of European identities have tended to be pragmatic rather than an expression of outright enthusiasm (see Herrmann et al., 2004). However, it is in moments of crisis that identities take root. Until June 2016 the European dimension of the identities of this second group were not in question. While EU membership was often claimed to be revisable, it was unthinkable for most people that Britain would leave the EU, and the Euroskeptical politicians were a minority within the Conservative Party. UKIP has succeeded in winning only one seat at Westminster.

The result of the Brexit referendum amplified the identities and values of this broadly pro-European group, whose assumptions about the world were suddenly challenged by a volatile medley of subterranean class politics, racist and xenophobic movements, and opportunistic politicians. The cosmopolitans were now united in a common front against the nationals, even though they are hardly a group in a politically clear-cut way. There are two main poles within the cosmopolitans: those with tangentially center-left and center-right inclinations. For many, the EU signals liberal individualism and is compatible with neoliberal love of globalization and the single market, while for others, the EU is an avenue for progressive politics, as reflected in human rights, the positive aspects of migration, environmentalism, and so on. Similarly, the ethos of the nationals cuts across left and right politics in its common distaste for radical cultural pluralism as exemplified by multiculturalism and migration. Islamophobia, anti-Semitism, and homophobia are the expressions of the new kind of cultural authoritarianism that is championed by the populist right. It would appear that this new cleavage of cosmopolitans versus nationals has considerably diminished the capital versus labor cleavage and has come to dominate political contestation in the public sphere.

Politically, then, the emerging cleavage can be defined in terms of (1) a stance on sovereignty, with European integration and more generally postnational politics viewed as threat to national sovereignty and (2) cultural pluralism and migration as an economic and cultural threat. In deeper cultural terms, the cleavage reflects a discord on the inherent value of the nation above all else. Brexit gave substance to this division, which has been mostly latent since it lacked a political event that might give it form. Cosmopolitanism has challenged the nation in ways that have mostly been latent. The public sphere is a conduit of many values and positions, which are often only latent. It takes a specific event, such as the referendum, to raise to a more conscious level of deliberation some of the latent currents, and as a consequence major reinterpretation occurs with new meanings attributed to older reference points, such as the idea of Europe or the notion of the nation. The intellectual and political elites all assumed a certain level of consensus on key issues that in the debate had a lesser focus for many than on hostility to cultural pluralism and the defining characteristics of the cosmopolitans.

In terms of social criteria, the outcome of the referendum offers fairly clear evidence of two large groupings, which I argue form the basis of an emerging cleavage. On the basis of the available information on the demographics of the voting areas, there are three striking and related patterns.[2] Leave and remain voters are noticeably defined in terms of education, professional occupation, and age. The second largely follows from the first. Areas with a high number of university-educated people tended to vote remain. This was also the case with professional occupations, with leave voters more numerous in low-income areas. Age was also a very significant factor. Far more young people voted remain than leave. It has also been observed that there were significantly higher leave voters in areas where large numbers of people do not have a passport. Not having a passport and thus not having traveled abroad in recent years correlates with cultural authoritarianism as expressed in hostility to other cultures.

Brexit, of course, also produced a strong regional divide and may herald the final breakup of the UK in the event of a second referendum in Scotland. However, the main force of the Brexit phenomenon is not a regional divide as such. Scottish independence and the subsequent end of the Union would undoubtedly be a hugely significant moment, not least for the implications it would have for Northern Ireland. However, unless and until such an event comes to pass, the regional dimension of Brexit is second to the emerging political–cultural cleavage, which certainly in Scotland plays out differently. Wales voted more or less along the same lines as England, and Northern Ireland voted unsurprisingly along partisan lines. Only in Scotland was there a strong pro-Europe vote, with 62 remain and 38 leave. The Scottish vote reflected the more general pattern in which age and education were the decisive forces, but certainly also Scottish specificity—which might be defined in terms of Scottish civic nationalism—and its generally pro-European inclination, some of which can be attributed to hostility to English nationalism. For these reasons, I argue that sociologically Brexit is an expression of a cultural cleavage that has taken an overt political form in an intensified conflict that cuts across all regions. Since the outcome has been a vote to leave, the defeated remain camp—the cosmopolitans—are now galvanized in their identity and in their opposition to those who voted leave. The result is that a latent cleavage has now surfaced as a pronounced division.

Does this mean the UK is a polarized society? The immediate aftermath of the referendum certainly suggested something more than a conflict over a divisive issue. In London, where the vote was overwhelming remain, somewhat unrealistically groups advocated the independence of London from the UK. In the medium to long term it obviously remains to be seen what the full implications are and how far reaching is the division within the country. The fact that neither side has a clear-cut political champion will undoubtedly undermine the capacity for political contestation. With the government apparently proceeding, however reluctantly, with the withdrawal of the UK from the

EU, the remain voters, despite having the support of the vast majority of MPs across the main parties, are politically silenced. For these reasons polarization may not necessarily ensue from the fact of a deeply cut cleavage. But a cleavage there is nonetheless. When the Brexit moment finally arrives—and at some point it will come to pass either one way or the other—the existing division may quite well develop into outright polarization that may be intensified by the eventual Scottish independence and a worsening economic situation.

My argument is that the new cleavage is an expression of major sociocultural and economic change and not that it derives explicitly from a political conflict as such. It is rather the case that the political conflict has drawn out the deep societal division that derives its force from divergent cultural processes and changing lifeworlds. As mentioned, the question of Europe was a relatively minor question for the British public, notwithstanding the fact that it had become an increasingly toxic issue within the Conservative party. UKIP arguably saw Europe as a trope for antimigration, and it can be anticipated that the party will evolve into a populist antimigration party, not least since it is unlikely that migration, which is demand driven, will simply vanish. The Brexit vote was motivated by the deepening of the cleavage between nationals and cosmopolitans. It gave voice to the predicament of the national sense of alienation with not only the political mainstream, but also their social and economic situation that has much to do with deindustrialization. The focus of much of this was migration, with which membership of the EU was associated. Underlying this focus on migration is a deep hostility to cultural pluralism. It is accompanied, on the other side of the now-divided fabric of the nation, by an increasingly frustrated body of cosmopolitans whose solidarity with the nationals has all but vanished.

There is nothing specifically British about this. However, what was different in the UK is that the EU was put to the test and failed. Other European countries could easily find themselves in a similar situation if a complex societal arrangement were put to the test in a referendum (for which no regulations were created concerning its constitutional status). Certainly the potent force of English nationalism made a difference, as did the incomplete decolonization of national consciousness. The relationship between elites and masses has changed everywhere due to new lines of division and a fundamental transformation of the European industrial societies in an era of hyper globalization and declining economic growth. The social and economic prospects of the working class and much of the middle class are no longer what they were in the 30 or so years after 1945. The very different positions and outlooks of the working class and the middle class can easily find common cause around issues such as migration and the EU, resulting in tirades against cultural pluralism and the reassertion of national sovereignty at a time when the notion is at best an anachronism. This is all occurring in the context of the declining power of the national culture to integrate an increasingly diverse society and when neoliberal regimes of techno-conservatism no longer offer a capacity for governance and in fact produce the context that leads to further contestation. Social and cultural differentiation has now reached such a point that it is no longer possible to say what defines British society. For these reasons it can be suggested that the strongest divisions today are within societies rather than between them. Brexit has both expressed and at the same time contributed to societal divisions, which, to sum up, play out along three lines: labor versus capital, radical cultural pluralism versus techno-conservatism, and cosmopolitanism versus national populism.

European Integration and Contradictions between Capitalism and Democracy

As a sociological phenomenon that is not specifically British, the term "Brexit" refers to an emerging cleavage that is present to varying degrees across European societies. The implications for the future of the EU are certainly significant, but it is unlikely that the EU will simply collapse into the specter of disintegration that Brexit signals at least for the UK. Yet, there can be no doubt that the project of European integration is at a critical point. British withdrawal, coupled with the ongoing crisis of Greece and the related systemic problems of the euro currency, the steady growth of xenophobic nationalism, the difficult relationship with Russia, and a volatile situation in Ukraine and Turkey along with the challenges of coping with the influx of large numbers of migrants from the Middle East are all a severe test for European integration. However, the integrative capacities of the EU should not be underestimated. In the 1980s the then-European Economic Community successfully integrated the southern European countries that had newly emerged from dictatorships and whose experience with parliamentary democracy was relatively limited. The eastern enlargement of the EU, which followed the German unification, was also relatively successful, despite a larger cultural difference. A greater problem is the post-2008 economic financial crisis, which has been exacerbated by the single currency and has led to a new division between the northern creditor countries and the southern debtor countries (Offe 2015). Despite the immense structural problems in solving the problems generated by the dysfunctional euro currency, which effectively locks much of the smaller and weaker economies into German capitalism, the Brexit phenomenon had different origins. This is not surprising since the UK is largely protected from the intractable problems of the single currency.

The changing nature of capitalism in Europe is clearly a factor in shaping the underlying conditions that underpin many of the problems of both the EU and of national societies. Through neoliberal orders of governance, an increasingly unregulated model of capitalism has become predominant and much of European integration is precisely a model for the opening of markets (see Streeck, 2014). This neoliberal model of integration as open markets has fueled Brexit fears, even if the causes are more likely to lie deep in the transformation of capitalism. It has enhanced the emerging cleavage between nationals and cosmopolitans. On the one side are those who are trapped within the social structures of decaying societies and declining economies and whose prospects are not served by increased integration. The fact that many areas of the UK heavily depended on EU support voted leave is a symptom of the social malaise that derives from a situation of social and economic decline. On the other side are those who through education and the mobility that it brings see their trajectory as less tied to the national community. In the case of the UK since June 24, this group is now increasingly denationalized. The paradox is that as a result of one momentum, the vision of an open

Europe is challenged by the reassertion of the national community, and from another and counter-momentum, the idea of Europe is affirmed. Cosmopolitanism has been in many ways strengthened by European integration, but so too have anticosmopolitan trends, which include increased xenophobic nationalism, homophobia, and hate crimes. Fligstein (2008) has analyzed a similar dynamic, which he sees as the source of a clash of identities that also take a generational form.

Capitalism was once the bedrock of European integration, which was originally conceived as a plan to integrate the economies of Europe. Its founders were driven by the desire for a lasting peace in Europe, especially between France and Germany. This utopian dream of a peaceful future for Europe was made possible by the booming postwar economies and the desire of the United States to tie Western Europe into its particular model of capitalism. Today capitalism in a postgrowth era no longer achieves this function, and not all benefit from wealth creation. Since 2008, new contradictions have become manifest between capitalism and democracy (see Delanty 2013, Offe 2015). Democratization has now become a major issue for the EU, which previously did not have to face such challenges and which has not offered any solutions to the post-2008 crisis.

The Brexit phenomenon is an interesting example of how democracy can challenge capitalism to the point of being an affront to the rule of capital. Capitalism and democracy form an uneasy balance, and for the greater part they tend to act upon each other. Capitalism must adjust to political orders in which democracy sets limits to economic forces, while democracy must also reconcile itself to the existence of capitalism (for example, through taxation, democracy can be enhanced and inequalities reduced). Democracy offers a critique of capitalism, but it also cannot exist without capitalism (in that while there are capitalist societies that are not democracies, there are no examples in modern society of democracies that are not capitalist). In a situation where social critique (emanating from the labor versus capital nexus) and the cultural critique (deriving from radical cultural pluralism) have been unable to bring about a fundamental transformation of capitalism, it is possible to see how the force of a democratic critique of capitalism can make considerable impact. However, in this case the target is as much the cultural critique, including the new cosmopolitan orientations, but due to its political impotence, in the end capitalism and the neoliberal cadres remain unscathed, even if they have to find technocratic solutions to Brexit.

To generalize, the post–World War II project of European integration sought the integration of capitalism in Europe, which it achieved through various positive and negative forms of what was largely systemic rather than integration. Social integration, including democracy, was achieved within the confines of the national welfare state. But it was inevitable that with the enhanced momentum toward integration that followed the Single Act (1986) and the consolidation of all previous integrative drives with the Maastricht Treaty in 1993 that problems of social integration would surface and challenge the dominance of systemic forms of integration, which could no longer rely on the bedrock of the national welfare state and its model of industrial capitalism.

What we are currently witnessing is a new contradiction between capitalism and democracy. The assertion of democracy voices a critique of capitalism and by implication a model of European integration that has given greater emphasis to capitalism in the form of the single market. The delicate balance of the era of European democratic capitalism is now more or less at an end. In the context of an emerging cleavage within European societies and the absence of a transnational political movement that could translate and mediate the different positions, we can expect to see increased divisions within many countries. It is one of many paradoxes of the current situation that it is only the populist right who are mobilizing the power of democracy in ways that are bringing about significant change.

The referendum of June 23 was a misguided attempt by the UK government to solve what was internal strife within the governing Conservative Party. A referendum is a blunt plebiscitarian instrument to make a democratic decision. Unless the rules are tightly defined and checks and balance put in place, undemocratic outcomes can easily be produced, in particular if the proposal is to end an existing arrangement rather than create a new one.

As an organ of popular democracy, a referendum is nonetheless an exercise of democracy, which in the case of Brexit, by taking the political mainstream off guard, led to a far-reaching critique of capitalism. British capitalism has been hit at a time when the national economy was under duress following the post-2008 crisis. This may have been a hollow victory for democracy, which is very unlikely to put in place an alternative economic model to the austerity regime.

Conclusion

The Brexit phenomenon is of significant interest to sociologists. It is difficult to think of another example of a country in recent times that through democratic means has undergone major systemic transformation whereby some four decades of institutional formation must be reversed. The case of the peaceful breakup of Czechoslovakia is a possible example of a process of institutional decoupling. The transition from state socialism to market societies and democracy in the other Warsaw Pact countries is, of course, an example of major societal transformation and in which popular democratization was an active element. However, in all these cases there was a prior collapse of the central state and in the external hegemon. Other examples might be the exit from colonization, but with the exceptions of Spain in the 1890s or Portugal in 1974 it is difficult to think of an example that led to the collapse of political authority or major societal transformation in the former imperial centers. The only country to have decoupled from the EU was Greenland in 1985, but this was a relatively simple level of dedifferentiation in view of the fishing-based economy and the tiny population of some fifty thousand within the Danish realm. The magnitude of the withdrawal of the UK from the EU is in itself a significant example of an attempt at societal dedifferentiation through an excess of democracy.

Perhaps its long-lasting legacy will be the contrary logic of denationalization, since in invoking the sovereign nation and the affirmation of a national Us versus Them, the national imaginary has been put to an even greater test. The belief that we are one nation was immediately buried the day after the referendum when the British public woke up to see that whatever might have bound the nation together has now disintegrated. The paradox in this is that Britain may now be a more Europeanized country due to the heightened politicization of the pro-Europe remain voters. The flip side is that it has also embellished xenophobic nationalism both in the UK and in Europe more generally.

One of the challenges for the future—for the UK it will be a very distant future—will be to overcome the emerging cleavage that sees societies moving in contrary directions. Democracy is central to that task, but it must be rescued from the populist right who have effectively fueled their destructive campaigns by widespread and unfounded fears about migration. It will be one of the most important challenges for a future progressive European left movement to gain possession of the democratic critique of capitalism. For this to be possible, cosmopolitans and nationals will need to find common ground. While it is unlikely that what is left of the nation-state can provide this, it is one platform, along with the shared European heritage of opposition to despotism and the rule of the market. The defense of Europe cannot be only in the name of mobility or, its flip side, the single market. The Brexit phenomenon is a call for cosmopolitans to find alternative arguments for the future of Europe. Whatever shape this may take, it is one that cannot afford to abandon entirely the category of the nation. It may then be that a new accord is needed between the idea of Europe and its nations.

Notes

1   It is possible that, in voting against their immediate economic interests—in the case of those rural areas of England and Wales dependent on the EU—their long-term interests might be served by the UK leaving the EU. However, the economic rationale by which that would be achieved is implausible in political terms and difficult to translate into interests.
2   I am freely drawing from various newspaper articles on voting trends. A particularly useful article is in the *Financial Times* blog, June 24, 2016, http://blogs.ft.com/ftdata/2016/06/24/brexit-demographic-divide-eu-referendum-results/

References

Boltanski, L., and E. Chiapello. 2012. *The New Spirit of Capitalism*. London: Verso.
Boltanski, L., and L. Thévenot. 2006. *Economies of Worth*. Princeton, NJ: Princeton University Press.
Bruter, M. 2005. *Citizens of Europe? The Emergence of a Mass European Identity*. London: Palgrave.
Campbell, J. 2016. *Polarized: Making Sense of a Divided America*. Princeton, NJ: Princeton University Press.
Delanty, G. 2013 *Social Theory in a Changing World: Conceptions of Modernity*. Cambridge: Polity.
Delanty, G. 2016. "A Crisis of Governability? Why the Brexit Referendum Undermines Democracy and Must Be Declared Illegitimate," *Studies in Social and Political Thought*. https://ssptjournal.wordpress.com/.
Eder, K. 1996. *The New Politics of Class*. London: Sage.
Favell, A. 2008. *Eurostars and Eurocities: Free Movement and Mobility in an Integrating Europe*. Oxford: Blackwell.
Fligstein, N. 2008. *Euroclash: The EU, European Identity, and the Future of Europe*. Oxford: Oxford University Press.
Herrmann, R. K., T. Risse, and M. B. Brewer, eds. 2004. *Transnational Identities: Becoming European in the EU*. Lanham, MD: Rowman & Littlefield.

Kumar, K. 2010. *The Making of English National Identity*. Cambridge: Cambridge University Press.
———. 2015. *The Idea of Englishness: English Culture, National Identity and Social Thought*. London: Routledge.
O'Mahony, P. 2014. "Europe, Crisis, and Critique: Social Theory and Transnational Society," *European Journal of Social Theory* 17 (3): 238–257.
Offe, C. 2015, *Europe Entrapped*. Cambridge: Polity.
Streeck, W. 2014. *Buying Time: The Delayed Crisis of Democratic Capitalism*. London: Verso.

Section 3

PROSPECTS FOR/AFTER BREXIT

Chapter Ten

THE EU AND BREXIT: PROCESSES, PERSPECTIVES AND PROSPECTS

Tim Oliver

Brexit is an unprecedented challenge for both Britain and the European Union (EU). Elsewhere in the EU the question of Britain's continued membership has often been crowded out by concerns about the unity of the eurozone, the stability of Schengen, of security relations vis-à-vis Russia and a wealth of other significant problems such as Europe's productivity and demographics. The idea of actively contemplating a member state withdrawing has also been a taboo. And like the boy who cried wolf in the Aesop fable, threats by British politicians to leave the EU had by the time of the referendum campaign become so commonplace that they sounded increasingly hollow. But as the fable teaches us, the wolf eventually appeared. It should therefore be no surprise that planning for Brexit on all sides was minimal.

To appreciate the impact Brexit is having on the EU, we need to examine the political and diplomatic processes Brexit has created or triggered. Since the 23 June vote the world has witnessed 13 interrelated negotiations and debates unfold in both Britain and the rest of the EU. From the start they have been dogged by questions about the future of the UK, the EU's own unity and direction of travel, leadership at both the national and international level, and trust and solidarity at and between the different actors. These processes by which Brexit is handled could easily see relations on all sides sour due to conflicting perspectives over the future political, economic and security relationships within the UK, between the UK and the EU and within the EU. The end result could be acrimony, division and damage to all sides. The prospect of a 'harsh Brexit' in which relations on all sides deteriorate should not be ruled out.[1] At the same time we should not rule out the prospect of a harsh Brexit helping create a crisis that in the longer run leads to a positive outcome by forcing necessary changes to the EU and European politics.

The lack of planning in the UK for Brexit was in part the result of British debates being largely focused on what new UK-EU deal would most benefit the UK. This myopic approach largely ignored how the rest of the EU might respond to Brexit and what a changed EU could mean for the UK. A question that will now define Brexit is what happens to the remaining EU from this point on. This will be a question especially pertinent to the UK. Without analyzing how the remaining EU might respond to British attempts to seek a new relationship outside the EU, it will be impossible to argue clearly that one new post-withdrawal relationship is more likely than others. Furthermore, the geopolitical stability of Europe has always been and will remain the first concern of the UK.[2] As Winston Churchill noted before World War I, Europe is where the weather comes from. As we discuss in the final part of the present chapter, the prospects for the UK and EU reaching an amicable agreement should not be taken for granted. A harsh Brexit could see relations break down within and between the various actors. However, this need not be catastrophic, and a positive outcome could unfold from a harsh Brexit. The EU has often integrated through facing crises. While Brexit alone is unlikely to be a significant enough challenge to bring about much-needed reforms and changes to the EU, if it combined with other challenges such as further problems in the eurozone, then they could create a large enough crisis that the EU might embrace some much delayed changes to itself and emerge as a stronger and more effective Union.

Processes

The challenge that lies ahead in managing Brexit has become increasingly apparent since the 23 June vote.[3] As a process, Brexit involves 13 interconnected debates, discussions and decisions at various levels and amongst a wide range of actors.[4] They can be divided into three groups: UK, EU-UK and EU.

United Kingdom

Five negotiations and debates began to unfold over the summer of 2016. The first defined a Brexit narrative, one explaining why the British people voted as they did and what they voted for. This has taken place in the media, academia and amongst international commentators. Political parties, not least the Conservative Party, have been an important focus in arguments about what happened and what should now take place. Various reasons have been given, ranging from anti-immigration through to a failure by young people to turn out and vote. The dominant narrative will define what exactly the British people voted for and what is therefore deemed acceptable in terms of implementing Brexit.

The second set of debates has therefore unfolded within the political parties as they have manoeuvred themselves to deal with the constitutional, political, political economy and identity questions Brexit will bring to the fore. This debate has been most clearly seen within the Conservative Party and its leadership race, but has also fuelled tensions within the Labour Party. Other parties such as the Liberal Democrats, Greens, Scottish National Party (SNP) and UK Independence Party (UKIP) are also trying to assess what Brexit means for their core beliefs and how to implement them in future.

The beliefs of the political parties will be most clearly tested in the third set of negotiations that surround Parliament and consultation with the British public. At some point the UK Parliament – Commons and Lords – will be called on to legally define Brexit in a vote. Arguments about who can trigger Article 50, the EU's withdrawal clause, have already drawn on an often-overlooked actor – the UK Supreme Court.[5] Even if attempts fail to stop the British Government deciding by Royal Prerogative when to trigger Article 50, votes will inevitably take place when any agreements reached with the EU have to be ratified by Parliament. The Conservative Party's slim majority, combined with tensions within it as to what Brexit should mean, could suggest that the UK is headed for a fraught series of votes that will look similar to those in 1992 over the Maastricht Treaty. Some parties have called for any eventual deal to require more than the consent of Parliament and so be put to the British people in a second referendum.

The possibility of a smaller referendum in Scotland will define the fourth set of negotiations that will surround the unity of the United Kingdom. The UK government has agreed to allow representatives of the devolved governments in Scotland, Wales and Northern Ireland, in addition to the mayor of London, to have some input into the negotiations with the EU. This not only reflects the fact that Scotland, London and Northern Ireland voted to remain in the EU but also constitutional requirements. The transfer of powers entailed in a UK withdrawal from the EU means the permission of the Scottish Parliament will be required (by what is known as the Sewell Convention) to repeal the European Communities Act 1972, because this would touch on matters that are devolved.[6] The potential for Brexit to damage the Good Friday Agreement in Northern Ireland has long been a concern in Ireland, but one that until the referendum was rarely heard about in Great Britain. Finally, the position of London, a global metropolis that, as the UK's economic heart, generates around 30 per cent of all UK taxes, will be one both the mayor of London and Her Majesty's (HM) Treasury will be watching to protect.[7] Absent from this list is England outside of London. The lack of an English Parliament or devolved government outside of London means England will lack a direct seat at the table. This will happen despite English nationalism being identified as one of the defining reasons why the UK voted for Brexit.[8]

Finally, the UK will need to think about where Brexit leaves its relations with the non-European world. Brexit has the potential to reshape the UK's bilateral relations with countries such as the United States, Commonwealth states and emerging powers.[9] As a result, a lot is going to be asked of HM Diplomatic Service and the new Department for International Trade.[10] After years of cutting representation in the EU, the Foreign and Commonwealth Office will need to increase its abilities to shape EU politics, which will remain of high importance for the UK. At the same time the UK's representatives will need to seek out new relations, negotiate long and complex trade deals and secure full membership of the World Trade Organization (WTO).

European Union–United Kingdom

Four negotiations are unfolding between the UK and the EU. The first surround the negotiations over a formal exit. The process by which this is handled is set out under Article 50.[11] However, this provides only for a two-year period and focuses on the details of an exit. There is some debate as to whether the exit and post-withdrawal relationship should be agreed at the same time.[12] The text of Article 50 states that any exit agreement the EU seeks should be negotiated while 'taking account of the framework for [the withdrawing state's] future relationship with the Union', and as such may not directly require such an agreement as part of the exit negotiations. If this is the case, then some form of transition period may be required to prolong the UK's membership, or some alternative more limited form of it such as membership of the European Economic Area (EEA), until full negotiations over a new relationship can be agreed and approved.[13] Whatever is agreed, the whole exit process and any transition arrangement would have to be approved by the 27 other EU member states, with the European Parliament also required to grant its consent. In addition to this the European Court of Justice may be asked to rule on the exit, potentially as the result of efforts brought by private individuals.

As noted, an exit agreement will not necessarily include agreement over a new UK-EU relationship. This will be the focus of the second set of UK-EU negotiations. Various models have been debated, largely within the UK and largely focused on what would or would not be best for the UK. What would be in the best interests of the remaining EU member states, each of which will have to agree the new deal, has rarely been given much thought.[14] Adopting relationships such as that held by Norway or Switzerland have often been the main focus of debate.[15] Brexit has brought with it a realization that neither is ideally suited to the UK nor potentially suitable to the EU. Nor may it be in the interests of Norway and Switzerland for the UK to replicate models that have increasingly become tailor-made for them. Attention has increasingly turned to some tailor-made deal for the UK, potentially creating a more ambitious version of the EU-Canadian Trade Agreement (CETA).[16] Such a deal would likely see the UK outside the EU's single market, a move that may prove controversial to some in the UK who would dispute whether the referendum sanctioned such a move. That CETA, and its bigger US-EU counterpart, the Transatlantic Trade and Investment Partnership (TTIP), have run into endless problems with ratification in various EU member states give a hint as to the potential difficulties that await negotiation and ratification of any UK-EU deal.

Often the debate about Brexit assumes that the only negotiations that matter will be those that take place between the UK and the EU. This ignores the third set of negotiations that will be between the remaining 27 EU member states over what to offer the UK in terms of an exit deal, a possible transition arrangement and a new relationship. For an organization of (currently) 28 member states, reaching agreement on issues is often a considerable challenge. The UK-EU relationship matters more to some states than to others. As the withdrawing member state, the UK has no right to participate in the discussions amongst the remaining 27 EU member states on what to offer the UK. These discussions will not be framed only by what is or is not good for the EU's relations with the UK. They will also be built with a view to how any new relationship fits with changes to the eurozone, Schengen and other ongoing changes to the Union's structures and policies.

Finally, if there is one area in which many have argued there is a strong possibility of the UK and the EU developing a close relationship, it is through cooperating over foreign, security and defence matters.[17] As the UK is one of Europe's two leading military powers, its absence from the EU threatens to diminish any remaining hopes for the EU to complement its economic power with military, foreign and security cooperation. The UK has been blamed for delaying such efforts, but it remains doubtful whether Brexit will pave the way for enhanced EU cooperation in this area, given ongoing differences between various states over issues such as relations between the EU and the North Atlantic Treaty Organization (NATO). Nevertheless, the potential for cooperation in this area remains strong given the likely desire by the UK to continue to influence debates and decisions over European security. Possibilities include forums such as an EU+1 arrangement; an EU2+1 involving France, Germany and Britain; or a modified version of the EU's current G6 (an unofficial group of interior ministers from the largest states).[18] Objections may be raised in Britain, where continued involvement with the EU's Common Foreign and Security Policy (CFSP) arrangements could be portrayed as Britain giving succour to efforts that some fear will undermine NATO.

European Union

Brexit is shaping four internal debates about the EU's future. The first revolves around debates about rebalancing the distribution of power and influence within the Union following the departure of one of its largest member states. The UK might be noted for being 'an awkward partner', but it has been a more effective shaper of EU politics than many, not least in Britain, have acknowledged.[19] The governments of the remaining 27 member states and institutions such as the European Parliament will each have views on how certain policy areas might be reshaped in a post-Brexit EU. Such debates will play heavily into debates about the future of the eurozone and European integration more broadly, something we return to further below. Manoeuvring can already be seen, with the European Parliament and Commission pushing for a significant role in Brexit negotiations, potentially because they fear the larger member states will agree a deal with the UK over Brexit, sidelining smaller states and Brussels institutions and pointing to how the governments of some larger states feel a post-Brexit EU should be run. Other concerns surround such fears as the EU becoming more inward looking and less liberal in its economic model.

Second, in addition to negotiations over the balance of power within the remaining EU, the EU will also need to negotiate its position within Europe. As noted, Britain's withdrawal could see changes to the EU's relationships with non-EU countries such as Norway or Switzerland. It also strengthens the idea of a multipolar Europe where the EU is surrounded by the poles of Britain, Russia and Turkey.[20] The need for the EU to rethink its position within Europe as a result of Brexit has led to calls for a setup with the UK that could be extended to cover wider EU-European relations.[21]

Third, while the EU is negotiating its place within a multipolar Europe, it will also be considering the impact of Brexit on its place in an emerging multipolar world.[22] Debate about Brexit and the United States has almost always focused on US-UK relations, despite President Barack Obama's warning that Brexit could change the wider transatlantic relationship.[23] The loss of the UK means China will have a larger economy than the combined economy of the EU. Brexit has already been seen in Russia as another sign of the EU's divisions and weakness. Again, this is in part a product of Brexit, but builds on existing problems. Going forward, these views will be shaped in no small part by how the remaining EU deals with problems in the eurozone or Schengen.

The problems facing the eurozone and Schengen will be the focus of the final set of negotiations over routine internal EU business. Technically, until an exit agreement is signed and ratified, the UK will remain one of 28 member states, excluded only from negotiations amongst the remaining EU member states over how to approach Brexit. However, Britain's exclusion or sidelining from internal business has already been noted, and continued a trend long obvious thanks to the UK's own imposed isolation and the focus of EU decision-making shifting increasingly to eurozone members.[24] Whether Brexit will therefore make for a more effective Union is open to debate, given that the UK's opt-outs from the euro and Schengen have limited its influence over two areas where the EU has struggled to find unity and solutions.

Perspectives

What perspectives have the rest of the EU begun to develop over Brexit? How the EU – collectively or as individual member states and EU institutions – responds to a Brexit will depend on a mix of five I's: Ideas, Interests, Institutions, International dimensions and Individuals.[25]

Ideas

Britain's vote to leave the EU means the population of an EU member state has democratically rejected the idea of 'ever closer union', challenging in an unprecedented way one of the EU's underpinning ideas. It was clear before the vote that in the event of a vote for Brexit the official message from the rest of the EU would be that the unity of the remaining EU would be their main concern.[26] When it did emerge, this message was intended firstly for the EU, and secondly for Britain, the rest of Europe and the wider world.[27] This focus was hardly surprising given the wider challenges the EU faces, challenges that the same leaders have made clear they remain committed to solving while not becoming focused solely on Brexit.

Despite this, Brexit has inevitably drawn the attention of the rest of the EU. Debate has focused largely on the political instability and economic pain Brexit has caused Britain. This has served as something of a deterrent, at least initially.[28] Even if things are not as bad as sometimes made out in the media, a narrative that Britain was going to shoot itself in the foot by voting to leave had already been established long before the referendum. Shifting that narrative will be an immense task for the British Government and will in large part rest more on what happens in the rest of the EU and in particular the eurozone. Despite the aforementioned increase in support for the EU, surveys before the referendum showed the EU had faced a widespread decline in support.[29] If this decline in support resumes then focus will inevitably shift from Britain to the EU, deflecting attention from some of the challenges facing Britain. As such it will not be Britain's efforts that define how well it does from Brexit but how well the rest of the EU performs. However, this should not be seen as a zero-sum game where the EU's loss and problems are Britain's gain and vice versa. Division in the EU looks bad around the world, carrying the risk of weakening perceptions of all European states. Loss of investment into Britain because of Brexit does not automatically mean that investment will go elsewhere in the EU. Similarly, a failing Eurozone does not mean Britain's economy will benefit from redirected investment.

Interests

Any zero-sum approach to the economic costs of Brexit is a reminder that economic interests could trump ideas in defining how the EU responds. Britain's place as one of the world's largest economies often leads some British Eurosceptics to argue that the EU needs the UK more than the UK needs the EU. Britain does run a trade deficit with the EU (£61.6 billion in 2014), meaning the rest of the EU has an economic incentive to find a new relationship.[30] However, from the perspective of the rest of the EU, it is the UK that is exposed. Trade with Britain represented somewhere around 16 per cent of the EU's total (admittedly excluding services), while the EU represented 44.6 per cent of the UK's exports of good and services in 2014.[31]

Nevertheless, economic, social and security interests will play a powerful role. To take a prominent example, fear amongst German car manufacturers at a bad UK-EU exit deal led immediately after the vote to pressure on the German and other governments to push for a relationship that avoids any disruption to trading links.[32] The potential costs for Ireland (including violence in Northern Ireland) could force it to put interests ahead of ideas of Irish commitment to European integration and efforts to resist being caught in the slipstream of British decisions.[33] The large EU population in the UK and the UK population elsewhere in the EU mean a mutually beneficial deal will need to be hammered out about their rights. Interests should also not be seen solely in economic terms. As noted above, Britain's place in foreign, security and defence matters means the rest of the EU has some interest in maintaining links over issues of common concern such as Iran, Russia or counterterrorism.

Institutions

As we have already covered in detail, the complex processes by which Brexit is handled offer numerous Pandora's boxes filled with cans of worms. Brexit will be defined by processes such as that set out in Article 50, or those that will be used to find a way through a potential ratification process involving 27 EU member states, the European Parliament and the UK's own internal processes, to say nothing of the potential legal constraints or involvement of the European Court of Justice. These will constrain both the UK and the EU, as will international structures. If no new relationship is agreed and the UK leaves in the way set out under Article 50, then the EU would still have to work within the limits of WTO rules, although Britain is highly unlikely to benefit much from a WTO-defined relationship.[34] Thanks to its complex processes for ratification of trade deals, the EU can be notorious for presenting offers to third parties with little room for compromise because the offer is itself a compromise worked out between 28 member states – with attention also paid to the European Parliament – which the EU is then loath to unpick. Whether the EU can find a way to a compromise on what to offer a departing Britain will be the focus of a great deal of the negotiations and play a significant part in deciding what form of deal Britain can expect.

International

As touched on earlier, international pressures on the UK and the EU could see them seek some means to cooperate more closely and so define how they manage Brexit. Efforts to negotiate a TTIP reflect a desire by the United States and the EU to use their interdependent economic relationship to shape global economics and politics.[35] While the UK could find itself excluded from the main TTIP negotiating processes (should TTIP survive growing opposition within EU member states and in the United States), Britain's long-term exclusion would contradict one of the aims of TTIP, which is to extend its reach beyond the EU and United States. The agreement will also frame how the UK attempts any trade deals of its own with countries such as China or Brazil.

International events will also define UK-EU cooperation. Terrorist attacks, aggressive behaviour by Russia (providing an 'other' against which UK and EU can be formed) and shared concerns about the environment or migration could provide a means by which the UK and EU build a new and close working relationship. That said, it must be recalled that international events have caused divisions and animosity between the UK and parts of the EU, the most obvious example being the 2003 Iraq War.

Individuals

Animosity could certainly be a problem when it comes to relations between individual leaders and decision makers. Theresa May, like her predecessors, faces a Conservative Party that retains some divisions over the EU, not least what Brexit is to mean. Reaching a compromise with the EU and a compromise within her party could prove a significant challenge. EU leaders might be in no mood to offer much by way of compromise, especially given the British people rejected a renegotiated relationship some of them were uneasy at offering. The attitude of Angela Merkel has already received much attention. For Merkel, a major concern will be the German elections due in 2017, which may give her little room to offer much by way of a compromise deal out of fear of how that may play out in German domestic politics. The absence of German support would more than likely doom any deal the UK seeks. This touches on a wider issue that many of the EU's leaders are struggling with in light of the vote: whether the vote for Brexit signals a wider shift in Western politics towards isolationism, populism and nationalism. Any shift will become clearer as elections take place, especially in the United States, France and Germany.

Prospects

These processes and perspectives mean Brexit could unfold as a 'soft Brexit' or a 'harsh Brexit'.[36] What will distinguish the two are the levels of trust shown between those involved. A harsh Brexit would see a collapse in trust between Britain and the remaining EU, an uncertain political situation develop within Britain and heightened tensions between the remaining EU that could aid European disintegration. This would happen because of difficulties within the remaining EU at reaching a withdrawal deal with Britain that balances the economic costs (especially as felt by some Member States compared to others) with protecting ideas of integration. Britain's own internal political and constitutional difficulties would leave it an unstable negotiating partner. Personal relations between leading politicians and decision makers in Britain and the EU would be strained. Most importantly, Brexit would align another crisis such as a Grexit or a collapse of Schengen that leaves the EU unable to continue muddling through, as opposed to solving, such problems.

For Britain the outcome of a harsh Brexit would see the initial economic and political shocks turned into longer-running challenges that shake the unity of the UK. The EU would also be hit economically, with negative social effects on all sides because of the British citizens living elsewhere in the EU and EU citizens resident in Britain. Geopolitically such a scenario would weaken transatlantic relations, aiding the collapse of TTIP and raising questions about NATO. One of the most radical prospects is the complete collapse of the EU. What mechanism would then be set up to manage relations between European states is rarely if ever discussed, albeit it is talked about on the fringes of the British Eurosceptic community. Disintegration could lead to a much reduced or reordered Union, perhaps focused on a few core countries in some rump eurozone. How European disintegration would unfold and what might trigger it has rarely been the subject of much analysis, a reflection in part of a view of European integration as a forward-moving, liberal internationalist project.[37] For Douglas Webber, author of one of the few pieces of literature on the subject, one of the most important aspects of any disintegration would be the response of the EU's predominant power and (reluctant) leader: Germany. The EU has never, as Webber argues, faced a 'crisis made in Germany', one where Berlin loses faith in the current EU project as a result of a widespread breakdown in EU solidarity and the increasing costs Germany is asked to carry in order to maintain the EU's unity. Brexit alone is unlikely to trigger this, but if it aligned with another crisis in the eurozone or Schengen then the EU's approach of muddling through each separate crisis could prove unsustainable. The eurozone continues to struggle on, Schengen faces mounting pressures from intractable conflicts in the Middle East and North Africa and heightened tensions with Russia show no signs of abating. Brexit adds another potential sticking point in efforts to manage or solve these ongoing crises.

This does not mean a 'soft Brexit' – where harmonious relations prevail – is the only hope. It is possible to sketch out a positive outcome from a harsh Brexit. It could be that having experienced the pain of a harsh Brexit, Britain and the EU eventually – perhaps after more than a decade – will find a more settled relationship with positive outcomes for their economics, politics and security. The EU has a long history of integrating through facing crises, and a Brexit could therefore drive integration forward. Rid of an often awkward partner, the EU could find it integrates further in the face of the costs of Brexit at the same time as facing a Grexit or other crisis. Instead of muddling through in the face of these ongoing crises, the EU could find it negotiates a new treaty that brings a degree of enhanced unity and a more stable EU. As Brendan Simms has argued, the EU has forlornly hoped that processes (many interminable and created with the aim of creating a reflex towards working together) will eventually lead to some moment or event that signals the creation of a functioning Union that may resemble that of a United States of Europe.[38] This is putting the cart before the horse. A major crisis that combines Brexit, a potential collapse of the eurozone and Schengen, and the possibility of war with Russia may be the moment or event that the members of the EU need to declare the creation of a functioning Union, after which the necessary processes would be put in place to support it.[39]

Notes

1 P. Morillas. 2016. *The Brexit Scenarios: Towards a New UK-EU Relationship*. Barcelona: CIDOB, June.
2 See B. Simms. 2016. *Britain's Europe: A Thousand Years of Conflict and Cooperation*. London: Allen Lane.
3 C. Grant. 2016. 'Theresa May and Her Six Pack of Difficult Deals'. London: CER, insight, 28 July, https://www.cer.org.uk/insights/theresa-may-and-her-six-pack-difficult-deals (accessed 4 September 2016).
4 Details of the 13 negotiations are based on evidence submitted by the author to the House of Commons Foreign Affairs Committee's inquiry, 'Implications of Leaving the EU for the UK's Role in the World'. See http://www.parliament.uk/business/committees/committees-a-z/commons-select/foreign-affairs-committee/news-parliament-2015/eu-results-launch-16–17/ (accessed 4 September 2016).
5 P. Gower. 2016. 'Brexit Article 50 Challenge to Quickly Move to Supreme Court', Bloomberg, 19 July, http://www.bloomberg.com/news/articles/2016-07-19/court-takes-brexit-challenge-very-seriously-judge-leveson-says (accessed 4 September 2016).
6 S. Douglas-Scot. 2014. *British Withdrawal from the EU: An Existential Threat to the United Kingdom?* London: Centre on Constitutional Change, 24 October, http://www.centreonconstitutionalchange.ac.uk/blog/british-withdrawal-eu-existential-threat-united-kingdom (accessed 4 September 2016).
7 L. McGough and G. Piazza. 2016. *10 Years of Tax: How Cities Contribute to the National Exchequer*. London: Centre for Cities, 7 July, http://www.centreforcities.org/wp-content/uploads/2016/07/16-07-05-10-Years-of-Tax-1.pdf (accessed 4 September 2016).
8 A. Barnett . 2016. 'It's England's Brexit'. *OpenDemocracy*, 4 June, https://www.opendemocracy.net/uk/anthony-barnett/it-s-england-s-brexit (accessed 4 September 2016).
9 D. Ransome. 2016. 'Brexit: What Next for the Commonwealth?' *The Round Table*, 27 June, http://www.commonwealthroundtable.co.uk/commonwealth/eurasia/united-kingdom/brexit-next-commonwealth/ (accessed 4 September 2016).
10 Foreign Affairs Committee. 2016. *Equipping the Government for Brexit*. London: House of Commons Foreign Affairs Committee, Second Report, HC 431, July.
11 A. Renwick. 2016. 'Does the Prime Minister Have to Trigger Brexit Talks under Article 50 after a Vote to Leave the EU?', *The UCL Constitution Unit blog*, 23 February, https://constitution-unit.com/2016/02/23/does-the-prime-minister-have-to-invoke-article-50-if-we-vote-for-brexit/ (accessed 4 September 2016).
12 R. Niblett. 2016. 'Preparing for the UK's Brexit Negotiations', *The World Today*, August, https://www.chathamhouse.org/publications/twt/preparing-uks-brexit-negotiation (accessed 4 September 2016).
13 D. Chalmers, and A. Menon. 2016. *Getting Out Quick and Playing the Long Game*. London: Open Europe Briefing, July, http://openeurope.org.uk/intelligence/britain-and-the-eu/3-step-brexit-solution/ (accessed 4 September 2016).
14 T. Oliver. 2016. *Brexit: What Happens Next?* London: LSE IDEAS.

15 S. Booth, and C. Howarth. 2012. *Trading Places: Is EU Membership Still the Best Option for UK Trade?* London: Open Europe.

16 A. Kassam. 2016. 'Canada's Trade Deal with EU a Model for Brexit? Not Quite, Insiders Say', *The Guardian*, 15 August, https://www.theguardian.com/world/2016/aug/15/brexit-canada-trade-deal-eu-model-next-steps (accessed 4 September 2016).

17 P. van Ham. 2016. *Brexit: Strategic Consequences for Europe*. Clingendael Institute.

18 N. von Ondarza. 2013. *Strengthening the Core or Splitting Europe? Prospects and Pitfalls of a Strategy of Differentiated Integration*. Berlin: SWP Research Paper, RP 2.

19 See O. Daddow, and T. Oliver. 2016. 'A Not So Awkward Partner: The UK Has Been the Champion of Many Causes in the EU', *LSE BrexitVote blog*, 15 April, http://blogs.lse.ac.uk/brexit/2016/04/15/a-not-so-awkward-partner-the-uk-has-been-a-champion-of-many-causes-in-the-eu/ (accessed 4 September 2016).

20 I. Krastev, and M. Leonard. 2010. *The Spectre of a Multipolar Europe*. London: ECFR, October, http://www.ecfr.eu/page/-/ECFR25_SECURITY_UPDATE_AW_SINGLE.pdf (accessed 4 September 2016).

21 J. Pisani-Ferry, N. Röttgen, A. Sapir, P. Tucker and G. Wolff. 2016. *Europe after Brexit: A Proposal for a Continental Partnership*. Bruegel, 29 August, http://bruegel.org/2016/08/europe-after-brexit-a-proposal-for-a-continental-partnership/ (accessed 4 September 2016).

22 T. Oliver. 2015. 'Europe's British Question: The UK-EU Relationship in a Changing Europe and Multipolar World', *Global Society*, 29 (3): 409–426.

23 T. Oliver, and M. J. Williams. 2016. 'Special Relationships in Flux: Brexit and the Future of the US-EU and US-UK Relationships', *International Affairs* 92 (3): 547–567.

24 J. Stearns. 2016. 'Brexit Is Already Making Britain a Lame Duck in Brussels', *Bloomberg*, 5 July, http://www.bloomberg.com/news/articles/2016-07-05/brexit-foretaste-already-on-menu-in-brussels-as-u-k-loses-perks (accessed 4 September 2016).

25 T. Oliver. 2016. 'Ideas, Interests, Institutions, International and Individuals: The Five I's of Brexit.' *E!Sharp*, July, http://esharp.eu/debates/the-uk-and-europe/ideas-interests-institutions-international-and-individuals-the-five-is-of-brexit (accessed 4 September 2016).

26 T. Oliver. 2016. 'European and International Views of Brexit', *Journal of European Public Policy* 23 (9) (published online May 2016).

27 'EU's Tusk says 27 EU Leaders Determined to Keep Unity after Brexit', 2016. *Reuters*, 24 June, http://www.reuters.com/article/us-britain-eu-reactions-tusk-idUSKCN0ZA0XN (accessed 4 September 2016).

28 Foundation for European Progressive Studies (FEPS). 2016. *Europeans and Brexit*. 18 July, http://www.feps-europe.eu/en/publications/details/412 (accessed 4 September 2016).

29 Bruce Stokes. 2016. *Euroscepticism beyond Brexit*. Pew Research Center, 7 June, http://www.pewglobal.org/2016/06/07/euroskepticism-beyond-brexit/ (accessed 4 September 2016).

30 Office for National Statistics (ONS). 2015. 'How Important Is the European Union to UK Trade and Unvestment?', 26 June, http://webarchive.nationalarchives.gov.uk/20160105160709/http://www.ons.gov.uk/ons/rel/international-transactions/outward-foreign-affiliates-statistics/how-important-is-the-european-union-to-uk-trade-and-investment-/sty-eu.html (accessed 4 September 2016).

31 J. Portes. 2015. 'After Brexit: How Important Would UK Trade Be to the EU?' *NIESR*, 2 November, http://www.niesr.ac.uk/blog/after-brexit-how-important-would-uk-trade-be-eu#.Vltjsd_hCb9 (accessed 4 September 2016); Office for National Statistics (ONS). 2015. 'How Important Is the European Union to UK Trade and Investment?', 26 June, http://webarchive.nationalarchives.gov.uk/20160105160709/http://www.ons.gov.uk/ons/rel/international-transactions/outward-foreign-affiliates-statistics/how-important-is-the-european-union-to-uk-trade-and-investment-/sty-eu.html (accessed 4 September 2016).

32 'Automakers Call for Tariff-Free Trade between UK and EU after Brexit Win'. 2016. *Automotive News*, 24 June, http://www.autonews.com/article/20160624/COPY01/306249977/automakers-call-for-tariff-free-trade-between-uk-and-eu-after-brexit (accessed 4 September 2016).

33 A. Barrett, A. Bergin, J. FitzGerald, D. Lambert, D. McCoy, E. Morgenroth, I. Siedschlag and Z. Studnicka. 2015. *Scoping the Possible Economic Implications of Brexit on Ireland*. Dublin: ESRI Research Series: The Economic and Social Research Institute, https://www.esri.ie/pubs/RS48.pdf (accessed 4 September 2016).

34 S. Booth, and C. Howarth. 2012. *Trading Places: Is EU Membership Still the Best Option for UK Trade?* London: Open Europe.

35 R. Korteweg. 2015. 'It's the Geopolitics, Stupid: Why TTIP Matters'. *CER Insight*, 2 April, http://www.cer.org.uk/insights/it%E2%80%99s-geopolitics-stupid-why-ttip-matters (accessed 4 September 2016).

36 P. Morillas. 2016. *The Brexit Scenarios: Towards a New UK-EU relationship*. Barcelona: CIDOB, June.

37 The two best examples are: H. Vollaard. 2014. 'Explaining European Disintegration', *Journal of Common Market Studies* 52 (5): 1142–1159; and D. Webber. 2014. 'How Likely Is It That the European Union Will Disintegrate? A Critical Analysis of Competing Theoretical Perspectives', *European Journal of International Relations* 20 (2): 341–365.

38 See B. Simms. 2016. *Britain's Europe: A Thousand Years of Conflict and Cooperation*. London: Allen Lane.

39 B. Simms. 2016. 'After Brexit, Should the Eurozone Pursue Full Political Union?' *New Statesman*, 11 July.

Chapter Eleven

THE IMPOSSIBILITY OF DISENTANGLING INTEGRATION

Antje Wiener

We make this report for debate.
    – House of Lords (2016, p. 3; emphasis in original text)[1]

Introduction

This chapter offers an analysis of the mid- to long-term effect of the Brexit referendum from the perspective of norms research in international relations theory and recognition theory.[2] To that end, it focuses on key *contestations* about fundamental norms that have been at the centre of the debate following the referendum vote on 23 June 2016, namely, fundamental human rights and sovereignty. It suggests that the contestations are *indicators* for potential mid- to long-term effects that the manifold debates about the referendum had on normative change both in the UK and, relatedly, in the European Union (EU). Contestations are defined as objections to norms. They are crucial for a society's normative structure of meaning. Contestations effectively mean the practices of 're-enacting normative meaning in use' (Milliken 1999): 132). Contestations obtain such a central role for politics because they are conducted by a diversity of involved stakeholders (that is, ranging from individual voters to government representatives) and therefore reveal the individual normative positions of individuals. As such, contestations are both indicative of the robustness of norms (i.e. reactive contestation) and constitutive for the revision of norms (i.e. proactive contestation). The argument developed in the present chapter maintains that the referendum debate is therefore a welcome opportunity to recall where British and European stakeholders stand on fundamental norms. Two norms stand out in the debate between the vote-leave campaign and the vote-remain campaign (hereafter: leavers versus remainers): the fundamental right of freedom of movement and sovereignty in Parliament. The former represents one of the four freedoms of the EU; the latter is the principal right of democracy in Britain. The chapter presents the argument about contestation and normative change and the related effects in three steps: step one presents the politico-legal and societal context of the UK within the EU, taking into account the four decades of European integration that the UK has shared with the other EU member states. Step two zooms in on the current scenario of fundamental norms in crisis, with reference to two fundamental norm contestations in the UK. And step three derives preliminary conclusions from that analysis with regard to the next stage of post-referendum and pre-Brexit political debate in Britain.

Step One: The Context

Family Resemblances

Why do we call something a 'number'? Well, perhaps it has a direct relationship with several things that have hitherto been called number; and this may be said to give it an indirect relationship to other things that we call the same name. And we extend our concept of number as *in spinning a thread we twist fibre on fibre. And the strength of the thread does not reside in the fact that some one fibre runs through its whole length, but in overlapping many fibres.*

– Wittgenstein (2005: 28; emphasis added)

Akin to Ludwig Wittgenstein's (Wittgenstein 2005) metaphor of a thread that gains its identity through the practice of twisting fibre on fibre, the EU's identity has emerged through the practice of integrating member states. While the thread was spinning, new members were included, strengthening the thread through enlargements in 1973, 1981, 1986, 1990, 1995, 2004, 2007 and 2013, with the UK joining in the first enlargement in 1973, along with Denmark and Ireland. This identity persists, despite many contestations regarding the EU's democratic deficit and the legitimation of the EU's political role in light of them. If we stick with the metaphor of a thread, spun fibre on fibre, it bears the footprints of all members that participated in the practices of 'spinning' the EU over time, through partaking in the multiple areas of integration. Many of these practices of integration have been overlapping, creating interfaces where norms have been re-enacted through the practices of the involved stakeholders to form common 'transnational' meanings (Wiener 2008). These meanings cannot be undone but require re-enacting to change. In the process, multiple areas in policy and politics have been changed to form common norms (standards, rules, principled procedures) through this practice. The result was the EU's *acquis communautaire*, that is, the shared set of EU primary and secondary law. Given that law is generated through practice and always re-enacted within a given sociocultural environment, it has been argued that this environment needs to be taken into account when assessing the robustness of a norm (Finnemore and Toope 2001). In the EU this environment is provided by the 'embedded *acquis communautaire*', which comprises the result of EU law making at any time (Wiener 1998). Over more than five decades of a steadily growing practice of law making, the EU has become more than an international organization of states. Despite its legal foundations as an – albeit considerably advanced and constitutionally sustained – international organization (Craig and De Burca 1998), its sociocultural foundations have long passed the stage of a 'naked' treaty.[3] In other words, it is impossible to withdraw from the EU as one might cancel membership in a club. If anything, the Brexit debates stand to demonstrate why and how the long-time club versus community debate among integration theorists comes down in favour of the community side.

Over the longer term, *disentangling* the UK from the substantial body of EU legislation which applies in the UK would be a massive task which would take many years to complete. (*Financial Times* 24 June 2016; emphasis in original)[4]

Taking account of the past two months, a preliminary analysis of the public contestations that have been unfolding with regard both to the referendum's result and regarding procedures to be followed (that is, political, regulatory and constitutional), the metaphor of a thread that is impossible to disentangle implies the following two scenarios. The first – retrospective – scenario suggests that, instead of getting Britain 'back', the referendum result is likely to trigger a process of disentanglement with no completion date in sight, despite the regulatory procedure stated in Article 50 Treaty on European Union (TEU) (more detail below). According to this scenario, the process following the required Article 50 procedure triggering Brexit will be complex and long-winded, if not cumbersome. As such it will be hard to follow, let alone understand, for those who are not directly involved. Given the anticipated duration and complexity, it should become a politician's nightmare, for voters will predictably feel even more alienated from the process than prior to the 'leave vote'. The expected 'gain' from voting to leave, that is, taking Britain back from the EU, will thus be turned into a disappointing 'loss'. This is echoed by David Davis, Secretary of State for Leaving the European Union, who warns British stakeholders that a 'frustrating' period lies ahead, until Prime Minister Theresa May triggers the Article 50 procedure.[5] This will become particularly embarrassing when it transpires that the UK has not only lost the power to direct its own exit from the EU but also that the completion of the Brexit procedure will take a long time in coming.

In turn, the second – prospective – scenario suggests that instead of removing the UK from an EU that is heralded by the leave campaign as an undemocratic supranational organization, the Brexit referendum is more likely to generate a boost for the EU. For the ongoing contestations create novel opportunities for a broad spectrum of stakeholders across all EU member states, including the UK, to engage with the EU's lingering democratic deficit narrative. This process generates a growing public awareness about the EU's principles and procedures that is generated through the contestatory practices of a growing number of stakeholders. According to this scenario, the post-referendum and pre-Brexit process has an effect on how the EU is perceived by a diversity of stakeholders (citizens and government representatives alike) both in the UK and beyond. It is therefore likely to ultimately contribute to a more positive image of the EU, making it stronger, and the UK weaker, as it were. Both scenarios are detrimental to what the British voters were promised by the leave campaign when it was set in motion by then Prime Minister David Cameron's decision to call for a referendum on the UK's membership of the EU in 2015 (see the European Union Referendum Act 2015). In the best case, these scenarios would be received as a caution to think, pause and rethink, prior to British prime minister May taking any decision to trigger the Article 50 procedure. As Alan Green wrote on the day following the June 23 referendum:

'The fact is that the longer the Article 50 notification is put off, the greater the chance it will *never be made at all*. This is because the longer the delay, the more likely it will be that events will intervene or excuses will be contrived.' And he added, 'In my view, if the Article 50 notification was not sent yesterday – the very day after the Leave result – there is a *strong chance it will never be sent*.' (See: Green 24 June 2016; emphasis added)[6]

This may be interpreted as a suggestion to move fast, which with hindsight does not appear to be May's preference, nor was it Cameron's, for that matter. As Cameron said in his resignation statement,

> A negotiation with the European Union will need to begin under a new Prime Minister, and I think it is right that this new *Prime Minister takes the decision about when to trigger Article 50* and start the formal and legal process of leaving the EU. (Downing Street, 24 June 2016)[7]

The new prime minister, May, on her first visit to Chancellor Angela Merkel in Berlin, was not in a hurry to trigger Article 50, saying that Britain needed to 'take *time* to determine its objectives' before initiating the Article 50 procedure as the procedure set by the Lisbon Treaty for any country to leave the EU (see: Reuters 20 July 2016; emphasis added AW).[8] It underlines the most likely path of action, namely, that the process leading up to the decision to trigger the Article 50 procedure, as well as the process following the decision – if it is made – will be accompanied by contestations involving stakeholders beyond the UK and all across the EU. To appreciate the time required for preparing the UK's potential exit, it is helpful to compare Greenland's exit in 1985, which did not come into effect until three years after its 1982 referendum. (At the time, fisheries policy was the main chapter to be negotiated).[9] In the British case, notably, the decision must be ratified by Parliament in the UK, once the Article 50 procedure has formally been completed and the exit vote has been taken by the EU's various political organs (including Council and Parliament).

> The withdrawal agreement is not subject to any of the constitutional safeguards in the EU Act 2011, but, *following the usual procedures for ratification, would have to be laid before Parliament* with a Government Explanatory Memorandum *for 21 sitting days before it could be ratified, in which time either House could resolve that it should not be.* Part 2 of the Constitutional Reform and Governance Act 2010 put the 21-sitting day 'Ponsonby Rule' on a statutory footing and gave legal effect to a resolution of the House of Commons that a treaty should not be ratified. If the Commons resolves against ratification, the treaty can still be ratified if the Government lays a statement explaining why the treaty should nonetheless be ratified and the House of Commons does not resolve against ratification a second time within 21 days (this process can be repeated *ad infinitum*). (See: House of Commons RB 2013: 13; emphasis added)

Notably, Article 50 (TEU) first refers to a member state's obligation to proceed according to its constitutional framework:

> Any Member State may decide to withdraw from the Union in accordance with its own *constitutional requirements.* (Article 50(1) TEU; emphasis added)

Just before going into publication, it is precisely this aspect, i.e. whether or not the fundamental norm of sovereignty in parliament must be brought to bear, enabling Parliament to contest the details of the Article 50 procedure or not, which is deliberated in the Supreme Court (see: Supreme Court, R (on the application of Miller and another) (Respondents) v Secretary of State for Exiting the European Union (Appellant) Case ID: UKSC 2016/0196, details: https://www.supremecourt.uk/live/ court-01.html) The decision to trigger Article 50 then is first of all a constitutional issue that stands to be handled with regard to the relevant constitutional norms by the government of the member state that wishes to exit the EU. Once this decision has been taken – taking constitutional norms into account – the following applies:

> A Member State which decides to withdraw shall notify the European Council of its intention. In the light of the guidelines provided by the European Council, the Union shall negotiate and conclude an agreement with that State, setting out the arrangements for its withdrawal, taking account of the framework for its future relationship with the Union. That *agreement shall be negotiated in accordance with Article 218(3)* of the Treaty on the Functioning of the European Union. It shall be concluded on behalf of the Union by the *Council, acting by a qualified majority, after obtaining the consent of the European Parliament.* (Article 50(2) TEU; emphasis added)

This exit decision will not enter into force until the Article 50 procedures are completed. Importantly, however, these negotiations stand to be conducted without the member state that triggers the exit procedure. This adds to the interest on the part of the British government to extend the pre–Article 50 process negotiations as much as possible.

> The Treaties shall cease to apply to the State in question *from the date of entry into force of the withdrawal agreement* or, *failing that, two years after the notification referred to in paragraph 2*, unless the European Council, in agreement with the Member State concerned, unanimously decides to extend this period. (Article 50(3) TEU)

At the time of writing of this chapter, a 'legal challenge bid to prevent the Government from triggering Article 50 of the Lisbon Treaty without the prior authorization of Parliament is due to be heard in the High Court in October'.[10] And the prime minister said that 'no attempt will be made to hold a "sort of backdoor" attempt to remain in the EU by holding a second referendum'.[11] Yet, as she added at the same press briefing, 'we will be looking for *opportunities*' (ibid.; emphasis added AW). Which opportunities she has in mind remains subject to specification through further debate. And, as is beginning to dawn on the politicians involved, Brexit is not a step but a 'process': in other words, there is ample time for post-referendum pre-Brexit contestations. As David Davis finds, leaving the EU will be the most 'complicated negotiation of all time'.[12] In light of the expected lengthy process, it is worthwhile for academic observers to 'zoom in' on the contestations (Hofius 2016) to analyse the Brexit crisis and identify its mid- to long-term effect on European politics in the UK and beyond. To that end, the following section sketches a practice-based approach.

Step Two: Fundamental Norm Contestations

'The UK legal system incorporates a vast body of EU law. *Disentangling* EU and domestic UK laws, to the extent required by the eventual terms of withdrawal, will be *an enormous task, and the practical and legal implications will vary* in each area of economic activity. There are *major and unresolved constitutional issues* concerning the relationships between different parts of the United Kingdom, and their future relationships with the European Union, which will have an important bearing on this.'[13]

The practice-based argument on the effect of Brexit that this essay advances, draws on norms research, broadly defined as a range of studies focusing on 'soft institutions' such as norms, principles and routinized practices, especially, though not exclusively, in the disciplines of European integration, international relations, recognition theory and legal anthropology (see, for example, Schmidt 2000; Merry 2011). Roughly, the approach centres on three leading assumptions. First, while norms may be qualified as legal or cultural, they are always by definition social; norms require prior social interaction in order to come into being (Morris 1956). Second, and relatedly, norms entail a dual quality as both socially constructed and structuring (Wiener 2007). That is, they acquire meaning within a social environment and they have an effect on behaviour (March and Olsen 1989). Third, and related to the two prior assumptions, the effect of norms depends on the way they are interpreted within a given societal environment (Finnemore and Toope 2001). It follows that, in order to examine the robustness of a norm, research needs to examine the practices of norm validation that are carried out at distinct stages of the process of norm implementation. Through studying these practices it becomes possible to identify normative change and to derive policy strategies to address the deeper moral issues of human rights obligations and constitutional principles. Both are at stake in current European politics.

In light of the referendum campaign claim that leaving the EU would re-establish democratic legitimacy in Britain, the practices that matter for the analysis are those that address the norms which lie at the core of liberal democracies such as the UK, namely, fundamental rights of individuals, sovereignty, democracy and the rule of law (Rosenfeld 1994). To evaluate the promises made by the vote-leave campaign, for example the claim to re-establish British sovereignty, three practices of norm validation matter. All contribute to the way normative meaning-in-use is re-enacted at distinct stages of norm implementation, each of which allows for contestation by the stakeholders involved. They include formal validation at the stage of treaty making (EU) or constitution making (UK) by the 'masters' of British fundamental norms. The second practice is habitual validation – known as 'social recognition' (March and Olsen 1989; Finnemore and Sikkink 1998). Social recognition reflects the degree of appropriateness assigned to the implementation of these norms by British stakeholders. When social recognition is high, a norm is by and large considered as 'taken for granted' (Price 2003). The third practice is cultural validation (Wiener 2008). It reflects the projection of individual background experience when re-enacting normative meaning. Carried out by individual stakeholders, it reveals, for example, how an individual voter validates a given norm. According to the vote-leave promise, following Brexit the changes listed below would need to be realized in order to match the promises made and, accordingly, the expectations that had been raised with the voters. This includes the following three claims: first, the UK government should be able to re-own its constitutional norms (as opposed to sharing them with other member states in the EU, for example, based on the organizing principle of 'pooled sovereignty'). Second, British stakeholders (that is, advocacy groups, nongovernmental organizations, trade unions, parties and the like) should converge on the social recognition of these fundamental norms (as opposed to having the shared interpretation of British fundamental norms challenged by a multiverse of Union citizens residing in the UK). And third, the degree of variation with regard to the individual validation of these fundamental norms should decline, given the rise in social recognition due to the process of 'renationaliza-tion' induced by Brexit. It follows that – quite different from the rest of the globalized world in the twenty-first century, the impact of cultural validation would be expected to cease in the UK, due to the decline of cultural diversity in light of enhanced thresh-olds vis-à-vis migration, and the declining tolerance vis-à-vis the acceptance of refugees. Contrary results would undermine the promise and hence cause political frustration among the supporters of the vote-leave campaign. Many indicators revealed by the post-referendum political discourse suggest that this is a likely scenario. The remainder of this section highlights some of these so as to provide a view on the likely mid- to long-term effects of the Brexit referendum and ensuing contestations.

In the post-referendum and pre-Brexit process two norm contestations stand out: the first is about the fundamental right of freedom of movement and whether it should be restricted for workers, while making exceptions for incoming bankers and outgoing capital as the leavers hold, or whether it should be implemented in compliance with the TEU as the remainers wish.[14] The second is about whether or not sovereignty in Parliament must be upheld as the remainers argue, or whether sovereignty lies with the voters, as the leavers hold. With regard to the former, the contestations ensuing from the two referendum cam-paigns disagreed on whether to restrict the fundamental norm of freedom of movement including all four (freedom of movement for goods, services, capital and labour) to capi-tal only, restricting the freedom of movement for labour. The latter effectively demands access to the EU market while at the same time restricting the freedom of movement of labour, thereby effectively undermining the fundamental right of free movement of persons, goods, services and capital that is stated in Article 45 (TEU). This contestation (#C1) evolved around the 'migration crisis' by a range of stakeholders including politi-cians, advocacy groups and most of the media in the UK, who sought to restrict migra-tion. Notably, the so-called migration crisis cuts deeper than market access. While market access is presented as a policy issue in the political arena, the crisis ultimately extends to the question about the UK's position on respecting its moral obligation to grant the fundamental human right of asylum (Ignatieff 2016). By presenting a poster of refugees waiting at the Austrian-German border in order to seek asylum in the EU, calling them 'migrants', Nigel Farage, the then-UK Independence Party (UKIP) leader and prominent leave campaigner, conjured up fear among British voters.[15] While this rhetoric was widely condemned as unfair and as adding to the canon of outright lies, its effect stood.[16]

While the contestations with regard to the 'migration crisis' have been a central point of discussion in the media, the 'sovereignty crisis' has only just begun to emerge as the post-referendum process begins to unfold, thereby raising questions about which political procedure and constitutional principles legitimate the decision to trigger the Article 50 procedure for exit negotiations with the EU. Here the contested issue is whether the ref-erendum vote suffices as a mandate for the prime minister to take the decision or whether a debate in Parliament is required. Effectively and fundamentally, this contestation (C#2) is about the location of sovereignty in the UK: with the individual voter or in Parliament. Both contestations address deeper issues of contested normativity in the UK and beyond. They are unlikely to be resolved quickly. As such, the manifold practices of contestation involved with regard to each norm offer important information regarding the contested meanings of fundamental norms. To 'disentangle' the body of legal regulations alone – notwithstanding cultural, societal, educational or constitutional changes that have been forged through four decades of 'spinning' the 'thread' together with the other EU members – has been rightly identified as a 'nightmare' that is likely to last decades.[17] In fact, as Simon Bulmer noted, the post-referendum contestations suggest a coming 'constitutional decade in the UK'.[18]

The decision to actually walk down the path towards leaving the EU, even though repeatedly confirmed, does not appear more doable or, for that matter, likely as the referendum day is further and further behind us. Academic research on the embeddedness of the *acquis communautaire* confirms this view. For the *acquis* entails the body of primary and secondary law that stands to be interpreted with reference to the social environment of its implementation (Joergensen 1998). The notion of the 'embedded *acquis communautaire*' (Wiener 1998; Merlingen et al. 2000) sustains the importance of the Wittgensteinian thread metaphor: in light of the previous practices of integration along multiple levels of government, layers of society and scales of goods (see, for example, Hooghe and Marks 2001; Cini 2003; Puetter 2012), by a multitude of actors, the task of disentangling will be difficult – arguably impossible. A repetition of the Greenland exit negotiations from 1982–1985 is ruled out in light of this massive difference in complexity on all dimensions of integration (that is, levels, layers and scale). It will be up to the negotiations between the UK and the EU, then, to forge a viable exit procedure. This is the challenge that lies ahead. The negotiations are performed by the involved stakeholders both in government and outside of government, both in the UK and outside the UK. The practices of these negotiations reveal potential pathways to participation. Based on detailed reconstructive research involving interviewing and more encompassing discourse analysis than this short essay is able to provide, these pathways stand to be traced, based on specific attention to what is actually said (or not) and done (or not).[19]

Step Three: Conclusions – Back to What and Where to Next?

(O)nce negotiations begin, they will be extremely complex. The UK will need to determine numerous transitional procedures for *disentangling* itself from EU regulations, settling the status of the millions of UK citizens residing in the EU and non-UK EU citizens in the UK, and deciding the future of UK-EU security cooperation. (Council of Foreign Relations; emphasis added)[20]

Most distinctively, the post-referendum pre-Brexit contestations demonstrate a clash among the vote-leave and vote-remain campaigns, respectively, based on exclusive preferences with regard to the fundamental norms of democracy and free movement. With regard to the sovereignty norm, the question is whether the 'referendum result must be respected', as the vote-leave campaign holds, or whether 'Parliament must have a say', as the vote-remain campaign would argue, with regard to free market access (UK to EU) vis-à-vis rejecting the fundamental EU principle of the right of free movement (EU to UK).[21] In each case, the contestations stand to reveal the stakeholders' preferred meaning attached to either of the alternative options. While the contestations about the funda-mental right of free movement that lie at the centre of the dispute over free market access to the EU's market for British citizens have been receiving ongoing publicity, given their prominence in the pre-referendum campaign of the vote-leave supporters, the second norm at stake, that is, sovereignty, has only begun to emerge after the referendum. The clashes of normative meaning have become visible with regard to the highly contested issue of the political, legal and constitutional follow-up of the referendum result. The key point regarding the norm of sovereignty consists in the dispute over the 'place' of sovereignty, that is, whether it resides with the individual voter (the referendum option) or ought to be located in Parliament (the constitutional option).

With regard to the parliamentary vote in connection with the decision to trigger the Article 50 procedure, *The Guardian* reports that the shadow international trade secretary, Barry Gardiner, spoke out against May's plans, saying that

> the logic of saying the prime minister can trigger article 50 without first setting out to parlia-ment the terms and basis upon which her government seeks to negotiate – indeed, without even indicating the red lines she will seek to protect – would be to *diminish parliament and assume the arrogant powers of a Tudor monarch*. (*The Guardian*, 27 August 2016; emphasis added)[22]

In effect, this Article 50-related contestation involves Members of Parliament who demand that

> Parliament cannot be side-lined from the *greatest constitutional change* our country has debated in 40 years. (Ibid.; emphasis added)

The bets are on, and at the time of writing, more weight is put behind the former by the vote-leave campaign and more behind the latter by those who favour remaining in the EU.[23]

Effectively and ironically, the unintended consequences of the referendum campaign consist in the most far-reaching contestations about the EU to this day. While originally cast by Cameron in 2013 as offering 'a simple choice' to the British people, ignoring warnings by the late and then German foreign secretary Guido Westerwelle that 'cherry picking' was not an option following that choice, the actual path after the referendum remains undecided.[24] Three years later, however, what had appeared to Tony Blair as if Britain were shooting itself in the head at the time (ibid.), now seems to entail a different option altogether. As the Brexit discourse reveals, through multiple contestations includ-ing stakeholders across the UK and Europe, the situation has unwittingly changed from a threat to the EU (that is, a weakening of the EU following a British exit) to a window of opportunity (that is, countering the EU's perceived legitimacy deficit through stake-holder involvement in contestations). This window of political opportunity needs to be activated, however. And, if used wisely, this shift from threat to opportunity represents a rather welcome development for the crisis-battered EU of the 2010s. From the perspective of recognition theory, it could be argued that this is the best possible outcome. As James Tully notes, for example, 'reasonable disagreement and thus dissent are inevitable and go all the way down in theory and practice'. As a result, there 'will be democratic agreement and disagreement not only *within* the rules [...] but also *over* the rules' (Tully 2002): 207; emphasis in original). After decades of 'permissive consensus' and the 'democracy deficit', Brexit has kicked off long-overdue contestations. This facilitates a welcome 'valve' for dissenters of all stripes to chime in. And as such it may create a novel 'site' for contestation to voice views that are more likely to be heard in light of the threat of further EU exits.[25]

Thus the actual effects of the practices that have been displayed by a multitude of stakeholders in the aftermath of the vote suggest that the ongoing contestations about when and how to trigger the Article 50 procedure contribute to (1) enhancing information about the EU, and yet at the same time they also (2) have an impact on the EU's democratic quality. In effect, then, (3) the complex practices of disentangling the UK from the EU are less likely to deliver on the promise of re-establishing British sovereignty vis-à-vis the EU than instead to strengthen the EU's legitimacy. In the end, the resignation of multiple political leaders in the UK might have been too early, and Prime Minister May in the long run if she reconsiders her decision in favour of Brexit and demonstrate to all voters in Britain (leave and remain) that the UK has triggered the most effective democratization process the EU has been confronted with since its inception. This insight would lead May to engage more fully with the spectrum of democratic practices and procedures available to her, beginning with a proper debate in Parliament, as it were. Yet, May preferred to do just the opposite. And, perhaps surprisingly, two former Prime Ministers, Sir John Major and Tony Blair have now activated this window of opportunity.

Much of the referendum campaign language claimed to get Britain 'back' from the EU. Getting something back suggests that the voters retain something that rightly belongs to them, and that had been occupied – unlawfully presumably – by someone else. The discourse is one of righting a wrong. Its public claim for legitimacy is high. In the aftermath of the referendum, 'disentangling' has become a central term. Now, the task is to identify the parts that actually belong to Britain at the end of the day when all areas of integration have been 'disentangled'. Whereas the leave campaign was outward oriented, boasting that it would re-establish the old ways (of what?) and through them political legitimacy, the direction of the process triggered by the leave-vote now became inward oriented, suggesting a degree of complexity difficult to comprehend for the non-involved voters. In fact, the looming complexity of the respective political and legal processes connected with triggering and carrying out the Article 50 procedure has begun to sound more like bringing the EU into Britain than taking Britain out of the EU. This was also quickly realized by the leaders of the remain campaign and the prime minister who had brought on the referendum in the first place. After the party, the vote-leave campaigners noted that delivering on the promise of getting Britain 'back' did not equal a pole position towards legitimacy. Instead, it was the beginning of a somewhat tedious long-term process, and, in addition, a process that might actually not result in getting back the Britain that had once joined the EU, but something rather different instead, namely, a Britain in its devolved parts. So far, the legitimacy promise has proved hard to deliver. Before the vote-leave supporters realized what was next, most of those with political responsibility for the referendum process had resigned. Clearly, not delivering on a promise of the proportions alluded to by the Brexit discourse would have meant political suicide.

The change in the Brexit discourse demonstrates the dawning realization, first, that, rather than getting back what had been put into the EU, the task entails the more detailed process of disentangling legislation, regulations, procedures and other details and, second, that, contrary to what the British voters were led to believe, the task is likely to be massive and time consuming. It may, in fact, not even lead to Britain's leaving the EU. In other words, instead of the frequently proclaimed clear-cut 'never-again' 'once-and-for-all' decision that was promised by Cameron, a murky and long-winded process stands to be expected. A process that was supposed to introduce a leaner politics with less interference from 'Brussels' begins with the creation of new administrative and political posts in the UK and in Brussels, such as the 'Brexit' portfolio in the new prime minister May's cabinet, and the post of chief Brexit negotiator for Michel Barnier of the European Commission[26] and Guy Verhofstadt for the parliament. As the shock of the referendum result is gradually replaced by day-to-day politics, the question of who actually won becomes increasingly hard to answer. Apart from lacking a clear-cut solution, the post-referendum landscape in Britain is marked by political turmoil, emotional exhaustion, regional division, economic loss and, not least, family drama (consider multinational European families that have grown and settled in Britain through European citizenship practice). The absence of joy and perspective in a country that conducted a referendum that few wanted, some thought necessary and now all have come to loathe is startling. As this essay's practice-oriented analysis suggests, the challenging situation for politics, voters and the economy alike is ultimately due to an underestimation of what the EU has become after more than five decades of integration and how the UK, and with it the British people, has changed through its taking part in this process over more than four decades.

Notes

1 See: House of Lords, 2016: Report on *The Process of Withdrawing from the European Union*, London: House of Lords, European Union Committee, HL Paper 138.

2 A first version of this chapter was presented at the University Association for Contemporary European Studies (UACES) annual conference at Queen Mary, University of London, 5–7 September 2016. The current version benefits from the discussions at UACES. Thanks for helpful comments are extended towards all participants, and especially to Brigid Laffan, Amanda Hadfield, Geoffrey Edwards, Willie Patterson, Simon Bulmer, Thomas Christiansen, David Phinnemore and Cahal McCall, and wonderful editorial guidance from William Outhwaite.

3 It is ironic that much of what the EU's quasi-constitutional quality entails today has been constituted through the practice of legal integration. The process reveals quite clearly how regulatory practices and cultural practices are interrelated and, as such, equally constitutive for political entities (compare Tully 1995). This is demonstrated by many of the regulatory practices of law making that have become closely intertwined with the cultural practices of everyday life. It is best revealed by the argument about 'European Citizenship' presented by the then-advocate general, Miguel P Maduro, in the *Rottmann* case (C-135/08 Janko Rottmann v Freistaat Bayern, judgment of 2 March 2010); see also Liste (2013).

4 Judith Aldersey-Williams, in: FT 24 June 2016, https://next.ft.com/content/81a4004e-3965-11e6-9a05-82a9b15a8ee7.

5 See: *The Telegraph*, 12 September 2016, at: http://www.telegraph.co.uk/news/2016/09/12/david-davis-says-process-for-leaving-the-eu-will-be-the-most-com/.

6 See reference to a blog by David Allen Green in *The Guardian* (details of the *Guardian* article here: http://www.theguardian.com/politics/2016/jun/26/who-will-dare-pull-trigger-article-50-eu; details of the blog entry, here: http://jackofkent.com/2016/06/why-the-article-50-notification-is-important/.

7 See details here: https://www.gov.uk/government/speeches/eu-referendum-outcome-pm-statement-24-june-2016.

8 See Reuters: http://www.reuters.com/article/us-britain-eu-may-time-divorce-idUSKCN1002DZ.

9 See: House of Commons, Research Briefings on Leaving the EU (2013: 12), details: http://researchbriefings.parliament.uk/ResearchBriefing/Summary/RP13-42.

10 See: *The Evening Standard*, at: http://www.standard.co.uk/news/politics/brexit-theresa-may-could-trigger-article-50-without-parliaments-approval-a3330951.html.

11 See: *BBCRadio4* News at Five, 31 August 2016.

12 See: *The Telegraph*, 12 September 2016, at: http://www.telegraph.co.uk/news/2016/09/12/david-davis-says-process-for-leaving-the-eu-will-be-the-most-com/.

13 See: Mayer Brown Legal Consulting at: https://www.mayerbrown.com/experience/Brexit-The-UK-and-the-EU/; emphasis added.

14 Here and throughout, references to the TEU are based on the publication of the treaties in the *Official Journal of the European Union*, C 202, Vol. 59, 7 June 2016.

15 For a rare comment on the distinction between the terms migrant, refugee and asylum seeker, see *The Guardian*, 28 August 2015, at: https://www.theguardian.com/world/2015/aug/28/migrants-refugees-and-asylum-seekers-whats-the-difference.

16 See: *The Huffington Post*, 16 June 2016 at: http://www.huffingtonpost.co.uk/entry/nigel-farages-eu-has-failed-us-all-poster-slammed-as-disgusting-by-nicola-sturgeon_uk_576288c0e4b08b9e3abdc483.

17 'It would have been relatively easy to persuade the EU to take another look at free movement – easy compared with sorting out the unknowable *nightmare* of disengagement. It should be the EU that provides funding for extra social housing, extra healthcare, extra school places, extra physical infrastructure, in places that are prosperous enough to attract migrant workers. It should be the EU that raises concerns when people are leaving one place in large numbers, and rolls up its sleeves to assist them in solving those problems locally. Europe will realise that soon enough, and we will be looking on as it does' (emphasis added). See: Deborah Orr, *The Guardian*, 1 July 2016: https://www.theguardian.com/commentisfree/2016/jul/01/brexit-britain-elites-run-amok.

18 See Simon Bulmer's contribution to the discussion at the roundtable 'The EU in Crisis', UACES conference, London, 5 September 2016.

19 In detail, this research would be carried out by applying the method of abductive reasoning (compare Bueger, 2014; Bueger and Gadinger, 2015; Hofius, 2016.

20 See Council of Foreign Relations, Backgrounders Series, at: http://www.cfr.org/united-kingdom/debate-over-brexit/p37747.

21 Compare, for example, the interview with Ian Begg on BBC Radio 4; News at Five on 31 August 2016.

22 For the report in *The Guardian* on 27 August 2016, see: http://www.theguardian.com/politics/2016/aug/27/theresa-may-acting-like-tudor-monarch-in-denying-mps-a-vote-over-brexit.

23 Compare for the most recent contribution to the latter position, ex-Prime Minister Tony Blair's intervention on 1 September, see: *The Guardian*, 1 September 2016.

24 See: BBC News, 23 January 2013, at: http://www.bbc.com/news/uk-politics-21148282.

25 Compare, for example, Marine Le Pen's call for a French exit referendum, 5 September 2016.

26 Compare *The Independent*, 27 July 2016, at http://www.independent.co.uk/news/uk/politics/
european-commission-appoints-chief-brexit-negotiator-but-says-he-wont-speak-to-uk-until-
article-50-a7157731.html.

References

Bueger, Christian. 2014. 'Pathways to Practice: Praxiography and International Politics', *European Political Science Review* 6 (3): 383–406.

Bueger, Christian, and Frank Gadinger. 2015. 'The Play of International Practice', *International Studies Quarterly* 59 (3): 449–460.

Cappelletti, Maurom Onica Seccombe and Joseph Weiler, eds. 1986. *Integration through Law: Europe and the American Federal Experience*. New York: De Gruyter.

Cini, Michelle, ed. 2003. *European Union Politics*. Oxford: Oxford University Press.

Craig, Paul, and Grainne De Burca. 1998. *EU Law – Text, Cases, and Materials*, 2nd ed. Oxford: Oxford University Press.

Finnemore, Martha, and Stephen J. Toope. 2001. 'Alternatives to "Legalization": Richer Views of Law and Politics', *International Organization* 55 (3): 743–758.

Hofius, Maren. 2016. 'Community at the Border or the Boundaries of Community? The Case of EU Field Diplomats', *Review of International Studies*, FirstView, 1–29. doi: 10.1017/S0260210516000085.

Hooghe, Lisbeth, and Garry Marks. 2001. *Multi-Level Governance and European Integration*. Lanham, MD: Rowman & Littlefield.

Joergensen, Knud Erik. 1998. 'The Social Construction of the *Acquis Communautaire*: A Cornerstone of the European Edifice'. Paper read at International Studies Association, Minneapolis, MN, 17–21 March.

Liste, Philip. 2012. *Speaking International Law*. Baden-Baden: Nomos.

March, James G. and Johan P. Olsen. 1989. *Rediscovering Institutions: The Organizational Basis of Politics*. New York: The Free Press.

Merlingen, Michael, Cas Mudde and Ulrich Sedelmeier. 2000. 'Constitutional Politics and the "Embedded Acquis Communautaire": The Case of the EU Fourteen against the Austrian Government', *Constitutionalism Web-Papers, ConWEB, ConWEB*, http://www.qub.ac.uk/ies/onlinepapers/const.html (4/2000): 17 pp.

Merry, Sally Engle. 2011. 'Measuring the World: Indicators, Human Rights and Global Governance', *Current Anthropology* 52 (3): 83–95.

Milliken, Jennifer. 1999. 'The Study of Discourse in International Relations: A Critique of Research and Methods', *European Journal of International Relations* 5 (2): 225–254.

Morris, Richard T. 1956. 'A Typology of Norms', *American Sociological Review* 21 (5): 610–613.

Price, Richard. 2003. 'Transnational Civil Society and Advocacy in World Politics', *World Politics* 55: 579–606.

Puetter, U. 2012. 'Europe's Deliberative Intergovernmentalism: The Role of the Council and European Council in EU Economic Governance', *Journal of European Public Policy* 19 (2): 161–178.

Rosenfeld, Michel. 1994. 'The Rule of Law and the Legitimacy of Constitutional Democracy', *Southern California Law Review* 74: 1307–1351.

Schmidt, Vivien A. 2000. 'Democracy and Discourse in an Integrating Europe and a Globalising World', *European Law Journal* 6 (3): 277–300.

Tully, James. 1995. *Strange Multiplicity: Constitutionalism in an Age of Diversity*. Cambridge: Cambridge University Press

Tully, James. 2002. 'The Unfreedom of the Moderns in Comparison to their Ideals of Constitutionalism and Democracy', *Modern Law Review* 65 (2): 204–228.

Wiener, Antje. 1998. 'The Embedded Acquis Communautaire: Transmission Belt and Prism of New Governance', *European Law Journal* 4 (3): 294–315.

———. 2007. 'The Dual Quality of Norms and Governance beyond the State: Sociological and Normative Approaches to "Interaction",' *Critical Review of International Social and Political Philosophy* 10 (1): 47–69.

———. 2008. *The Invisible Constitution of Politics: Contested Norms and International Encounters.* Cambridge: Cambridge University Press.

Wittgenstein, Ludwig. (1953) 2005. *Philosophical Investigations, translated by G. E. M. Anscombe.* Oxford: Blackwell.

Chapter Twelve

NO EXIT FROM BREXIT?

Simon Susen

Introduction

The main purpose of this chapter is to examine the concept of Brexit. To this end, the analysis is structured as follows. The first part provides a shorthand *definition* of the concept of Brexit. The second part reflects on the historical *context* in which, on 23 June 2016, the UK referendum on European Union (EU) membership took place and which, arguably, had a profound impact on its outcome. The third part sheds light on the various sociological *implications* of the result of this referendum, paying specific attention to the principal reasons that led to the triumph of the Leave campaign over the Remain campaign. The fourth part offers some critical reflections on the *legitimacy* – or, as some may argue, illegitimacy – of the referendum's outcome. The fifth part makes some tentative remarks on the *prospects* of different Brexit scenarios – not only in relation to the UK, but also in relation to the EU in particular and the wider international community in general. Based on the preceding considerations, the chapter concludes by making a case for a 'critical sociology of Brexit'.

I. What Is Brexit?

In the most general sense, the term 'Brexit' refers to the withdrawal of the United Kingdom from the European Union. It remains to be seen whether Brexit constitutes a potential or an actual, an abrupt or a gradual, a reversible or an irreversible process. Irrespective of the question of what the exact nature of Brexit turns out to be, however, there is a wide-reaching consensus – among both its advocates and its opponents – that its consequences are of major historical significance. Of course, one may scrutinize the numerous implications of Brexit on different levels, particularly the following: social, political, economic, cultural, institutional, ideological, scientific, demographic, military, geostrategic and environmental – to mention only the most obvious ones. Notwithstanding the question of what specific role these levels may, or may not, play in the unfolding of a Brexit scenario, it is the *confluence of multiple factors* that will determine what *life in the UK outside the EU*, as well as *life in the EU without the UK as a member state*, will look like.

Brexit has been pursued by numerous individual and collective actors – most radically by the UK Independence Party (UKIP), but also by Eurosceptics of other political parties, notably those of the Conservative Party. Ever since the UK joined the European

Economic Community (EEC) in 1973, and despite the fact that the continuation of the UK's membership of the EEC was agreed to by 67 per cent of voters in the 1975 referendum[1], the UK's relationship with 'continental Europe' has always been fraught with difficulties. From the beginning, the UK's EU membership has been characterized by high levels of Euroscepticism – among its citizens in general and its political elites in particular, especially among those situated on the right of the political spectrum. In essence, the UK's fiercest critics of the European project make the following argument: initially, the UK committed to joining a merely *economic* project. As EU countries grew closer and closer together, however, it found itself immersed in a *political* project, to which – according to most British Eurosceptics – the UK had not signed up when it decided to become a member of the EEC in 1973.

From a historical point of view, it is worth remembering that numerous treaties were signed (and called into force) that led to the consolidation of the EU: the Brussels Treaty (signed 1948, in force 1948); the Paris Treaty (signed 1951, in force 1952); the Modified Brussels Treaty (signed 1954, in force 1955); the Rome Treaty (signed 1957, in force 1958); the Merger Treaty (signed 1965, in force 1967); the European Council Conclusion (signed 1975); the Schengen Treaty (signed 1985, in force 1995); the Single European Act (signed 1986, in force 1987); the Maastricht Treaty (signed 1992, in force 1993); the Amsterdam Treaty (signed 1997, in force 1999); the Nice Treaty (signed 2001, in force 2003); and the Lisbon Treaty (signed 2007, in force 2009). This gradual movement towards 'an ever closer union' of the EU's member states constitutes a historical development of which Eurosceptics, not only in the UK but also in other European countries, tend to be highly suspicious.

Under Article 50 of the Lisbon Treaty, member states have the right to withdraw from the EU at any time. Yet, given that Article 50 has never been invoked in the past, the details of the UK's withdrawal process – if it goes ahead – are subject to a considerable degree of *uncertainty*. In principle, the time frame for withdrawing from the EU is two years from the date that a particular country wishing to leave – in this case, the UK – gives formal and official notice of this intention, although an extension may be granted if the negotiations turn out to take longer than expected. Thus, the immediate question that poses itself in this context is as follows: presupposing that it actually intends to do so, *when* will the UK trigger Article 50? It is generally assumed that new agreements between the EU and the UK will be negotiated in this two-year period, although the divorce procedure may go ahead without any definite arrangements.

The Brexit vote appears to be a historical irony, considering that the UK applied to join the EEC twice (in 1963 and in 1967, respectively) and that, on both occasions, its applications were vetoed by Charles de Gaulle, the then-President of France. The main reason for this was that the UK was perceived as *largely incompatible* with continental Europe, not least due to the former's deep-seated hostility to any unifying project envisaged by the latter. After de Gaulle ceased to hold the French presidency, however, the UK's (third) application for membership was successful. When, on 1 January 1973, the UK joined the EEC, British scepticism towards the idea of a pan-European project had far from disappeared, indicating that it had become a member, above all, for economic – rather than for political – reasons. As both 'Bremainers' and 'Brexiteers' will concede, this *lack of enthusiasm for the political, let alone the cultural, dimensions underlying the European project* can be regarded as one of the primary reasons for the outcome of the 2016 UK Referendum.

The linguistic creation 'Brexit' is, evidently, a portmanteau of the words 'Britain' and 'exit'. One may speculate whether or not further national exits from the EU – such as 'Grexit' (Greece), 'Bexit' (Belgium), 'Nexit' (Netherlands), 'Frexit' (France) or 'Dexit' (Germany) – will follow. These are only a few potential scenarios related to what many interpret as the increasing unpopularity of the EU in some of its key member states. The voting result of the 2016 UK Referendum was as follows: 51.89 per cent voted to leave and 48.11 per cent voted to remain. In other words, the outcome was remarkably close, adding to the uncertainty concerning the democratic mandate of the referendum result.

It remains to be seen what both the short-term and the long-term consequences of the UK's withdrawal from the EU will be. There is no doubt, however, that Brexit – if it *is* implemented – will have a major impact on (a) the UK, (b) the EU and (c) the world. Those *favouring* Brexit tend to assume that, in the long term, the UK will be in a *stronger* position, regaining a robust sense of national sovereignty in relation to the EU in particular and the world in general. Those *rejecting* Brexit tend to believe that, in the long term, the UK will be in a *weaker* position, reduced to an increasingly marginalized player on the world stage, with a shrinking economy and significantly curtailed political influence on both regional and global decision-making processes – the irony being, of course, that all of this has been self-inflicted.

Arguably, the most controversial issue in this respect concerns the so-called 'Four Freedoms' of the European Union: (a) the free movement of *goods*; (b) the free movement of *services and freedom of establishment*; (c) the free movement of *persons* (and citizenship), including the free movement of workers; and (d) the free movement of *capital*. One thorny point of contention, on both sides of the argument, is the extent to which the UK – after having invoked Article 50 and, eventually, withdrawn from the EU – may, or may not, be able to continue to enjoy these freedoms. It is widely estimated that, on average, 45 per cent of the UK's exports go into the European Economic Area (EEA). Thus, notwithstanding the exact outcome of the negotiations between the UK and the EU, access to the latter's Single Market will be crucial to the former's future prosperity.

II. Historical Context

It is vital to examine the historical context in which, on 23 June 2016, the UK referendum on EU membership took place, since the constitution of the former had a profound impact on the outcome of the latter. From a historical perspective, the Brexit vote can be explained in terms of 'the conjunction of three phenomena: a *world problem*, a *European or EU problem* and a *British* (or, more properly, English and Welsh) *problem*'[2]. Let us, therefore, consider each of these problems.[3]

1.

The *world problem* is reflected in the prevalent disillusionment with and alienation from mainstream political parties, political leaders, political institutions and political systems.

Symptomatic of this widespread disaffection and frustration with, if not hostility towards, what many perceive as the 'business as usual' of conventional political actors and structures is the rise of populist agendas, especially of those associated with right-wing politics. Surely, new social movements – notably those whose participants pursue progressive aims and objectives – have expressed a profound sense of discontent with traditional social and political arrangements for several decades.[4] For these arrangements tend to contribute to reproducing and legitimizing mechanisms of domination, which, due to their disempowering implications for large parts of the population, leave little room for individual or collective forms of emancipation. Right-ring populism, however, is not driven by the ambition to replace representative models of democracy with deliberative or grass-roots modes of collective decision-making. Rather, it is motivated by the attempt to blame not only 'the system' – including the political, cultural and economic elites by which it is sustained – but also minority groups – such as immigrants – for social crises and dysfunctionalities.

There are numerous examples illustrating this recent trend: the rise of Donald Trump and his victory in the 2016 US presidential election; the prominent (and almost triumphant) role of the far-right (*FPÖ*[5]) candidate Norbert Hofer in the Austrian presidential election; the 'mainstreamization' of the Front National's leader Marine Le Pen in France; and, last but not least, the increasing influence of UKIP, previously led by Nigel Farage, in Great Britain. These are only some – rather obvious – examples of a wider sociopolitical transition towards the normalization of right-wing populism in 'the West'. Given that debates on immigration played a major role in the run-up to, as well as in the outcome of, the 2016 UK Referendum, it is hardly surprising that right-wing anti-immigration rhetoric shaped the agenda of political forces advocating Brexit to a significant, if not decisive, degree.

2.

The *European problem* is reflected in the prevalent disillusionment with and alienation from the structures, practices and actors of the EU. Certainly, this sense of dissatisfaction with the EU is more pronounced in some European countries than in others. As the most enthusiastic defenders of the EU are obliged to concede, however, it can be detected across the entire continent – that is, not only in *'weaker' countries*, which have been severely affected by the recent financial crisis, neoliberal austerity programmes and high rates of unemployment as well as, in the Mediterranean context, the migration crisis (especially Greece; in addition: Italy, Spain, Portugal and – in the North Atlantic – Ireland), but also in *'stronger' countries*, which, despite facing enormous endogenous and exogenous problems, continue to be *relatively* stable and prosperous (such as France) or may even have benefited from recent developments (such as Germany). Arguably, Euroscepticism, although being far from absent, is less pronounced in the 'newcomer' EU countries – such as Bulgaria (since 2007), Croatia (since 2013), Cyprus (since 2004), the Czech Republic (since 2004), Estonia (since 2004), Hungary (since 2004), Latvia (since 2004), Malta (since 2004), Poland (since 2004), Romania (since 2007), Slovakia (since 2004) and Slovenia (since 2004). Within these 'newcomer' countries, the EU tends to be perceived as a *transnational project of opportunities* – not least by those who have settled in the territories of other EU member states, but also by their citizens in general, who tend to believe that, at least in the long term, their country will be better off within a union of largely wealthy nations.

Yet, across Europe, this collective sense of optimism has considerably weakened in recent years, especially since the global financial crisis that peaked in 2008. One may argue about, and hold different opinions on, the main reasons for this fading of popularity of the EU on a large scale, but it appears that the following factors are particularly important:

(a) the EU's alleged incapacity to find an adequate response to, let alone to prevent, the *financial crisis of 2008*;

(b) the EU's alleged inability to deal with the recent *migration crisis*, combined with its general lack of success in controlling *migration flows*;

(c) the EU's alleged failure to combat, let alone to eliminate, *terrorism*;

(d) the EU's alleged tendency towards undemocratic, out-of-touch, self-referential and cumbersome bureaucratic *centralism*;

(e) the EU's alleged propensity towards undermining its member states' national *sovereignty* – above all, in political, judicial and territorial terms.

Extreme versions of this Eurosceptic view can be found not only in public opinion, shared by ordinary people 'from below', but also in populist statements, made by high-profile politicians 'from above'. Within the context of the UK referendum debate, Boris Johnson's explicit and provocative comparison of the EU's integration strategy of an 'ever closer union' with the expansionist politics of Napoleon and Adolf Hitler can be interpreted as an extreme attempt to qualify the EU's policies as authoritarian, dictatorial and ultimately undemocratic. To be sure, social-scientific analysts may hold different views on whether Euroscepticism was generated 'from below' (by ordinary European citizens) and then taken up and reinforced 'from above' (by European politicians), or whether it occurred the other way around. There is no doubt, however, that, over the past decades, a toxic ideological climate has developed in various sectors of European society – that is, a climate that has made the EU increasingly unpopular, so unpopular that it has been going through a genuine *legitimacy crisis* on a grand scale.

3.

The *British* problem – which may be more accurately described as the English and Welsh problem – is reflected in the pervasive reluctance of UK citizens and politicians to conceive of their EU membership as a largely positive condition, as illustrated in their tendency to embrace a deeply ambivalent attitude towards the EU. The British state's role in the EU and British society's role in Europe have always been a matter of contention, as expressed in the relatively even balance of opinion in the run-up to the referendum campaign, culminating in the narrow victory of the Leave campaign. The obvious question that poses itself in the wake of the referendum result is what the UK's role in a post-Brexit European scenario will be. Two European countries existing within Europe but outside the EU, namely Norway and Switzerland, are often mentioned in this context. Both of them are part of the Schengen Area and, effectively, part of the EEA: Norway is a member of the European Free Trade Association (EFTA), and Switzerland has numerous bilateral agreements with the EU. The UK's withdrawal from the EU will present uncharted territory, in the sense that Brexit – once Article 50 has been invoked and all negotiations that form part of the divorce procedure have been completed – will involve a large-scale disentanglement from the deep structural ties it has built with, within and through the EU ever since it became a member.

Arguably, the most likely scenario – although, at this stage, it is far from certain – is that the UK will choose to go down the EEA path, in order for it to retain its vital access to the European market. Even if it does not formally join the EEA, however, its official representatives – who, along with their EU counterparts, will be sitting at the Brexit negotiating table – will do everything they can to ensure that the UK preserves its access to the European market. This almost certainly means that, in one way or another, the UK will have to accept the rules of the game underlying the aforementioned 'Four Freedoms' of the EU. The irony of such a post-Brexit scenario, of course, lies in the fact that it illustrates that many of those who voted for the UK to leave the EU were systematically *misled* when making them believe that, in the Promised Land of a 'truly' independent UK, they could realistically expect a substantial fall in EU immigration. Eventually, the UK will have to choose from a range of relatively uncomfortable options, before being confronted with deeply painful and ultimately negative, albeit not necessarily catastrophic, outcomes. Most EU member states – in particular, France and Germany – will insist that, within the European market, there can be no free movement of *goods*, *services* and *capital* without the free movement of *persons* and *workers*. In other words, it is not even a matter of cherry picking: *either* 'you are in' *or* 'you are out', but you cannot have it both ways. Thus, once the UK is no longer a member of the EU and, within a post-Brexit framework, chooses to accept the free movement of *goods*, *services* and *capital* within the EEA (and does so either as a member or as a non-member of the EEA), it will almost certainly have to accept the free movement of *persons* and *workers* too.

Whatever the result of the Brexit negotiations turns out to be, the devil *will* lie in the detail and, undoubtedly, the detail *will* matter, since the ramifications are highly significant – not only for the UK itself, but also for other European countries and, indeed, for the world. The last thing that the member states of the EU – notably its most powerful players, such as Germany and France – wish to trigger is a domino effect, whereby Brexit would be succeeded by other national exits from the EU – such as 'Grexit' (Greece), 'Bexit' (Belgium), 'Nexit' (Netherlands), 'Frexit' (France) or 'Dexit' (Germany). At the moment, none of them may seem likely, but we must not forget that, a few years ago, not many people would have predicted a Brexit scenario. Time will tell what the numerous – potential and actual, short-term and long-term, minor and major – consequences of the Brexit-related opening of the Pandora's box will be. Surely, the societal effects will have different shapes and forms, while carrying different weight at different local, national, regional, continental and global levels. It seems inevitable, however, that other EU member states will not grant the UK 'special treatment', let alone endow it with a 'special position', given that its government called the referendum and its population voted to leave. From the beginning of its EU membership, the UK has been perceived as, at best, a 'difficult customer' or, at worst, a 'trouble maker', most of whose citizens and representatives, from the point of view of other EU members, have been hard to please within the family of European nations. It is no surprise, then, that even an *à la carte* approach (no Schengen, no euro, in addition to the EU deal that the then-Prime Minister, David Cameron, struck in February 2016 in Brussels) was not enough to satisfy the majority of UK voters that remaining in the EU was the most sensible option for their country.

Another potential, but highly significant, domino effect of the 2016 UK Referendum is of *domestic* nature: the possible break-up of the UK, due to Scotland's and Northern Ireland's vote to remain within the EU (62 per cent and 55.8 per cent, respectively). In light of the outcome of the 2016 UK Referendum, Scotland is in a strong position to make a case for holding another referendum on independence, and calls for a reunified Ireland have also been on the agenda since the result has been announced (although the former is far more likely to occur than the latter). Even if a second referendum in Scotland turned out to back independence, it would be far from clear to what extent such a scenario would be a desirable, let alone a viable, option for Scotland for a number of reasons: the fall of the oil price; the question of the currency (the pound sterling versus the euro); the uncertainty about EU membership (given that France, Belgium and – most forcefully – Spain are unlikely to back a separatist movement's twofold ambition to gain independence and, once this goal has been achieved, to join the EU); the insecurity arising from the question about the details of Scotland's disentanglement from the UK, considering the former's deep social, political, cultural, economic, military and historical ties with the latter. In short, even if a second referendum on Scottish independence *were* to be held and even if, this time, Scotland's population voted *for* independence, it would be far from a done deal that this 'stateless nation'[5] would be in a sufficiently strong position to convince all EU member states that it should be allowed to join the club as an independent country.

Furthermore, it remains to be seen what impact Brexit will have on the status and role of Northern Ireland – crucially, in terms of its border with the Republic of Ireland, which, if it came to Brexit, would effectively become the border between the UK and the EU. The reintroduction of border controls on the basis of strict police, if not military, surveillance systems and checkpoints seemed almost unimaginable *before* the referendum. *After* the referendum it represents a serious question that those in charge of putting Brexit into practice not only have to confront but also have to resolve. One may legitimately argue that the UK's non-inclusion in the Schengen Area and non-inclusion in the eurozone should make its exit from the EU slightly more straightforward than the hypothetical exit pursued by any of the EU countries that have signed up to Schengen and/or are fully fledged members of the EU's monetary union.

Whatever a Brexit scenario will turn out to look like, however, it is unquestionable that – as even the most optimistic Brexiteers will have to concede – the implications and ramifications are mind-bogglingly complex: in the *best-case scenario*, it will involve the UK's cumbersome renegotiation of its relationship with the EU, for which it will be forced to pay a high price, not only economically but also symbolically; in the *worst-case scenario*, it will lead to the UK's break-up, which, long before the 2016 UK Referendum, had been so famously predicted by Tom Nairn, one of the most prominent Scottish political theorists of nationalism.[6] If Cameron goes down in history as the British Prime Minister who may be regarded as directly or indirectly responsible not only for the UK's withdrawal from the EU but also for the UK's dissolution, this will be a legacy that, in terms of its far-reaching significance, will be hard to trump.

III. Sociological Implications

Let us confront the task of shedding some light on the various sociological *implications* of the result of the 2016 UK Referendum, paying particular attention to the principal reasons that led to the triumph of the Leave campaign over the Remain campaign. The key word that has been, and continues to be, mentioned by both experts and laypersons commenting on the result of the 2016 UK Referendum – and doing so from all sides of the political spectrum – is *divisions*. Hence, the obvious question that poses itself is what kind of divisions they have in mind.

What is striking in this respect is that especially those who are opposed to the outcome of the 2016 UK Referendum tend to stress that, in their judgement, the Brexit vote was, above all, a *protest vote* and, hence, primarily a vote *against* various issues, rather than a vote *for* a set of desired results. This interpretation is ironic insofar as Brexiteers commonly accused those in charge of the Remain campaign of relying on 'Project Fear' – that is, on a collective endeavour embedded in a political discourse based on scaremongering and incapable of making a positive case for UK's membership in the current, or in a reformed, EU. From the point of view of most Brexiteers, it was not their own project but the project of the Bremainers that was predominantly about making a case *against*, rather than a case *for*, a post-referendum scenario – namely, against social, political and economic uncertainty and decline. The Brexiteers, in the eyes of their supporters, succeeded in making a *positive* case for their desired goal, notably 'UK's independence'. This bold political objective was expressed in various catchphrases – such as 'Let's take back control!', 'We want our country back!', 'Put Britain first!' and 'This Thursday [23 June 2016] can be our country's Independence Day' – all of which, as cynics may point out, can be interpreted as socio-hermeneutic manifestations of the collective narcissism pervading crucial elements of the 2016 UK Referendum debate.

The outcome of the referendum suggests that the rhetoric of the Leave campaign was far more effective than that of the Remain campaign. In the opinion of a vast number of voters, the former came across as far more *positive* and *optimistic* than the latter. The Bremainers seemed to offer little more than a largely *passive* attitude, concerned with preserving the status quo in an uninspiring and pragmatic, if not technocratic, manner. The Brexiteers, by contrast, appeared to transmit – and, if successful, to be able to deliver on – a fundamentally *active* attitude, oriented towards the construction of a bright future in an inspirational and idealistic, if not utopian, fashion.

> The 'remain' campaign relied heavily on trying to scare people into voting for the status quo. Indeed, it was foolish of the Cameron government to allow the seemingly *passive* term 'remain' to define the potential future of the UK in Europe rather than asserting an *active* goal for building a better future. Hardly anyone in the 'remain' camp presented an idealistic argument for a European future (Gordon Brown made an attempt).[7]

It would be erroneous, however, to overlook, let alone to deny, the *negativity* permeating the Brexit campaign: caught up in a deep sense of national nostalgia, combined with a romanticizing celebration of a glorious past, implicitly connected to the worldwide influence of the British Empire, the Leave campaign lacked any concrete and thought-through proposals for an alternative future, informed by a clear, detailed and viable game plan.

> The vote was grounded in *nostalgia*. The Brexit campaign was *almost entirely negative* and *devoid of plans for an alternative future*. It played on an old idea of sovereignty, old English ideas about the difference between the island nation and the mainland of Europe, alarm over immigrants and claims that the UK was somehow subsidizing Europe.[8]

Another irony of Brexit, then, consists in the following paradox:

- On the one hand, the Remain campaign – in the eyes of many voters – lacked electoral appeal because it *appeared* largely *negative, pessimistic* and *passive*, whereas the Leave campaign – in the eyes of many voters – possessed electoral appeal because it *appeared* largely *positive, optimistic* and *(pro-)active*.
- On the other hand, the Remain campaign sought to stick to a *pragmatic* and *realistic* strategy, referring to the 'hard' European reality of which the UK was already part and obeying, with some exceptions due to EU concessions, the rules of the game with which it was already familiar, whereas the Leave campaign endorsed an *obscure* and *unrealistic* vision, lacking a coherent and feasible outline of what British life outside the UK would look like and, more importantly, how exactly it would be organized.

The paradox described above is symptomatic of another significant problem attached to the 2016 UK Referendum: voters were confronted with a *binary choice* (Remain versus Leave), but could vote either way for *very different* – and, on several levels, diametrically opposed – reasons:

- For those on the *radical left*, the EU is essentially a *market-driven* project of transnational capitalism, in which, under the hegemonic influence of Germany and France, the pursuit of financial profit and the free movement of capital can be guaranteed and, in fact, maximized. Most defenders of this position, however, tend to be willing to accept the historic achievements of the EU – such as its commitment to the progressive ideals of the Enlightenment as well as its contributions to securing peace and cooperation between European political powers.
- For those on the *radical right*, the EU is essentially a *pan-European* project, that is, an expression of the historic attempt to build a United Europe, which, under the hegemonic influence of Germany and France, is oriented towards the construction of a 'European Federation', a 'Federal Europe', a 'Federal Republic of Europe', a 'United States of Europe' or a 'European state or superstate' – that is, a Europe in which national sovereignty ceases to exist.
- For those on the *centre-left*, the EU is essentially a *civilizational* project shaped by Enlightenment ideals – 'such as progress, tolerance, liberty, equality, solidarity, dignity, sovereignty, and autonomy'[9] – and, ultimately, a political endeavour capable of

providing a cosmopolitan framework in which 'social processes of liberation, self-determination, and unification'[10] predominate, peace and prosperity are guaranteed, pluralism and multiculturalism are celebrated, while transnational cooperation and deliberation preponderate.

- For those on the *centre-right*, the EU is essentially a *pragmatic* project, permitting European nation states to reach an unprecedented degree of social, political and economic stability, not only by protecting but also by fostering the free movement of (a) goods, (b) services, (c) persons/workers and (d) capital – all of which, by virtue of the 'invisible hand' of the European market, contribute to the enhancement of the standards of life across the continent, demonstrating that the advantages and benefits outweigh the disadvantages and costs of being a fully fledged member of this organization.

In light of their largely *favourable* view of the EU, those on the *centre-left* and those on the *centre-right* were likely to vote in favour of *Remain* (Blairites, Cameronites and so on). In light of their largely *critical* view of the EU, those on the *radical right* were likely to vote in favour of *Leave* (Goveites, Farageites and so on). In light of their deeply *ambivalent* view of the EU, the case of those on the *radical left* is more complicated: while many of them abstained from voting or simply cast a blank vote, most of them were more likely to vote in favour of *Remain* as 'the lesser of two evils' option (Corbynites and so on).

The ideological scheme outlined above is, of course, a reductive account of what is, in reality, a far more multifaceted picture. Even this four-dimensional simplification of the motivational background against which politicians made their case and citizens cast their vote, however, illustrates the complexity that permeates the decision-making process of the 2016 UK Referendum – a degree of complexity to which, in terms of both the act of voting itself and the far-reaching consequences of the overall result, a binary choice between Remain and Leave cannot do justice.

If, however, it is true that, as various commentators have argued and large numbers of voters have openly admitted, the Brexit vote was, to a considerable degree, a *protest vote*, then we need to ask *what* many, if not most, of those who voted in support of Brexit actually voted *against*.

Brexit was a vote *against London, globalization and multiculturalism* as much as a vote *against Europe*.[11]

Arguably, Brexit was also a vote *for some version of the past*. Fully 75 percent of those aged 18 to 24 voted for a future in Europe. Sixty-one percent of those over 65, along with a majority of all those over 45, voted against.[12]

Brexit was manifestly a vote *against multiculturalism* and *for English nationalism*.[13]

The Brexit campaign wasn't driven by arguments about costs and benefits. It was driven by *resentment, frustration and anger*. It was *emotional and expressive*. And the grievances expressed had real foundations, even if the EU was a partially misplaced target and *no practical solutions* were offered.[14]

The main question with which we are confronted in this respect concerns the afore-mentioned *divisions* that, presumably, exist in contemporary Britain and have shaped the outcome of the referendum in a decisive manner.

In a schematic, and admittedly simplifying, fashion, these divisions can be described as follows:

Remain:	Leave:
empowered	disempowered
winners	losers
wealthy	poor
employed	unemployed
highly educated	poorly educated
university-educated	non-university-educated
white or pink collar	blue collar
tertiary sector	primary and secondary sectors
young	old
18–44-year-olds	45–65-plus-year-olds
urban	rural
Scotland/Northern Ireland	England/Wales
South-East/North-West England	North-East/South-West England
centre-left/centre-right	radical right (some radical left)
progressive	conservative
Labour/Liberals/Greens	UKIP/right-wing Conservatives
'Modern Conservatives'	'Traditional Conservatives'
cosmopolitan/globalist	parochial/nationalist
modern(ist)	traditional(ist)
multicultural	monocultural
outward-looking	inward-looking
non-white (Asian/black) British	white British
multilingual	monolingual
Muslim	Christian
Catholic	Anglican/Protestant

From the Remain perspective:

prudent	imprudent
status-quo-affirmative	status-quo-resentful
risk-averse	risk-taking

From the Leave perspective:

boring	exciting
lacklustre	inspiring
unimaginative	imaginative

From both perspectives:

pessimistic	optimistic
optimistic	pessimistic
negative	positive
positive	negative
past-oriented	future-oriented
future-oriented	past-oriented

For the right or the wrong reasons, these are widely considered the *key divisions* to which commentators across the board – that is, from different angles, with different emphases and within different explanatory frameworks – refer in their various analyses and assessments of the Brexit vote.[15] Of course, one may engage in endless debates concerning both the role and the significance of each of these (real or alleged) divisions in British society. Irrespective of how one chooses to interpret their roots and ramifications, it is difficult to deny – regardless of one's view of the relationship between the UK and the EU – that they played a pivotal role in shaping the outcome of the referendum. In essence, these divisions may be classified as follows:

- *social* divisions
  (empowered versus disempowered, winners versus losers)
- *economic* divisions
  (wealthy versus poor, employed versus unemployed)
- *educational* divisions
  (highly educated versus poorly educated, university-educated versus non-university-educated)
- *professional* divisions
  (white- or pink-collar workers versus blue-collar workers, tertiary-sector workers versus primary- and secondary-sector workers)
- *generational* divisions
  (young versus old, 18–44-year-olds versus 45–65-plus-year-olds)
- *geographic* divisions
  (urban versus rural, Scotland/Northern Ireland versus England/Wales, South-East/North-West England versus North-East/South-West England)
- *political* divisions
  (centre-left/centre-right versus radical right, progressive versus conservative, Labour/Liberals/Greens versus UKIP/right-wing Conservatives, 'Modern Conservatives' versus 'Traditional Conservatives')
- *ideological* divisions
  (cosmopolitan/globalist versus parochial/nationalist, modernist versus traditionalist)
- *cultural* divisions
  (multicultural versus monocultural, outward-looking versus inward-looking)
- *ethnic* divisions
  (non-white British versus white British, multilingual versus monolingual)
- *religious* divisions
  (Muslim versus Christian, Catholic versus Anglican/Protestant)
- *attitudinal* divisions
  (*Remain perspective:* prudent versus imprudent, status-quo-affirmative versus status-quo-resentful, risk-averse versus risk-taking)
  (*Leave perspective:* boring versus exciting, lacklustre versus inspiring, unimaginative versus imaginative)

(*Remain perspective:* pessimistic versus optimistic, negative versus positive, past-oriented
   versus future-oriented)

(*Leave perspective:* optimistic versus pessimistic, positive versus negative, future-oriented
   versus past-oriented)

The types of division to which most commentators, notably those on the left of the political
spectrum, tend to attribute the greatest importance are (1) social, (2) economic, (3) educational, (4) professional, (5) generational, (6) geographic, (7) political and (8) ideological
divisions. Surely, one needs to treat all figures used in support of this division-focused interpretation of the Brexit vote with caution, in order not to fall into the trap of relying on
reductionist explanations as to why particular sectors of the UK population voted one way
or another. At the same time, however, it is crucial to recognize the role that each of these
divisions played in influencing the outcome of the referendum, insofar as they are indicative of the extent to which UK citizens' *attitudes* towards the EU in particular and towards
Europe in general are profoundly shaped by the *positions* that they occupy within British
society. More importantly, the question that poses itself is why the Remain campaign failed
(whereas the Leave campaign managed) to appeal to particular sectors of the population,
especially to those who – had they been convinced not only by the benefits and advantages
of staying in the EU, but also by the more universal and long-term historical implications
of continued UK membership – could have easily swung the result the other way.

   It has become a cliché to compare the current situation to the historical period of
the 1930s in continental Europe, but it is indeed worrying, and potentially disastrous,
that progressive political forces – not only in the UK, but also in other countries – tend
to disregard the counterintuitive truth that the marginalized, excluded, deprived, disenfranchised and disempowered sectors of the population do not necessarily hold opinions
and subscribe to normative discourses, let alone cast their vote, in accordance with what
critical sociologists – notably, those who examine the social world in Marxist, feminist,
Bourdieusian or Chomskyan terms – would consider their *real* interests. The 'like turkeys
voting for Christmas' idiom – although it certainly applies to the Brexit vote, because
those who have been misled will ultimately have to pay the bill – is not sufficiently radical
in that it misses one vital point: turkeys do not have a vote, whereas citizens – including
the most underprivileged among them – do have a vote and, more importantly, will have
to face the consequences of 'Christmas' as *living*, rather than dead, beings. It remains to
be seen how lively life after (or, possibly, without) Brexit will be for them.

IV. Legitimacy

This part shall offer some critical reflections on the *legitimacy* – or, as some may argue,
illegitimacy – of the 2016 UK Referendum's outcome. The result of the 2016 UK
Referendum has triggered one of the most serious political crises in Europe since the end
of World War II. In public discourse, one of the most striking words used to describe the
post-referendum situation in the UK is *uncertainty*.

   It appears, then, that the post-referendum scenario constitutes a historical context characterized by an enormous – and, in many ways, unprecedented – degree of social, political

and economic uncertainty. In the best-case scenario, it will lead to the temporary *weakening* of the UK's position in Europe; in the worst-case scenario, it will result not only in the gradual *decline* of the UK's influence on the world stage but also in its *break-up*. Of course, supporters of Scottish and Irish independence are unlikely to conceive of the UK's shrinking to a binational union between England and Wales as a 'worst-case scenario', given that their formal and definitive separation from these two British 'home nations' is what they have been striving for all along. The issue of the different possible post-Brexit scenarios put aside, an important question that needs to be addressed concerns the very legitimacy – or, as some may conclude, illegitimacy – of the 2016 UK Referendum's outcome. In this respect, we need to take into account a number of key dimensions, on the basis of which the legitimacy of this referendum can – or, perhaps, must – be called into question.

1.

Large proportions of the electorate were *misled* by the Leave campaign, whose main slogans, propositions and promises were based on lies, gross inaccuracies, major misrepresentations and populist sound bites.

2.

The electoral choice between Remain and Leave was unjustifiably *simplistic*. The issues at stake – notwithstanding the question of whether or not they could be grasped by the average voter – were too significant, too complex and too far-reaching to be decided in terms of a choice between two options.

3.

The binary electoral choice between Remain and Leave was unduly, as well as deceptively, *polarizing*. Both in ideological and in sociological terms, the reasons why electors voted one way or another were sufficiently *diverse* to suggest that the reduction of the profound heterogeneity of normative positions on the EU to a polarized and polarizing choice between Remain and Leave was not only procedurally inadequate but also politically treacherous. It is simply absurd that both politicians and voters who, in many cases, held *radically different views* found themselves 'in the same boat' by having their opinions and voices reduced to one of the two options. There were far more than two sides to the argument.

4.

Referenda in the UK – especially if they are of major national and international significance, with vast long-term consequences, not only for the home population but also for Europe in particular and the world in general – are *consultative*, rather than decisive. A striking feature of the UK political system – ever since it came into existence during the Glorious Revolution in 1688 – is that it prescribes that *Westminster* possesses *sovereign* decision-making power. It is the legislative force of representative democracy embodied in the UK parliament, rather than the advisory function of referenda, by virtue of which decisions are taken to govern the country. Whatever one makes of the UK's political system, which, in many respects, is shaped by the anachronistic legacy of the late seventeenth century and several features of which may be interpreted as an obsolete hangover from the past, the country remains a *representative democracy*, in which *sovereign power lies with, and is exercised by, Parliament*. In other words, Parliament needs to debate, and to vote on, the result of the referendum. Bearing in mind the magnitude of the numerous issues that are at stake, it would be democratically legitimate for the Westminster Parliament to decide *not* to invoke Article 50, if the majority of its members came to the conclusion that the consequences of withdrawing from the EU would be too severe, if not catastrophic, not only in the short term but also, more importantly, in the long term.

5.

Unlike other countries (such as Switzerland) in which referenda are common practice, the UK does *not* have any clear, detailed and explicit *rules and regulations* about the decision-making power of referenda, that is, about the premises that define whether or not they are binding. Particularly important issues in this regard are the *size* of the majority vote as well as the *distribution* of the votes across different regions and the four 'home nations'. Given that the overall result was extremely close (51.89 per cent in favour of Leave and 48.11 per cent in favour of Remain), and given that it was evenly split between the four 'home nations' (England and Wales in favour of Leave versus Scotland and Northern Ireland in favour of Remain), it is far from obvious that the Leave campaign has a democratic mandate to go ahead with Brexit. If just above half a million (approximately six hundred thousand) UK electors had voted Remain instead of Leave, the result would have been the opposite. Two 'home nations' have (in the case of Scotland, resolutely and overwhelmingly) voted in favour of remaining within the EU. Dragging them, against their will, out of the EU would not only be *undemocratic* but also, most likely, lead to the *break-up* of the UK. Considering the extensive scope of the consequences triggered by Brexit, it is difficult to see how those engaging in the formal procedure of taking the UK out of the EU could claim to possess a legitimate, let alone a solid, democratic mandate. Assessing the legitimacy of the 2016 UK Referendum, the two key issues at stake are 'the *matter* put to referendum and the actual *procedure* of holding the referendum'[16]: the latter was highly inappropriate for dealing with, let alone doing justice to, the enormity of the former.

6.

Constitutional democracies must have rules and regulations in place that prevent the *misuse* of referenda as mere instruments to push through normative agendas that, if they are implemented, have vast social, political and economic consequences – especially if these, at least in the medium term, are irreversible. It is no accident that, for example, the Federal Republic of Germany – in light of the German experience with referenda in the Weimar Republic (1918–1933) and, subsequently, in the consolidation of Nazi fascism (1933–1945)[17] – substantially limited the decision-making power of referenda within its own territory (both in its pre-reunification period, 1949–1990, and in its post-reunification period, 1990–present) and practically confined their role to the federal level of the *Länder*.[18] Surely, one can engage in enlightening debates on the pros and cons of referenda. There are strong arguments in favour of referenda – such as their tendency to spark political engagement, discussion and controversy at the grass-roots level and, thus, their potential contributions to the realization of radical, direct and participatory forms of democracy.[19] Yet, referenda are politically dangerous to the degree that they tend to *polarize* opinion and foster the emergence of *populist* discourses, based on reductive rhetoric and catchy slogans, rather than on in-depth critical analysis. Referenda may be suitable for case-specific policies and/or legislative matters, although even at such an issue-focused level they are far from unproblematic. When electorates are asked to voice their opinion, or to make a judgement or a choice, on *a large and complex range of interconnected societal issues* by virtue of *one single binary-choice vote*, referenda are largely inappropriate as reliable instruments for democratic, informed and responsible decision-making processes.

7.

It is true that, as previously examined, the 2016 UK Referendum is indicative of numerous deep *divisions* that exist within British society. Of course, one may rightly add that, to a greater or lesser extent, such an epiphenomenalist analysis of the electorate applies to *every* parliamentary election in British history. In this case, however, we are dealing not only with a referendum, rather than with a parliamentary election, but also with a large-scale scenario – the possibility of Brexit – the consequences of which may be not only profoundly damaging, if not catastrophic, but also, in several respects, irreversible.

- When reflecting on *social* divisions (empowered versus disempowered, winners versus losers) and on *economic* divisions (wealthy versus poor, employed versus unemployed), it is important to concede that it is widely acknowledged that, for a large number of electors, the Brexit vote was – and was meant to be – a *protest vote*. 'Ironically many of those who voted Brexit will bear the worst costs of economic decline and financial crisis and in the end the elites win.'[20]
- When reflecting on *educational* divisions (highly educated versus poorly educated, university-educated versus non-university-educated) and on *professional* divisions (white- or pink-collar workers versus blue-collar workers, tertiary-sector workers versus primary- and secondary-sector workers), it is important to account for the fact that, for a large number of electors, the Brexit vote was based on *misinformation* and *deception*. Ironically, many of those who voted Brexit were those who lacked accurate information on what it actually meant in terms of its far-reaching consequences.[21]
- When reflecting on *generational* divisions (young versus old, 18–44- year-olds versus 45–65-plus-year-olds), it is important to note that the age group that voted overwhelmingly in favour of Leave – that is, the 45–65-plus-year-old electors – is constituted by those British citizens whose future will be affected by the Brexit vote for the *shortest* time span,

whereas the age group that voted overwhelmingly in favour of Remain – that is, the 18–44-year-old electors – is constituted by those British citizens whose future will be affected by the Brexit vote for the *longest* time span. Ironically, the majority of the 45–65-plus-year-old voters decided over the long-term future – and against the will – of the majority of the 18–44-year-old voters.

- When reflecting on *geographic* divisions (urban versus rural, Scotland/Northern Ireland versus England/Wales, South-East/North-West England versus North-East/South-West England), it is important to face up to the intricacy permeating the Brexit-vote situation: if the UK were to go ahead with Brexit, the two 'home nations' that voted in favour of Leave – that is, England and Wales – would drag those two 'home nations' that voted in favour of Remain – Scotland and Northern Ireland – into a future that, while it might be desired by the majority of the former's electorate, was *not* desired by the majority of the latter's electorate. Ironically, what was, in the eyes of the Brexiteers, meant to be a collective political act oriented towards the re-establishment of 'national' sovereignty, independence and autonomy, and thus towards the strengthening of the UK's position on the world stage, might turn out to be a *divisive* political act resulting in *national break-up* – and, hence, not only in the weakening of the UK's position on the world stage, but also in its dissolution or at least its shrinking to 'an ever smaller union' between England and Wales.

- When reflecting on *political* divisions (centre-left/centre-right versus radical right, progressive versus conservative, Labour/Liberals/Greens versus UKIP/right-wing Conservatives, 'Modern Conservatives' versus 'Traditional Conservatives'), it is important not to underestimate the long-term consequences of the Brexit vote on the *UK parliamentary system*. What was meant to be little more than Cameron's attempt to resolve an internal conflict in the Conservative Party turned out to lead to the most severe constitutional crisis in modern British history. Ironically, the Eurosceptic and Europhobic supporters of the right wing of the Conservative Party and those of UKIP – who, overall, represent a relatively small minority at Westminster – were given the opportunity to mobilize ill-informed preconceptions, prejudices and resentments about the EU, to such an extent that *pro-European and Europhile Members of Parliament (MPs)* – who, overall, represent a considerable *majority at Westminster* (modern/moderate Conservative MPs, most Labour MPs and literally all Liberal MPs) – are forced into a situation in which they have to implement, and to legitimize, a political project that they did not support in the first place and in which the only room for manoeuvre appears to be the option of translating 'hard Brexit' into 'soft Brexit', rather than into 'no Brexit' at all.[22]

- When reflecting on *ideological* divisions (cosmopolitan/globalist versus parochial/nationalist, modernist versus traditionalist), it is important to spell out that, no matter how hard most Brexiteers – and so-called reluctant Bremainers – try to reassure both UK citizens and the international community that Brexit is not about taking the UK out of *Europe* but only about liberating it from the alleged chains of the *EU*, it does represent a *major paradigm shift* from a cosmopolitan and outward-looking *United* Kingdom to an increasingly parochial and inward-looking *Divided* Kingdom, reduced to an alliance of 'Little England' and 'Little Wales', whose future may be shaped by the hegemony of neoliberal austerity, law-and-order and anti-immigration policies. Ironically, the imaginary of 'an even greater (and more British) Great Britain' may translate into the reality of 'an even smaller (and more English) Small Britain'.

- When reflecting on *cultural* divisions (multicultural versus monocultural, outward-looking versus inward-looking), it is important to highlight that the UK has always been, and will always remain, a *multicultural* society. As such, it is made up not only of four 'home nations' – that is, England, Wales, Scotland and Northern Ireland – but also of inhabitants with diverse cultural backgrounds from different parts of the world. In fact, ever since it came into existence, 'there has been no independent Britain, no "Island nation" '[23] – at least not in the strict sense of an economically self-sufficient, politically disconnected and culturally homogenous entity. Ironically, the Brexit campaign gave the misleading impression that a Brexit vote would pave the way for the construction of an independent Brexitania, whose citizens' identity would be based on a monoculturally defined sense of pure, pristine and patriotic Britishness, thereby repudiating its multiculturally constituted constitution and socially eclectic heritage.

- When reflecting on *ethnic* divisions (non-white British versus white British, multilingual versus monolingual), it is important to point out that the UK has always been, and will always remain, a *multi-ethnic* society. In the run-up to the 2014 referendum, 'the most visceral attacks'[24] launched by the Brexit campaigners 'came in relation to a sense of that national community having been betrayed by a metropolitan elite that appeared to care more for the situation of "non-British" others than it did for the "legitimate" citizens of Britain'.[25] Ironically, the rise of discursive (and, in some cases, physical) assaults on ethnic minorities before and after the Brexit vote is not primarily an expression of the divisions between the UK and the EU but, above all, a manifestation of the ethnic – and, on many levels, racialized – divisions within British society itself.[26]

- When reflecting on *religious* divisions (Muslim versus Christian, Catholic versus Anglican/Protestant), it is important to stress that, according to most statistics available on this matter[27], the religious groups that, for the right or the wrong reasons, are often perceived as 'backward-looking', namely Catholics and Muslims, voted overwhelmingly in favour of Remain, whereas the religious groups that, for the right or the wrong reasons, are frequently perceived as 'forward-looking', namely Anglicans and Protestants, tended to vote in favour of Leave.[28] Ironically, then, the parameters of 'regressive' and 'progressive' appear to have been turned upside down by the motivational infrastructure of religious electors casting their votes at the 2016 UK Referendum.

- When reflecting on *attitudinal* divisions (*Remain perspective:* prudent versus imprudent, status-quo-affirmative versus status-quo-resentful, risk-averse versus risk-taking; *Leave perspective:* boring versus exciting, lacklustre versus inspiring, unimaginative versus imaginative; *Remain perspective:* pessimistic versus optimistic, negative versus positive, past-oriented versus future-oriented; *Leave perspective:* optimistic versus pessimistic, positive versus negative, future-oriented versus past-oriented), it is important to remark that, in a somewhat stereotypical way, the two camps were caricatured *by each other* on the basis of diametrically opposed mindsets.

   – According to the Bremainers, the Leave campaign was imprudent, status-quo-resentful and unnecessarily risk-taking.

- According to the Brexiteers, the Remain campaign was boring, lacklustre and unimaginative.
- On some levels, both campaigns accused one another of very similar, if not the same, limitations, but they did so for diametrically opposed reasons.
  - According to the Bremainers, the Leave campaign was pessimistic, negative and past-oriented: it painted a misleadingly bleak – and, arguably, distorted – picture of the UK's annual financial contribution to the EU as well as of the EU-based immigrants freely moving to the UK, and it mobilized a nostalgic collective imaginary promising the restoration of national sovereignty, comparable to the era of the British Empire, in a post-Brexit reality.
  - According to the Brexiteers, the Remain campaign was pessimistic, negative and past-oriented: it painted a misleadingly bleak – and, arguably, distorted – picture of the UK's life outside the EU, underestimating its ability to govern itself and to break out of the straitjacket of the EU's bureaucracy and lack of accountability as well as to challenge the EU's structural incapacity to deal with, let alone to prevent, the financial and the migration crises. In their view, Brexit is, above all, about the UK's right to reconvert itself into the protagonist of its own future.
  - From the point of view of the Bremainers, the Brexiteers *overstated* the advantages and *understated* the disadvantages of leaving the EU.
  - From the point of view of the Brexiteers, the Bremainers *overstated* the advantages and *understated* the disadvantages of staying in the EU.
- Ironically, then, Bremainers and Brexiteers accused one another of very similar – if not nominally equivalent – limitations, but when doing so they made their respective cases on the basis of diametrically opposed reasons.

V. Prospects

The primary aim of the following reflections is to make some tentative remarks on the prospects of different Brexit scenarios – not only in relation to the UK, but also in relation to the EU in particular and the wider international community in general. One may speculate about what exactly is going to happen in the UK over the next few months, years and decades. As illustrated in the preceding sections, the UK is a country characterized by profound *divisions* – notably, by social, educational, generational, geographic, political, ideological, cultural, ethnic, religious and attitudinal divisions. Paradoxically, these divisions make it both relatively easy and relatively difficult to formulate hypotheses about future developments.

- On the one hand, it does not take a genius to predict that these *divisions* – owing to their deep, multilayered and far-reaching constitution – are *unlikely to disappear any time soon.* If anything, the degree of their significance and intensity will increase, meaning that – both within and outside the EU, both in the short term and in the long term – the governability of the UK will be highly complex and the country's overall development, as a society, will suffer from a *lack of cross-sectional unity and cohesion.*
- On the other hand, we have to accept that it is far from certain how exactly these divisions – which are tension-laden, contradictory and potentially destructive at many levels – will

evolve and how precisely they will manifest themselves in *political trends and developments of the future*. It sounds like a cliché, but, faced with the numerous variables shaping the current situation in the UK, the only real certainty is the presence of a *profound sense of uncertainty*.

Despite the seriousness of the limbo in which the UK finds itself in the aftermath of the 2016 Referendum, it is possible to identify – broadly speaking – *six scenarios*, some of which are more likely, and some of which are less likely, to emerge within the near future.

Scenario 1: 'Straight Hard Brexit'

The first possibility is the *'straight hard Brexit' scenario*. In this scenario, Article 50 will be triggered in early or mid-2017, the negotiations between the UK and the EU about the details of Brexit will commence and last for approximately two years, and by the end of 2019 the UK will have completely withdrawn from the EU, without being a member of the EEA and without continuing to subscribe to the 'Four Freedoms' principle. This scenario would do justice to the slogans 'out means out' and 'Brexit means Brexit'.

Scenario 2: 'Straight Soft Brexit'

The second possibility is the *'straight soft Brexit' scenario*. In this scenario, Article 50 will be triggered in early or mid-2017, the negotiations between the UK and the EU about the details of Brexit will commence and last for two to three years, and by 2019/2020 the UK will have formally withdrawn from the EU, but it will remain a member of the EEA and will effectively continue to subscribe to the 'Four Freedoms' principle. In formal terms, the UK will cease to be a member of the EU; in practical terms, however, it will continue to have access to the European Single Market, paying a heavy price for this privilege, in addition to not being able to sit at the EU decision-making table.

Scenario 3: 'Relegitimized Hard Brexit'

The third possibility is the *'relegitimized hard Brexit' scenario*. In this scenario, Article 50 will be triggered in early or mid-2017, the negotiations between the UK and the EU about the details of Brexit will commence and last for two to three years, by 2019/2020 the UK government – after having presented the main aspects of the proposed deal with the EU (which will consist in the UK formally withdrawing from *both* the EU *and* the EEA) to the general public – will call a general election and/or hold a referendum, and – with the democratic mandate of a newly elected Leave government and/or a Leave referendum result – the UK will officially accept the deal on offer and, consequently, cease to be a member not only of the EU but also of the EEA.

Scenario 4: 'Relegitimized Soft Brexit'

The fourth possibility is the *'relegitimized soft Brexit' scenario*. In this scenario, Article 50 will be triggered in early or mid-2017, the negotiations between the UK and the EU about the details of Brexit will commence and last for two to three years, by 2019/2020 the UK government – after having presented the main aspects of the proposed deal with the EU (which will consist in the UK formally withdrawing from the EU, but maintaining its EEA membership) to the general public – will call a general election and/or hold a referendum, and – with the democratic mandate of a newly elected Leave government and/or a Leave referendum result – the UK will officially accept the deal on offer and continue to be a member of the EEA, but cease to be a member of the EU.

Scenario 5: 'Autocratic No Brexit'

The fifth possibility is the *'autocratic no Brexit' scenario*. In this scenario, Article 50 will be triggered in early or mid-2017, the negotiations between the UK and the EU about the details of Brexit will commence and last for two to three years, and by 2019/2020 the UK government, *without* holding another referendum and *before* calling another election, will officially reject the deal on offer and decide to remain a member of the EU.

Scenario 6: 'Legitimized No Brexit'

The sixth possibility is the *'legitimized no Brexit' scenario*. In this scenario, Article 50 will be triggered in early or mid-2017, the negotiations between the UK and the EU about the details of Brexit will commence and last for two to three years, by 2019/2020 the UK government – after having presented the main aspects of the proposed deal with the EU (which will consist in the UK formally withdrawing from both the EU and the EEA) to the general public – will call a general election and/or hold a referendum, and – with the democratic mandate of a newly elected Remain government and/or a Remain referendum result – the UK will officially reject the deal on offer and remain a member of the EU.

*** *** ***

What is the likelihood of one of these scenarios becoming reality? Arguably, there are strong reasons to believe that a realistic predictive assessment – in the order *from 'least likely' to 'most likely'* – looks roughly as follows:

Scenario 5: 'Autocratic No Brexit'

The *'autocratic no Brexit' scenario* is the *least likely* scenario, not only because it would be difficult to sell to the British electorate, but also because it would be difficult to sell to the international community, including the EU. It would deprive the UK government of both internal and external legitimacy. Although it would prevent both the UK's withdrawal from the EU and the break-up of the four-nation state from happening, it would be extremely damaging to the country's future.

Scenario 1: 'Straight Hard Brexit'

The *'straight hard Brexit' scenario* is the *second-least likely* scenario, not only because it would be difficult to sell to the British public, but also because it would simply not be in the long-term interest of the UK to find itself not only outside the EU but also outside the EEA and, thus, detached from the European Single Market, with which its economy is deeply entangled and upon which it is profoundly dependent.

Scenario 3: 'Relegitimized Hard Brexit'

The *'relegitimized hard Brexit' scenario* is the *third-least likely* scenario, not only because leaving *both* the EU *and* the EEA would be almost tantamount to political and economic suicide, but also because this radical Leave option would be unlikely to obtain a democratic mandate on the basis of a newly elected government and/or another referendum. Still, a 'relegitimized hard Brexit' scenario is slightly more likely than a 'straight hard Brexit' scenario, because even a Conservative government will do everything it can (including holding an election and/or another referendum) to avoid any kind of 'hard Brexit' scenario, given that leaving *both* the EU *and* the EEA is not in the UK's strategic interest.

Scenario 2: 'Straight Soft Brexit'

The *'straight soft Brexit' scenario* is the *third-most likely* scenario, not only because it would minimize the disadvantages of leaving the EU by maximizing the advantages of remaining in the EEA, but also because this option would allow the current government to 'get on with the job' without having to obtain another democratic mandate on the basis of an additional election and/or referendum.

Scenario 4: 'Relegitimized Soft Brexit'

The *'relegitimized soft Brexit' scenario* is the *joint most likely* scenario, not only because it would minimize the disadvantages of leaving the EU by maximizing the advantages of remaining in the EEA, but also because this option could reasonably find public support on the basis of a general election and/or another referendum.

Scenario 6: 'Legitimized No Brexit'

The *'legitimized no Brexit' scenario* is the other *joint most likely* scenario, not only because it would permit the UK to enjoy the advantages of remaining in both the EU and the EEA, but also because, on the basis of another general election and/or another referendum, it would bestow the government with sufficient political legitimacy to keep the UK in the EU.

Wishful Thinking?

Those of us who harbour the hope that the Brexit referendum result was just a bad dream tend to suggest that the *'legitimized no Brexit'* scenario may well become reality. Granted, wishful thinking can be the source – or, indeed, the product – of fallacious reasoning, but there are strong grounds for the view that the 'legitimized no Brexit' scenario is *not* an impossible scenario – far from it. It is difficult to know what is currently going on 'behind the scenes' of the Westminster establishment and what kind of short-term and long-term strategies are *really* being adopted by the government's key players. It seems to me that, for the reasons outlined above, the current UK administration is likely to be preparing (and aiming) for one of the following three scenarios: *'straight soft Brexit' (scenario 2)*, *'relegitimized soft Brexit' (scenario 4)* and/or *'legitimized no Brexit' (scenario 6)*. None of these scenarios is ideal, and all of them (including the 'autocratic no Brexit' and 'hard Brexit' scenarios) are fraught with difficulties. It is probable, however, that the only way in which the UK can guarantee that, in the long run, it will survive both as a *strong* player (in Europe in particular and on the world stage in general) and as a *united* player (representing not only England and Wales but also Scotland and Northern Ireland) will be by ensuring that Brexit does not become a *real* reality. Even the softest and most (re-)legitimized forms of Brexit will involve the substantial risk of triggering the break-up of the UK – a price that no UK government is likely to be willing to pay.

Conclusion

This chapter has sought to contribute to a critical understanding of the concept of Brexit. It has done so by addressing a number of key issues, all of which are crucial to a comprehensive analysis of Brexit – notably, with regard to its meaning, its historical conditioning, its sociological implications, its wider legitimacy (or lack thereof) and the different scenarios in which it may (or may not) be implemented.

The first part has provided a shorthand *definition* of the concept of Brexit, stating that, in essence, it refers to the withdrawal of the UK from the EU. As explained above, advocates and opponents of Brexit tend to agree that, if Brexit is implemented by the UK government, its multiple consequences are of major historical significance – not only for the country itself, but also for the EU and, arguably, for the entire world.

The second part has reflected on the historical *context* in which, on 23 June 2016, the UK referendum on EU membership took place, arguing that the former had a profound impact on the latter's outcome. In this respect, the conjunction of three phenomena – which have contributed to the triumph of the Leave campaign – are especially important: a *world problem*, a *European or EU problem* and a *British problem*. These problems are indicative of the prevalent disillusionment with and alienation from mainstream political structures, practices and actors at the global, continental and national levels. Arguably, these are not limited to the UK. In fact, the Brexit scenario may be succeeded by further national exits from the EU – a domino-effect situation that the EU will seek to avoid at all cost and that, although it may seem unlikely to occur, cannot be ruled out.

The third part has shed light on the various sociological *implications* of the result of the 2016 UK Referendum, paying particular attention to the principal reasons that led to the triumph of the Leave campaign over the Remain campaign. As illustrated above, numerous *divisions* that exist in contemporary Britain appear to have shaped the outcome of the referendum in a decisive manner. In this respect, the following types of division are particularly significant: (1) social, (2) economic, (3) educational, (4) professional, (5) generational, (6) geographic, (7) political, (8) ideological, (9) cultural, (10) ethnic, (11) religious and (12) attitudinal. As stressed in the preceding inquiry, all figures used in support of this division-focused interpretation of the Brexit vote need to be treated with caution. It would be erroneous to rely on reductionist explanations as to why particular sectors of the UK population voted one way or another – not least because, with the exception of the *geographic* distribution of the Brexit vote, the validity of most of the division-focused data is extremely difficult to verify. Determinist explanations of voting patterns can hardly be illuminating when trying to explore why particular sectors of the electorate voted one way or another. *Different citizens vote differently not only for many different reasons but also because they themselves, as individual electors, may be motivated by a variety of reasons and influenced by a variety of factors, irrespective of whether or not these fall into division-specific patterns.* It is nonetheless crucial to recognize that these divisions *substantially* affected the outcome of the referendum, indicating the extent to which UK citizens' *attitudes* towards the EU in particular and towards Europe in general are profoundly shaped by the *positions* that they occupy within British society. There is no point in speculating about the future of a Brexit (or, indeed, a non-Brexit) scenario if we, as critical sociologists, fail to grapple with both the causes and the consequences of these numerous, and arguably profound, divisions. When making assumptions about prospective developments in the UK, however, it is imperative not to underestimate the *complexity* permeating the confluence of, and tensions between, central issues and interests that are at stake in the gradual consolidation of specific Brexit scenarios. Whatever may, or may not, happen at the governmental level cannot be dissociated from what may, or may not, happen at the societal level. It remains to be seen what life in the UK after (or, possibly, without) Brexit will look like.

The fourth part has offered some critical reflections on the *legitimacy* – or, as some may argue, illegitimacy – of the 2016 UK Referendum's outcome. From a historical perspective, it is difficult to understate, let alone to overlook, the fact that the result of the 2016 UK Referendum has triggered one of the most serious political crises in Europe since the end of World War II. Thus, it does not come as a surprise that, in contemporary public discourse, the term 'uncertainty' is widely employed to describe the post-referendum situation in the UK. The post-referendum scenario constitutes a historical context characterized by an enormous – and, in many ways, unprecedented – degree of social, political and economic uncertainty. From the point of view of the British government, this unparalleled state of affairs will – in the best-case scenario – lead to the temporary *weakening* of the UK's position in Europe or – in the worst-case scenario – result not only in the *decline* of the UK's influence on the world stage but also in its *break-up*. Notwithstanding one's assessment of the different possible post-Brexit scenarios, an important question that needs to be addressed concerns the very legitimacy – or, as some may conclude, illegitimacy – of the 2016 UK Referendum's outcome. As elucidated above, there are several key considerations on the basis of which the legitimacy of this referendum can – or, perhaps, must – be called into question, notably the following:

1. Large proportions of the electorate were *misled* by the Leave campaign.
2. The binary electoral choice between Remain and Leave was unjustifiably *simplistic*, taking into account both the magnitude and the complexity of the issues at stake.
3. The electoral choice between Remain and Leave was unduly, as well as deceptively, *polarizing* – that is, it was not only procedurally inadequate but also politically treacherous.
4. In the UK, where the Westminster Parliament possesses *sovereign* decision-making power, referenda are *consultative*, rather than decisive.
5. Unlike countries in which referenda are common practice, the UK does *not* have any clear, detailed and explicit *rules and regulations* about the decision-making power of referenda.
6. Constitutional democracies must have rules and regulations in place that prevent the *misuse* of referenda as mere instruments to push through normative agendas that, if implemented, have vast social, political and economic consequences – especially if these, at least in the medium term, are irreversible.
7. In light of the numerous and profound *divisions* that substantially influenced the outcome of the 2016 UK Referendum, we are confronted with a number of ironies – or, rather, harsh realities – that undermine its legitimacy. Those who least wanted to trigger, and/or least deserved to be affected by, the potentially harsh consequences of Brexit are those who may be hit hardest by the long-term effects of its implementation.

The fifth part has made some tentative remarks on the *prospects* of the Brexit scenario – not only in relation to the UK, but also in relation to the EU in particular and the wider international community in general. As argued in this chapter, the numerous and profound divisions that exist in contemporary British society will be crucial to the unfolding of any future scenario. More specifically, the chapter has maintained that it is possible to identify *six scenarios*, some of which are more likely, and some of which are less likely, to unfold within the near future: (1) 'straight hard Brexit', (2) 'straight soft Brexit', (3) 'relegitimized hard Brexit', (4) 'relegitimized soft Brexit', (5) 'autocratic no Brexit' and (6) 'legitimized no Brexit'. The chapter has argued that the options 'autocratic no Brexit', 'straight hard Brexit' and 'relegitimized hard Brexit' are the *least likely* scenarios to become reality – mainly because of their immensely damaging long-term consequences. In addition, the chapter has maintained that 'straight soft Brexit', 'relegitimized soft Brexit' and 'legitimized no Brexit' are the *most likely* scenarios to become reality – essentially because of their capacity to minimize the damage caused by the Brexit vote, while avoiding its most detrimental long-term consequences.

It must be emphasized, however, that none of the 'most likely' scenarios can be regarded as ideal and that, furthermore, all of them (including the 'least likely' scenarios) are fraught with difficulties. Before the Brexit vote, it did not enter many intellectuals' minds 'that populism would defeat capitalism in its country of origin'[29] and that, eventually, 'identity questions would prevail against interests'[30]. After the Brexit vote, however, it has become abundantly clear that, for large proportions of the population living in the UK, life outside the EU may be even more 'solitary, poor, nasty, brutish, and short'[31] than it already was before. The prospect of more neoliberal austerity, more law-and-order policy and more anti-immigration sentiment (and strategy) in an even more isolated United (or, possibly, Divided) Kingdom does not sound like a future to which progressive forces, broadly defined, will be looking forward.

Whatever may (or may not) happen in (and with) the UK's short-term and long-term future, however, the pursuit of a 'critical sociology of Brexit' will be vital. Such a collective undertaking is crucial not only for assessing and, if possible, influencing the impact of Brexit on academic life, but also, more importantly, for ensuring that social scientists, irrespective of their disciplinary identity, play a constructive role in shaping society for the better, even – or, perhaps, especially – if history does not appear to be on their side and prospects are, on balance, dire. The first step towards realizing such an ambitious endeavour is to recognize that it is, above all, the divisions *within* European societies, rather than those *between* them, to which we need to face up before taking on the challenging task of building a worthwhile future.

Notes

1 See, for instance: Baimbridge (2006); Baimbridge, Whyman and Mullen (2006); Butler and Kitzinger ((1975) 1996).

2 Outhwaite (2016b), p. 1 (italics added).

3 I owe the main argument underlying this tripartite analysis to William Outhwaite. See ibid. On key issues in the *sociology of contemporary Europe*, see, for instance: Delanty and Rumford (2005); Favell and Guiraudon (2011); Gerhards and Lengfeld (2015); Outhwaite (2006c); Outhwaite (2006a); Outhwaite (2006b); Outhwaite ((2000) 2006); Outhwaite (2008); Outhwaite (2012); Outhwaite (2016a); Sakwa and Stevens ((2000) 2012); Therborn (1995); Triandafyllidou and Gropas (2015).

4 On this point, see, for instance: Basconzuelo, Morel and Susen (2010a); Basconzuelo, Morel and Susen (2010b); Browne and Susen (2014), pp. 224–228; della Porta, Andretta, Mosca and Reiter (2006); Hamel, Lustiger-Thaler, Nederveen Pieterse and Roseneil (2001); Jogdand and Michael (2003); Laraña, Johnston and Gusfield (1994); Mayo (2005); Melucci (1980); Melucci (1994); Nederveen Pieterse (1992); Sklair (1995); Smith and Johnston (2002); Susen (2010a); Susen (2010b), pp. 268–271; Susen (2015), pp. 127, 129, 134, 135, 176, 177, 186, 187, 188, 189 and 272; Touraine ((1992) 1995); Waterman (1998); West (2013).

5 See McCrone (1992). See also Davidson, McCafferty and Miller (2010).

6 On this point, see Nairn ((1977) 1981) and Nairn (2002).

7 Calhoun (2016), p. 54 (italics added).

8 Ibid., p. 50 (italics added).

9 Susen (2015), p. 17.

10 Ibid., p. 17.

11 Calhoun (2016), p. 50 (italics added).

12 Ibid., p. 50 (italics added).

13 Ibid., pp. 50–51 (italics added).

14 Ibid., p. 53 (italics added).

15 See, for example: Abbott, Cressey and van Noorden (2016); Ahluwalia and Miller (2016); Bard-Rosenberg (2016); Bhambra (2016); Calhoun (2016); Clery (2016); Delanty (2016); Dorling

(2016); Edwards (2016); Finlayson (2016a); Finlayson (2016b); Habermas and Assheuer (2016); Horton (2016); Laconangelo (2016); Matthews (2016); McGowan (2016); Outhwaite (2016b); Qvortrup (2016); Reid (2016); Rose (2016); Shuster, Stewart and Walt (2016); Siva (2016); van-den Heuvel (2016); Younge (2016).

16 Delanty (2016), p. 2 (italics added).

17 On 19 August 1934, only 17 days after the death of President Paul von Hindenburg (1847–1934), a referendum on merging the posts of Chancellor (*Reichskanzler*) and President (*Reichspräsident*) was held in Nazi Germany. In essence, the referendum was the German leadership's way of seeking to gain formal and official approval for Adolf Hitler's supreme and unquestionable power. Owing to the crushing outcome of this referendum in favour of his leadership, Hitler was able to claim public support, and arguably 'legitimacy', for his political agenda and future actions.

18 Referenda can be regarded as an integral component of direct democracy in Germany. In practice, however, both their application and their influence are relatively limited. Two types of mandatory and binding referenda exist on the federal level: referenda that can change the *constitution* and referenda that can change the *state territories*. In essence, the German referendum system contains three levels:

(a) *Volksbegehren* (literally, 'people's request'), which is a citizens' initiative; if the government ignores such a request, this can result in a *Volksentscheid* (literally, 'people's decision');

(b) *Volksbefragung* (literally, 'people's inquiry'), which is based on a non-binding facultative ballot question and, in Germany, the most widely used type of referendum;

(c) *Volksentscheid* (literally, *people's decision*), which is, in principle, a binding plebiscite, but which is, in practice, used only if the constitution requires it.

On this point, see, for example: Heussner and Jung ((1999) 2009); Jung (1994); Troitzsch (1979).

19 For excellent discussions of *direct and deliberative models of democracy*, see, for example: Cooke (2000); Eriksen and Weigård (2003); Festenstein (2004); Habermas ((1992) 1996); Habermas (2005); Pellizzoni (2001); Young (1997). See also, for instance: Susen (2015), pp. 75, 106, 109, 187, 212 and 295*n*43.

20 Delanty (2016), p. 3. On this point, see, for instance, Ashcroft (2016), p. 2: 'A majority of those working full-time or part-time voted to remain in the EU; most of those not working voted to leave. More than half of those retired on a private pension voted to leave, as did two thirds of those retired on a state pension.'

21 On this point, see, for instance, Ashcroft (2016), p. 2: 'A majority (57%) of those with a university degree voted to remain, as did 64% of those with a higher degree and more than four in five (81%) of those still in full time education. Among those whose formal education ended at secondary school or earlier, a large majority voted to leave.'

22 On this point, see, for instance, ibid., p. 3: 'A majority of those who backed the Conservatives in 2015 voted to leave the EU (58%), as did more than 19 out of 20 UKIP supporters. Nearly two thirds of Labour and SNP voters (63% and 64%), seven in ten Liberal Democrats and three quarters of Greens, voted to remain.'

23 Bhambra (2016), p. 1.

24 Ibid., p. 1.

25 Ibid., p. 1.

26 On this point, see, for instance, Ashcroft (2016), p. 2: 'White voters voted to leave the EU by 53% to 47%. Two thirds (67%) of those describing themselves as Asian voted to remain, as did three quarters (73%) of black voters.'

27 See, for example, ibid., esp. p. 2.

28 On this point, see, for instance, ibid., p. 2: 'Nearly six in ten (58%) of those describing themselves as Christian voted to leave; seven in ten Muslims voted to remain.'

29 Habermas and Assheuer (2016), p. 1.
30 Ibid., p. 1.
31 Hobbes ((1651) 1996), p. 171.

References

Abbott, Alison, Daniel Cressey and Richard van Noorden. 2016. 'UK Scientists in Limbo after Brexit Shock', *Nature* 534 (7609): 597–598.

Ahluwalia, Pal, and Toby Miller. 2016. 'Brexit: The Way of Dealing with Populism', *Social Identities* 22: 453–454.

Ashcroft, Michael. 2016. 'How the United Kingdom Voted on Thursday … and Why', *Lord Ashcroft Polls*, 24 June, http://lordashcroftpolls.com/2016/06/how-the-united-kingdom-voted-and-why/, 1–14.

Baimbridge, Mark, ed. 2006. *The 1975 Referendum on Europe. Volume 1: Reflections of the Participants.* Exeter: Imprint Academic.

Baimbridge, Mark, Philip Whyman and Andrew Mullen, eds. 2006. *The 1975 Referendum on Europe. Volume 2: Current Analysis and Lessons for the Future*, Exeter: Imprint Academic.

Bard-Rosenberg, Jacob. 2016. 'On Brexit', *Studies in Social and Political Thought*, 30 June, https://ssptjournal.wordpress.com/2016/06/30/jacob-bard-rosenberg-on-brexit/.

Basconzuelo, Celia, Teresita Morel and Simon Susen, eds. 2010a. *Ciudadanía territorial y movimientos sociales: Historia y nuevas problemáticas en el escenario latinoamericano y mundial.* Río Cuarto: Ediciones del ICALA.

———. 2010b. 'Prólogo', in *Ciudadanía territorial y movimientos sociales: Historia y nuevas problemáticas en el escenario latinoamericano y mundial*, edited by Celia Basconzuelo, Teresita Morel and Simon Susen. Río Cuarto: Ediciones del ICALA, 7–10.

Bhambra, Gurminder K. 2016. 'VIEWPOINT: Brexit, Class and British "National" Identity', *Discover Society*, 5 July, http://discoversociety.org/2016/07/05/viewpoint-brexit-class-and-british-national-identity/.

Browne, Craig, and Simon Susen. 2014. 'Austerity and Its Antitheses: Practical Negations of Capitalist Legitimacy', *South Atlantic Quarterly* 113 (2): 217–230.

Butler, David, and Uwe W. Kitzinger. (1976) 1996. *The 1975 Referendum*, 2nd ed., Basingstoke: Macmillan.

Calhoun, Craig. 2016. 'Brexit Is a Mutiny against the Cosmopolitan Elite', *New Perspectives Quarterly* 33 (3): 50–58.

Clery, Daniel. 2016. 'EUROPE "Brexit" Casts Pall on Future of U.K. Science', *Science* 353 (6294): 12–13.

Cooke, Maeve. 2000. 'Five Arguments for Deliberative Democracy', *Political Studies* 48 (5): 947–969.

Davidson, Neil, Patricia McCafferty and David Miller, eds. 2010. *Neoliberal Scotland: Class and Society in a Stateless Nation.* Newcastle: Cambridge Scholars.

Delanty, Gerard. 2016. 'A Crisis of Governability? Why the Brexit Referendum Undermines Democracy and Must Be Declared Illegitimate', *Studies in Social and Political Thought*, 30 June, https://ssptjournal.wordpress.com/2016/06/30/a-crisis-of-governability-why-the-brexit-referendum-undermines-democracy-and-must-be-declared-illegitimate/.

Delanty, Gerard, and Chris Rumford. 2005. *Rethinking Europe: Social Theory and the Implications of Europeanization.* London: Routledge.

della Porta, Donatella, Massimiliano Andretta, Lorenzo Mosca and Herbert Reiter. 2006. *Globalization from Below: Transnational Activists and Protest Networks.* Minneapolis: University of Minnesota Press.

Dorling, Danny. 2016. 'Brexit: The Decision of a Divided Country', *BMJ – British Medical Journal* 354: 2.

Edwards, Jim. 2016. 'It Is Time to Accept the Fact that Brexit May Never Actually Happen', *Business Insider*, 21 July.

Eriksen, Erik O, and Jarle Weigård. 2003. *Understanding Habermas: Communicative Action and Deliberative Democracy*. London and New York: Continuum.

Favell, Adrian, and Virginie Guiraudon, eds. 2011. *Sociology of the European Union*, Basingstoke: Palgrave Macmillan.

Festenstein, Matthew. 2004. 'Deliberative Democracy and Two Models of Pragmatism', *European Journal of Social Theory* 7 (3): 291–306.

Finlayson, Gordon. 2016a. 'First Time as Farce', *Studies in Social and Political Thought*, 30 June, https://ssptjournal.wordpress.com/2016/06/30/first-time-as-farce/.

Finlayson, Jon. 2016b. 'EU Referendum Petition', *Studies in Social and Political Thought*, 2 July, https://ssptjournal.wordpress.com/2016/06/30/first-time-as-farce/.

Gerhards, Jürgen, and Holger Lengfeld. 2015. *European Citizenship and Social Integration in the European Union*, London: Routledge.

Habermas, Jürgen. (1992) 1996. 'The Sociological Translation of the Concept of Deliberative Politics', in Jürgen Habermas, *Between Facts and Norms: Contributions to a Discourse Theory of Law and Democracy*, translated by William Rehg, Cambridge: Polity, 315–328.

———. 2005. 'Concluding Comments on Empirical Approaches to Deliberative Politics', *Acta Politica* 40 (3): 384–392.

Habermas, Jürgen, and Thomas Assheuer. 2016. 'The Players Resign – Core Europe to the Rescue: A Conversation with Jürgen Habermas about Brexit and the EU Crisis', translated by David Gow, *ZEIT ONLINE* 26, 12 July, http://www.zeit.de/kultur/2016-07/juergen-habermas-brexit-eu-crises-english.

Hamel, Pierre, Henri Lustiger-Thaler, Jan Nederveen Pieterse and Sasha Roseneil, eds. 2001. *Globalization and Social Movements*. Basingstoke: Palgrave.

Heussner, Hermann K., and Otmar Jung, eds. (1999) 2009. *Mehr direkte Demokratie wagen – Volksentscheid und Bürgerentscheid: Geschichte, Praxis, Vorschläge*, 2nd (rev.) ed., Munich: Olzog.

Hobbes, Thomas. (1651) 1996. 'Leviathan', in *Modern Political Thought: Readings from Machiavelli to Nietzsche*, edited by David Wootton. Indianapolis: Hackett, 122–302.

Horton, Richard. 2016. 'Offline: The Meanings of Brexit', *The Lancet* 388 (10039): 14.

Jogdand, Prahlad Gangaram and S. M. Michael. 2003. *Globalization and Social Movements: Struggle for a Humane Society*, Jaipur: Rawat Publications.

Jung, Otmar. 1994. *Grundgesetz und Volksentscheid: Gründe und Reichweite der Entscheidungen des Parlamentarischen Rats gegen Formen direkter Demokratie*. Opladen: Westdeutscher Verlag.

Laconangelo, David and Rosie Scammell. 2016. 'Is Brexit Cause or Effect of Rise in Hate?', *Christian Century*, July 6, 12–13.

Laraña, Enrique, Hank Johnston and Joseph R. Gusfield, eds. 1994. *New Social Movements: From Ideology to Identity*. Philadelphia: Temple University Press.

Matthews, Owen. 2016. 'Brexit Wounds', *Newsweek Global*, 7 August, 12–16.

Mayo, Marjorie. 2005. *Global Citizens: Social Movements and the Challenge of Globalization*. London: Zed.

McCrone, David. 1992. *Understanding Scotland: The Sociology of a Stateless Nation*. London: Routledge.

McGowan, John. 2016. 'Brexit – How Do We Go Forward?', *Psychologist* 29 (8): 590–591.

Melucci, Alberto. 1980. 'The New Social Movements: A Theoretical Approach', *Social Science Information* 19 (2): 199–226.

———. 1994. 'A Strange Kind of Newness: What's "New" in New Social Movements?', in *New Social Movements: From Ideology to Identity*, edited by Enrique Laraña, Hank Johnston and Joseph R. Gusfield. Philadelphia: Temple University Press, 101–130.

Nairn, Tom. (1977) 1981. *The Break-Up of Britain: Crisis and Neo-Nationalism*, 2nd, expanded ed. London: NLB.

———. 2002. *Pariah: Misfortunes of the British Kingdom*. London: Verso.

Nederveen Pieterse, Jan, ed. 1992. *Emancipations, Modern and Postmodern*. London: Sage.

Outhwaite, William. 2006a. 'The EU and Its Enlargements: "Cosmopolitanism by Small Steps"', in *Europe and Asia beyond East and West*, edited by Gerard Delanty. London: Routledge, 193–202.

————. 2006b. 'Is There a European Society?', in William Outhwaite, *The Future of Society*. Malden, MA, and Oxford: Blackwell, 108–124.

————. 2006c. 'European Transformations', in *Handbook of Contemporary European Social Theory*, edited by Gerard Delanty. London: Routledge, 279–288.

————. (2000) 2006. 'Social Structure', in *Contemporary Europe*, edited by Richard Sakwa and Anne Stevens, 2nd ed. Basingstoke: Palgrave Macmillan, 138–159.

————. 2008. *European Society*. Cambridge: Polity.

————. 2012. *Critical Theory and Contemporary Europe*. New York: Continuum.

————. 2016a. *Europe Since 1989: Transitions and Transformations*. London: Routledge.

————. 2016b. 'Game Over (for England and Wales)', *Studies in Social and Political Thought*, 6 July, https://ssptjournal.wordpress.com/2016/07/06/game-over-for-england-and-wales/.

Pellizzoni, Luigi. 2001. 'The Myth of the Best Argument: Power, Deliberation and Reason', *British Journal of Sociology* 52 (1): 59–86.

Qvortrup, Matt. 2016. 'Referendums on Membership and European Integration 1972–2015', *Political Quarterly (London. 1930)* 87 (1): 61–68.

Reid, Graeme. 2016. 'Science and Brexit', *Science* 353 (6294): 7–7.

Rose, Elliot. 2016. 'Show, Don't Tell', *Studies in Social and Political Thought*, 7 July, https://ssptjournal.wordpress.com/2016/07/07/show-dont-tell/.

Sakwa, Richard, and Anne Stevens, eds. (2000) 2012. *Contemporary Europe*, 3rd ed., Basingstoke: Palgrave Macmillan.

Shuster, Simon, Dan Stewart and Vivienne Walt. 2016. 'Europe's Crisis of Faith', *Time*, 7 November, 11–16.

Siva, Nayanah N. 2016. 'UK Researchers Digest the Fallout from Brexit', *The Lancet, British* ed., 388 (10040): 115–116.

Sklair, Leslie. 1995. 'Social Movements and Global Capitalism', *Sociology* 29 (3): 495–512.

Smith, Jackie, and Hank Johnston, eds. 2002. *Globalization and Resistance: Transnational Dimensions of Social Movements*, Lanham, MD: Rowman & Littlefield.

Susen, Simon. 2010a. 'Los movimientos sociales en las sociedades complejas', in *Ciudadanía territorial y movimientos sociales: Historia y nuevas problemáticas en el escenario latinoamericano y mundial*, edited by Celia Basconzuelo, Teresita Morel and Simon Susen. Río Cuarto: Ediciones del ICALA, 149–226.

————. 2010b. 'The Transformation of Citizenship in Complex Societies', *Journal of Classical Sociology* 10 (3): 259–285.

————. 2015. *The 'Postmodern Turn' in the Social Sciences*. Basingstoke: Palgrave Macmillan.

Therborn, Göran. 1995. *European Modernity and Beyond: The Trajectory of European Societies, 1945–2000*. London: Sage.

Touraine, Alain. (1992) 1995. *Critique of Modernity*, translated by David Macey. Oxford: Blackwell.

Triandafyllidou, Anna, and Ruby Gropas. 2015. *What Is Europe?* Basingstoke: Palgrave Macmillan.

Troitzsch, Klaus G. 1979. *Volksbegehren und Volksentscheid. Eine vergleichende Analyse direktdemokratischer Verfassungsinstitutionen unter besonderer Berücksichtigung der Bundesrepublik Deutschland und der Schweiz*, Meisenheim am Glan: Hain.

vanden Heuvel, Katrina. 2016. 'Brexit's Benefits', *The Nation*, 19 May, 5–6.

Waterman, Peter. 1998. *Globalization, Social Movements, and the New Internationalisms*. London: Mansell.

West, David. 2013. *Social Movements in Global Politics*. Cambridge: Polity.

Young, Iris Marion. 1997. 'Communication and the Other: Beyond Deliberative Democracy', in *Intersecting Voices: Dilemmas of Gender, Political Philosophy, and Policy*, edited by Iris Marion Young. Princeton, NJ: Princeton University Press, 60–74.

Younge, Gary. 2016. 'The Great Brexit Lie', *The Nation*, 18 July: 10–11.

Chapter Thirteen

CRITICAL THEORY, BREXIT AND THE VICISSITUDES OF POLITICAL ECONOMY IN THE TWENTY-FIRST CENTURY

Harry F. Dahms

Introduction

In a very short time, much has been written by social scientists, philosophers, journalists, and other well-informed commentators about the lead-up to and the outcome and aftermath of the Brexit referendum. Most of it is highly insightful and provides a public searching for explanations of what happened, and why, with probing, compelling, and sobering analyses.[1] Brexit has been illuminated from a multiplicity of angles, at many different levels of social, political, and cultural complexity, so much so that it is easy to be overwhelmed by what may resemble a baffling cacophony of both consonant and conflicting voices and a disorienting kaleidoscope of (in)sights.

With sociology as the discipline that has been accompanying, analyzing, and reflecting on the history and transformations of modern society since the second half of the nineteenth century, the contributions of sociologists to illuminating Brexit should be especially valuable. Yet, since sociology is the most pluralistic and diverse as well as fragmented social science, sociologists may well run the risk of amplifying further the impression that the issue of Brexit simply is too complicated to penetrate in a manner that leads to discernible lessons for the future.

Presently, the event of the Brexit referendum is of interest above all for three reasons. First, what does Brexit signify, sociologically? Secondly, what contribution can (and should) sociology make to illuminating Brexit as a social phenomenon? And thirdly, what does Brexit tell us about, and mean for, sociology as a discipline? In the interest of providing preliminary answers to these questions, we first need to delineate a cursory diagnosis of what may have contributed to the outcome of the Brexit referendum, then take a step back both from the continuing turmoil caused by Brexit *and* today's understanding (and self-understanding) of sociology with regard to its subject matter, modern society, and return to the discipline's origins in the nineteenth and the early twentieth century.

The Sociological Significance of Brexit

From several angles, Brexit is the most visible recent instance pointing away, in an emphatic fashion, from established perspectives on the developmental trajectory of modern society as they came to be accepted during the post–World War II era. Earlier instances that chipped away at the confidence that modern society is following a desirable evolutionary path into the future were the oil shock and the subsequent recession and "crisis of confidence" (Bensman and Vidich 1976) during the 1970s; the rise of neoliberalism during the 1980s as spearheaded by the Margaret Thatcher and Ronald Reagan administrations; the concurrent proliferation of postmodern critiques of the ideological character of modern society, especially in the English-speaking world; the public acknowledgment and rapid acceleration of globalization during the 1990s; the 9/11 terrorist attacks in 2001; the financial crisis in 2008; and the euro crisis in 2010.

It has become apparent for some time that there is a growing disjuncture between the notions about and perspectives on modern society that prevail, especially as members of society must subscribe to them in order for it to maintain stability and function, and the nature and underlying logic of societies of this type. These notions and perspectives took hold during the decades following World War II, and the disjuncture appears to go beyond what is typical and to be expected regarding the tension between the representations and realities of any form of social organization, even and especially in the social sciences, including sociology. Many of these notions, perspectives, and corresponding claims about the nature of modern society, especially as they are relevant with regard to Brexit, pertain to political economy (including constellations of business, labor, and government). Francis Fukuyama's (1992) well-known claim about the "end of history" identified two of these notions, in particular that liberal democracy and market economies are among the greatest achievements of human civilization, and that – considering the alternatives (especially planned economies and one-party rule) – they are the best arrangements for confronting political and economic challenges. These and related notions and perspectives have persisted for more than half a century, were given further impetus by the collapse of European communism, turned out to be astonishingly stable, and have informed and inspired research agendas in the social sciences. With the rise of neoliberalism, the perspective – that realistically as well as philosophically speaking - there are no viable or desirable alternatives to liberal democracy and market economies, has become petrified to the point at which the horizon of the future, and of possible *futures*, has narrowed to a condition of collective retardation (Block and Somers 2014).

Yet, in various ways, and from an increasing number of vantage points, the perspectives and notions that have sustained the post–World War II regime of business-labor-government relations have come under attack. On the one hand, claims about life in modern society that have informed politics, economic policy, and – paradoxically – sociological research, are in contradiction with the reality of modern society, to varying degrees. As time goes by, the tension between the desire to interpret patterns of social change in terms of the notions and perspectives that have been integral to the stability of modern societies and their ability to function, and the feasibility of doing so, has been intensifying. Willingness to organize one's life around "a hard day's work" no longer reliably leads to economic security. Participation in processes of democratic will formation no longer are conducive to political institutions and the political process reflecting the intent of voters (rather, in fact, vice versa), or to approximating strategies to address problems in terms of the nature of those problems. Instead, neoliberalism, and austerity policies in particular, are being superimposed onto a broad range of problems, with regard to how the latter are being defined and interpreted and how to conceive of related "solutions."

What came to the surface before, during, and after Brexit had been building for years, for example, growing resentment vis-à-vis political elites, including elected officials, civil servants, and experts generally; similar resentment regarding economic and especially financial elites (though not necessarily to the same extent, or in the same way); a general distrust in politics; partly as a consequence of the latter, a fractured relationship with democracy; indications that even in so-called democratic countries, democracy is not as broadly cherished and deeply supported as generally assumed; a willingness to assign blame and responsibility for undesirable developments to "others" – immigrants, minorities, outsiders, politicians, lawyers, and so forth; growing economic inequality; and the experience of greater stress in personal and social life, such as a feeling of not being able to keep up with job expectations and requirements, work acceleration, or even individuals' own expectations of themselves (Ehrenberg 2009).

Concurrently, feelings of dissatisfaction and betrayal with regard to the promises of post–World War II constellations of business, labor, and government also have been building for decades. Recovery from the catastrophe of World War II required mass loyalty (Habermas 1989) and good faith on the part of the citizenry, but the exceptional circumstances that arose after 1945 and that produced the kind of continuous economic and political benefits that were conducive to stabilizing mass loyalty lasted only for a few decades, with economic and political elites further monopolizing prosperity starting in the 1980s.

As the preliminary culmination of and reaction to these and related trends, Brexit highlights the need for sociologists to revisit, reexamine, and scrutinize basic assumptions, notions, and concepts about social, political, cultural, and economic life, as well as structures that corresponded with a historically unprecedented period of social and political stability and economic prosperity, especially in Western Europe and North America. Do these assumptions and notions still apply, and if so, how? Is it justifiable to continue to rely on them implicitly, as if the precepts and constellations (for example, with regard to business, labor, and government) continue to characterize the societal framework within which individuals, as well as decision makers, endeavor to confront an array of old and new challenges?

Toward a Sociological Perspective on Brexit: Political Economy in the Twenty-First Century

In this context, the purpose of this outline is to suggest a broader perspective on Brexit, in an effort that harkens back to and is informed by the research agendas of three of the classics of social theory who, in more or less equal measure, albeit in different ways, both *inspired* and *burdened* the development of sociology as the social science of modern society: Karl Marx, Émile Durkheim, and Max Weber. Their writings influenced the self-understanding of sociologists and provided the discipline with complementary research programs centered on three distinct processes that shaped the development and form of modern societies: capital accumulation, differentiation, and rationalization, respectively. For the classics, the challenge of illuminating the novelty of modern societies was to address and examine explicitly how their functioning and stability depended on a peculiar and particular linkage between cause and effect, and between the highly elusive forces that shape the appearances of social life, and how those appearances are interpreted by people in everyday life.

Specifically, the processes of capital accumulation, differentiation, and rationalization combine with modern society's adaptive imperative to maintain stability and function, despite the myriad costs those processes exact in multitudinous ways, to shape social forms from individual identity to global civilization as well as interpretations of the motivations behind individual or collective actions, institutional responses, and how humanity relates to nature. Yet, both in everyday life and in mainstream sociology, the systemically mediated social, political, and cultural consequences of these processes tend to be interpreted as indicative of the nature of social life and human existence in the twenty-first century, beyond the processes with which Marx, Durkheim, and Weber were concerned.[2]

The stability and functioning of modern societies is contingent on individuals remaining oblivious to these societies' machinations and to how they shape precisely those individual identities that then endeavor to grasp how the forces without which modern societies would be impossible, and which distinguish them from premodern, traditional societies. Yet many individuals still are determined to understand the conditions of their existence. In the absence of adequate (sociological) means to do so successfully, individuals construct linkages between cause and effect that remain at the surface level of social life and reality; they try to explain events at the same level of social complexity, even though – according to the insights provided by the classics of social theory, with regard to what matters most about the link between cause and effect in modern societies – effects occur at the level of surface appearances, whereas causes stay hidden from view and are accessible only as the result of rigorous critical *and* empirical analysis (if at all).

Marx, Durkheim, and Weber were sources of *inspiration* for sociologists inasmuch as they stressed the imminent need to examine and rigorously scrutinize modern society, especially with regard to the tension between everyday life and the underlying forces shaping it, in order to engender an entirely novel type of critical reflexivity. This reflexivity was necessitated by strong indications suggesting that modern society evolves according to highly complementary and mutually reinforcing, yet distinct, imperatives that, paradoxically, sustain a dynamic without which modern society as a nexus of social and political organization and economic process would not be able to maintain stability and function. Moreover, these imperatives occur at the level of society as a *totality*, rather than at levels that are directly accessible, observable, or conceivable to members of society. To complicate matters further, modern society must successfully compels a large segment of its population to subscribe implicitly to a set of notions and perspectives about the nature of the social world they inhabit. In many instances, these notions and perspectives are necessary for and conducive to society maintaining order and functioning sufficiently well for its stability – especially the stability of specific social structures – not to be threatened, but frequently they are *not* related to the ideas and categories members of society employ to make sense of their lives or to construct meaningful personal life histories. In fact, typically, the ideas and categories that frame members' efforts to live their lives are necessary for the functioning of modern society, but not conducive to illuminating its functioning to members.

Yet, Marx, Durkheim, and Weber also in a sense *burdened* the history of sociology in that the steps they took toward scrutinizing the underlying logic of modern society were so revolutionary in nature that many sociologists, especially those not theoretically inclined, were tied too strongly to traditional modes of thinking to fully appreciate the gravity of the classics' contributions, especially the critical thrust of their analyses as compared to traditional perspectives on society, including modern society. As the discipline was established at universities in Europe and North America, a lacuna formed between the standards the classics had tried to delineate for rigorous analysis, respectively, and the limited readiness and ability of most sociologists to acknowledge the revolutionary nature of the classics' contributions and the difficulties in studying modern society. There were several reasons for this lacuna.

First, to appreciate the enormity of the challenge to illuminate the underlying, complementary "logics" of modern society, sociologists needed to be willing to recognize themselves as products of processes that are supposed to be conducive to, but which also subvert in key regards, the validity of ideas like freedom, individual autonomy, self-determination, and so forth, as they guide individuals' sense of self and choices in everyday life. Yet such recognition was (and continues to be) highly unpleasant and threatening to more or less carefully crafted identities, and many sociologists preferred to sidestep acknowledgment and execution of this requirement as laid out by the classics. Secondly, most sociologists were ready and even eager to concede the importance to the discipline of the classics' contributions, but many were not willing to comprehend the analytically radical and revolutionary character of the latter. Thus, in order to acquire the skills and knowledge required for a professional career in sociology, the ability to be familiar with and conversant regarding any of the classics, their writings were appropriated in ways that made them more manageable. In many different ways, the result was a reduction of truly astonishing bodies of work provided by the classics, to a set of lifeless categories and concepts that could be employed and applied more or less arbitrarily, as served the need to legitimate research programs by referring to well-established theoretical frames, without grasping the depth and breadth of the impetus of each or any of those theories. As a consequence, thirdly, the establishment and professionalization of the discipline during the twentieth century – and especially after World War II, in the context of the Cold War – went hand in hand with the progressive domestication of the classics' theoretical works, theories, concepts, and categories.

If the normalization of the domestication of the classics, during the second half of the twentieth century, could have been avoided, sociology might have recognized that Marx, Durkheim, and Weber delineated in different ways a kind of inquiry directed at underlying patterns that is essential to the study of modern society, and which should have provided sociologists with a research orientation concerned with how unseen forces transform, on an ongoing basis, not just what we call "society", but also who we are as social beings and what it means to be human. Along such lines, the classics' theories should have served as *foils* for tracing and tracking how everyday life (with the requisite notions and perspectives individuals need to be able to rely upon) ever is in danger of concealing further the forces that shape it and social life more generally. It is necessary to circumscribe the processes that, successively, reconfigure constellations of business, labor, and government, and the tension between political economy and society, in a manner that remains concealed, without sociologists explicitly and doggedly making sure that they are being brought to light. Domesticating the contributions of the classics through modes of interpretation directed at normalizing what were revolutionary theories, oriented persistently toward shining a light on the forces shaping the observable manifestations of social life, further concealed those forces, thus hampering efforts to actualize sociology's somewhat half-hearted claim to be the social science of modern society.

Thus it is high time to reactivate the distinction between surface appearances and underlying forces (Postone 2007). In line with postwar sociology and the liberal perspective on human nature, this distinction was considered condescending, when applied to individuals in everyday life, misapprehending how its implications applied to sociologists just as much as to any member of modern society, as it highlighted the need for a specific mode of reflexivity and analysis, rather than a stance about the difference between social scientists and others. The liberal perspective on modern society is overly (and unduly) political, problematic, and in conflict with the very idea of sociology as systematic analysis, for example, as it makes assumptions about members of modern society that clearly do not apply to the extent to which the promulgators of this view would prefer: there are many people who are not in favor of values related to progress, freedom, equality, and justice for all, in modern societies and elsewhere (Adorno, Frenkel-Brunswik, Levinson, and Sanford 1950).

As we are being overwhelmed by far too much information, the assumption of self-possessing, autonomous actors making prudent choices certainly would be desirable, but it appears to be increasingly unrealistic. Systems of manipulation have become far too sophisticated – both by design and as a consequence of adaptive processes not driven by decision makers, but by this or that computer algorithm – for the notion of individual autonomy even in this limited sense to be a defensible stance. More and more individuals have a hard time (if time at all, under the regime of neoliberalism) responding to, not to mention reflecting on, issues of public interest and importance, such as Brexit and its ramifications. Thus, in certain regards, the classics may well apply much more today than they did when they made their observations. Processes they described have accelerated and become much more aggravated, while many sociologists who address, for example, phenomena illustrating deepening forms of alienation, anomie, and disenchantment, would prefer to think that because such developments are highly undesirable and incompatible with life in modern democratic societies, they also must not be occurring, empirically speaking.

Critical Theory and the Significance of Brexit for Sociology

Brexit is a multilayered and multidimensional phenomenon, at the intersection of many social, political, economic, and cultural forces, processes, and corresponding fault and conflict lines, so much so that to suggest the possibility of identifying clearly and unambiguously its overall sociological significance, as well as its significance for sociology, would be frivolous at best.[3] However, it *is* possible (as well as *necessary*) to view Brexit as an opportunity to revisit some central claims pertaining to the mission and responsibility of sociology in and to the modern age, in general, and in the twenty-first century, in particular. In fact, to appreciate fully the significance of Brexit, and why it came as a shock to many (including many sociologists), it is necessary to examine how sociology may have neglected to assess the current condition of modern society, despite countless studies concerned with specific aspects of, and phenomena in, modern society, and whether the discipline may be prone to cultivating blind spots in areas that warrant close attention. Thus, Brexit should not have come as a shock to sociologists.

Indeed, it is possible that both the *event* of Brexit, and reactions to it, highlight the need to confront an array of more or less unpleasant facts about the condition of modern society (or, as some would have it, to confirm that in key regards, we live in *post*modern society), in the United Kingdom and beyond. If so, depending on the scope and pervasiveness of those facts, it may be high time to call sociologists to task, to accede to the application of focused critical scrutiny, after failing to do so in the face of several other "events" in recent years (ongoing processes, really), including the 2008 financial crisis, the euro crisis, the spread of terrorism, and the resurgence of right-wing politics in societies with democratic political institutions and strong liberal or progressive traditions.[4] Specifically, sociologists would be well advised to embrace the contributions and modes of analyses supplied by the tradition of critical theory and to consider the role of political economy today, at a more penetrating level of analysis than is provided by politicians, policy wonks, journalists, and even (and especially) economists.

Critical theory is one tradition in sociology whose orientation, while remaining rather marginal, has been more consistent with the impetus of the classics of social theory, especially in this tradition's early incarnation, as it formed during the 1930s. Pursuing an explicitly interdisciplinary approach to studying the modern social world, including especially philosophy, sociology, psychoanalysis, and political economy, this tradition has continued to be inspired by the classics' radical impetus to a greater extent than professional sociology. Critical theory applies a rigorously formulated and focused understanding of critique directed at how concrete historical and social conditions influence, mold, have bearing on, and are reflected in research agendas that social scientists typically presume implicitly and do not try to explicate.

The frequency of the above-mentioned types of events and crises appears to be increasing, highlighting the growing de facto fragility of modern societies. The study of the latter, especially with regard to their stability and functioning, has been a prime concern of sociology since the mid-nineteenth century, especially since its establishment as a social science at universities around 1900. It would appear that at the current historical juncture, sociologists must endeavor to illuminate the social circumstances, patterns, processes, and forces that promote the proliferation of incidents and developments which are threatening confidence in the resilience and ability of modern societies to protect and secure myriad gains that have been made in recent decades, and to prepare for proliferating challenges we should expect to be forced to face before long, such as the consequences resulting from natural resource and food depletion, rapid climate change, and massive overpopulation in the context of conspicuously inert social and political structures.

Sociology has many blind spots, and largely is, in terms of established practice, sociology *in* modern society, rather than sociology *of* modern society. Sociologists tend to be tied up with the values that prevail in society and are prone to be guided by principles akin to what has been called "politically correct" – in the positive sense. Yet this outlook comes at the price of potentially neglecting difficult questions, or questions that could lead to undesirable insights. Repressed aspects of modern society are forcing themselves into the forefront of social, political, cultural, and public life, a process that is likely to intensify for the foreseeable future. As a consequence, the sociology of modern society that sociologists have been working to establish may be hampered by what many of those who engage in sociology would prefer to see. Thus, the "dark side" of modern society has been neglected to too great an extent (Alexander 2013; Mignolo 2010).

While mainstream sociology continues to refer to the processes of capital accumulation, differentiation, and rationalization and to employ them for framing purposes, the radical theoretical impetus (at the intersection of epistemology and ontology, rather than in terms of practical politics) behind interest in these processes, in Marx, Durkheim, and Weber, has largely vanished from the work, imagination, and moral principles of most social scientists, including sociologists. In fact, considering the ever greater distance between sociology and philosophy, this radical impetus is likely to never have been part of the self-understanding of many sociologists, with evidence suggesting that the majority of the latter either consider *all* forms of sociology to be critical at its core, or critique – except when applied to the structure of theories or the design of methods – anathema to sociology. In order for sociology to be up to its challenge of analyzing modern society, it is necessary and indispensable for sociologists to include critical theory as an approach, especially in the sense of the early Frankfurt School of Max Horkheimer, Theodor W. Adorno, and Herbert Marcuse (Dahms 2011).

Brexit: Taking Sociology to Task

Despite the discipline's beginning, much of sociology operates in the realm of surface manifestations of modern social phenomena, and remains in the mode so common in everyday life, of trying to explain such surface manifestations (for example, election campaigns) with reference to other surface manifestations and processes (for example, voters' economic interest, voter's resentment regarding the establishment, techniques of manipulating voters employed by politicians, competition among politicians, and so on). To be sure, there are many reasons that explain the appeal of staying at the surface, of not digging further, of confining oneself to the upper layers of the surface, and of not reaching for the level of underlying forces that produce and maintain the surface. To illustrate, in traditional and mainstream interpretations of Marx's writings, the distinction between material "base" and ideological "superstructure" (Thompson, 2014) was taken to signify that modern societies' material economic underpinnings matter most, and that the social, political, cultural, artistic, and philosophical forms are merely expressions of the former, so that Marx was purported to have contended that all we needed to study was the "base," which at different stages of societal evolution produces the corresponding ideological "superstructure," with the latter being entirely dependent on the former. Yet, ironically, this traditional/mainstream reading of Marx is a manifestation of thinking on the surface, in the sense that in the case of the inclusion of presumably mysterious underlying forces in considerations of causality, the latter is absolute and inevitably must go in one direction only.

As efforts in recent years have demonstrated, especially since the end of Soviet communism, conventional perspectives on the divide between base and superstructure are just as problematic as interpretations of Marx as a "class theorist" or "conflict theorist" (for example, Dahrendorf 1959). In these and many other instances, with corresponding flaws in established interpretations and applications of the works of Durkheim and Weber, social scientists frequently inferred that even though their theories were revolutionary as far as illuminating the link between individual identity and social reality was concerned, the concepts and categories they introduced to advocate the need for critical perspectives on causality in modern societies were compatible with how these concepts and categories were used, in terms of "common sense" and everyday life. The stated purpose of their theories was precisely to stress and elaborate how modern societies engendered modes of socialization and education that compel individuals to subscribe to notions about the workings and nature of modern societies that the majority of individuals must subscribe to in order for modern society to be stable and function, but that are not conducive to enabling individuals to understand the mechanisms that sustain modern society. In short, individuals are conditioned to experience their lives, reality, and each other as a function of how we all are embedded in our social worlds. The classics of social theory took steps toward visualizing how social analysts must break with such perspectives, which impede appreciation of how modern societies are located in, and indeed form, a field of tensions between economic opportunity (the "pursuit of prosperity" proceeding according to the "logic of capital"; Dahms 2015) and social, political, and cultural (as well as environmental) costs necessitated by the shift from largely static, feudal subsistence economies to increasingly dynamic, capitalist growth economies. Since the early nineteenth century, the intensity of these tensions has been growing, and their scope spreading around the entire planet, thus both normalizing and "naturalizing" the resulting socioeconomic order (Dahms, in preparation).

Notes

1 Especially Balibar et al. (2016); Runciman et al. (2016).
2 Regarding the issue of "mainstream" sociology, see Dahms (2011), ch. 6.
3 When employing the term "Brexit," I refer to the larger event of Brexit, that is, the campaigns for leave and for remain, the referendum itself, and for the – now open-ended – aftermath, including the latent turmoil that is the result of the referendum brought forth by the Conservative Party, and the more manifest crises that have ensued for Labour, especially the conflict over party leader Jeremy Corbyn.

4 Mirowski (2013) has provided an intriguing analysis of how neoliberalism reconfigured itself after the financial crisis of 2008. In a similar fashion, but with an entirely different thrust and motivation, sociology, too, would benefit from not letting major crises "go to waste."

References

Adorno, T. W., Else Frenkel-Brunswik, Daniel J. Levinson, and R. Nevitt Sanford. 1950. *The Authoritarian Personality*. New York: Harper and Brothers.

Alexander, Jeffrey. 2013. *The Dark Side of Modernity*. Malden, MA: Polity.

Balibar, Etienne et al. 2016. *The Brexit Crisis: A Verso Report*. London: Verso.

Bensman, Joseph, and Arthur. J. Vidich. 1976. "The Crisis of Contemporary Capitalism and the Failure of Nerve." *Sociological Inquiry* 46 (3–4): 207–217.

Block, Fred, and Margaret Somers. 2014. *The Power of Market Fundamentalism: Karl Polanyi's Critique*. Cambridge, MA: Harvard University Press.

Dahms, Harry F. 2011. *The Vitality of Critical Theory*. Current Perspectives in Social Theory 28. Bingley, UK: Emerald.

———. 2015. "Toward a Critical Theory of Capital in the 21st Century: Thomas Piketty between Adam Smith and the Prospect of Apocalypse." *Critical Sociology* 41 (2): 359–374.

———. In preparation. *Modern Society as Artifice: Critical Theory and the Logic of Capital*. London: Routledge.

Dahrendorf, Ralf. 1959. *Class and Class Conflict in Industrial Society*. Stanford, CA: Stanford University Press.

Ehrenberg, Alain. 2009. *The Weariness of the Self: Diagnosing the History of Depression in the Contemporary Age*. Montreal: McGill-Queen's University Press.

Fukuyama, Francis. 1992. *The End of History and the Last Man*. New York: Free Press.

Habermas, Jürgen. 1989, "The New Obscurity: The Crisis of the Welfare State and the Exhaustion of Utopian Energies." In *The New Conservatism: Cultural Criticism and the Historians' Debate*. Cambridge, MA: MIT Press, 71–99.

Mignolo, Walter. 2011. *The Darker Side of Western Modernity: Global Futures, Decolonial Options*. Durham, NC: Duke University Press.

Mirowski, Philip. 2013. *Never Let a Serious Crisis Go to Waste: How Neoliberalism Survived the Financial Meltdown*. London: Verso.

Postone, Moishe. 2007. "Theorizing the Contemporary World: Robert Brenner, Giovanni Arrighi, David Harvey." In *Political Economy and Global Capitalism: The 21st Century, Present and Future*, edited by R. Albritton, B. Jessop, and R. Westra. London: Anthem, 7–24.

Runciman, David et al. 2016. "Where Are We Now? Responses to the Referendum." *London Review of Books* 38 (14) (14 July): 8–15.

Thompson, Michael. 2014. "The Base-Superstructure Hypothesis and the Foundations of Critical Theory." In *Mediations of Social Life in the 21st Century*, edited by H. F. Dahms. Current Perspectives in Social Theory 32. Bingley, UK: Emerald, 161–194.

Chapter Fourteen

EUROPEAN UNION VERSUS EUROPEAN SOCIETY: SOCIOLOGISTS ON 'BREXIT' AND THE 'FAILURE' OF EUROPEANIZATION

Adrian Favell

It is, of course, an almighty cliché that sociology, like the Owl of Minerva, only takes flight at dusk. Sociology – of the kind that focuses on power distortions, social conflicts, inequalities, the fragility of social order – only ever seems to find its vocation alongside political science and law when things are falling apart and the centre cannot hold. Brexit!? Good Lord! How did that happen? ... Send in the clowns.

During the golden years of the European Union (EU) – the heyday of Jacques Delors, the expansive drive after the Single European Act (1986), and even more after the fall of the Berlin Wall (1989) and Maastricht (1992) – sociology was, as George Ross has said, signally absent from the EU studies party. The study of the EU was dominated by theoretically minded political scientists and lawyers concerned with explaining and justifying the emergence of a complex post-national political/legal system, grounded mostly in rationalist economic reasoning and/or the Kantian vision of a kingdom of ends. In writing about a Europe of high-flying politicians, bureaucrats and lawyers and their institutions, the everyday mass of European society was invisible. What sociology there was, came across as baldly utopian, and barely sociological: the 1990s flowering of cosmopolitan social theory led by the ungrounded speculations of Ulrich Beck and Jürgen Habermas. Nobody was interested in whether there needed to be an actual European society underpinning the political/legal construction, at least, not in what empirical evidence there might be found for it.

As the clouds then gathered over the EU, political science and international relations (IR) theory in particular started to edge towards sociological-style claims. Ideas and institutionalism – summarized in the massively cited work of Peter Hall and Rosemary Taylor (1996) – started to be invoked as the explanation for the ongoing dynamics of the European construction; more critical scholars took a 'constructivist turn', which, albeit 20 years off the intellectual pace in the postmodern humanities, started to bring power, discourse and ideology into the mix (Thomas Risse, 'Exploring the Nature of the Beast' (1996); Thomas Christiansen, Knud Erik Jørgensen and Antje Wiener, *The Social Construction of Europe* (1999)); and eventually the mainstream itself, led presciently by Gary

Marks and Liesbet Hooghe ('A Postfunctionalist Theory of European Integration', 2009), started more and more to turn to public opinion measures of actual existing Europeans, as it realized that the iceberg was melting – glossed in a new anxious terminology of declining 'output legitimacy', 'democratic deficit', 'Euroscepticism', and 'the end of the permissive consensus'.

Where was sociology when the political scientists were (re)discovering, after all, the usefulness of a social foundation – however shaky – to politics, law and economics? Marginal, as ever. The most widely recognized work to fill this society-shaped hole was Neil Fligstein's *Euroclash* (2008), an earnest attempt by a mainstream US sociologist in dialogue with political scientists to lay out what might be known from existing secondary sources about the social foundations of the EU. Fligstein's honest and Euro-friendly assessment – the object of several pages of withering scorn in Perry Anderson's antithetical *The New Old World* (2009) – charted with sober empiricism the basic evidence for why and how the Europe that had been constructed reflected the interests, lifestyles and social patterns of a particular tranche of the European upper and middle classes, leaving out a disaffected minority – that could quite easily become an electoral majority. Although a simplistic reading of European dynamics, it was an academic message ripe for the times in that it was an obviously valid general argument and an easy-to-understand picture.

Fligstein was notable for turning EU studies back towards Karl Deutsch (not Karl Marx or Carl Schmitt), and towards behavioural evidence that had to be there for all the identity talk about Europe – the obsession of the European Commission in those years – to have any grounding. Works coming out of the constructivist wing of IR, as with theoretical anthropology before it, without this sociological savoir faire, have been inevitably limited to reading European 'identity' as purely discursive and imagined (in the Benedict Andersonian sense): an elite fabrication, spun out of such things as European anthems, flags and branding devices, as seen in the work of Cris Shore (*Building Europe*, 2000) or, more recently, Kathleen McNamara's (2015) *The Politics of Everyday Europe*. Other literature on 'Europeanization' tried to limit this term, sometimes aggressively, to the study only of policy processes and policy diffusion, operationalized via national-level policy actors implementing or initiating European norms. They did not look at European society below – European social relations and the everyday behaviour of 'Europeans' (if they indeed existed) – but, rather, policy constructions of 'Europe': it was politics and policy without society.

The point was, and is, that it is not easy to do sociological work on sociological Europeanization – that is, on the varieties of ways in which the everyday lives, communications, networks, behavioural patterns and, ultimately, worldviews of *ordinary* locals and (European) nationals have become 'Europeanized' as part of, but distinct from, how they have also become (routinely) 'globalized'. Eurobarometer and similar sources, such as the European Social Survey, are a gold mine for today's leading social scientists looking for a quick data set to turn into a five-star article in a top journal, without ever needing to leave the office. But they are a weak and disappointing excuse for sociological research, when all they provide are stylized, one-shot question and answers on complex questions such as European 'identity' (whatever that is). Inevitably they flatten behaviour to public opinion research formulae as well as reproduce an unthinking methodological nationalism. More disturbingly, the fishing for public opinion measures is uncomfortably reminiscent of the 'clapometer' mode of electoral politics that, with ubiquitous referenda settling unresolvable issues, is becoming the alpha and omega of European democracy.

Yet, all along, there has been a sociology available to EU studies, with real methodological innovation and empirically (that is, fieldwork) based studies reaching parts of social reality that Eurobarometer, like cheap Euro lager, could never reach. A brief trawl through this literature might also have revealed something about why the EU was coming apart, and why Britain would lead the way in destroying Europe's future.

A pioneer in many ways, Juan Diez Medrano's *Framing Europe* (2003) was the first step in a thoroughgoing Weberian programme that has pinpointed the shortfall in the emergence of hegemonic European social classes. His brave fieldwork, cycling around in the mid-2000s to interviews in a mid-sized UK city – a few miles from the depressing midland small town where I was born – already showed in some detail why the good folk of Northampton, England, would never be part of the same Europe as their German or Spanish counterparts (an equally thoroughgoing Durkheimian counterpart can now be found in Hans-Jörg Trenz's recent *Narrating European Society*, 2016).

Up in the North West, Mike Savage and associates in Manchester had been pursuing similarly rich research on British local, national and international identities and behaviour, through interviews and community research (*Globalization and Belonging*, 2004). Their portrait of middle- and working-class lives in Manchester revealed a genuinely cosmopolitan, globally minded and ethnically/racially diverse society, not just 'grim up north' but one that was integrating into the world beyond these shores in a way quite distinct to the routine 'social transnationalism' of ordinary Germans foregrounded by Steffen Mau in the book of that name (*Social Transnationalism: Lifeworlds beyond the Nation-State*, 2010), based on the first similar survey of the globalization of the German population over the last decades. Savage's and Mau's findings could also be contrasted to the portraits culled across a wide section of the bourgeoisie in the cities of Milan, Madrid and Paris found in Alberta Andreotti, Patrick Le Galès and Javier Moreno's *Globalized Minds, Roots in the City* (2015). The EUCROSS project, led by Ettore Recchi, also put together (2012–2015) an unprecedented large-scale survey with follow-up biographical research about the everyday transnational behaviour of ordinary nationals in six countries, providing further databases that explode the national focus of routine empirical sociology and two-dimensional measurements.[1]

Perhaps most brilliantly conceived of all, Sophie Duchesne, Elizabeth Frazer, Florence Haegel and Virginie van Ingelgom's *Citizen's Reactions to European Integration Compared: Overlooking Europe* (2015), noting the excessive focus on middle classes in all the other work, constructed contentious, repeated focus groups, of ordinary, largely working-class Belgians, Britons and French, to reveal in their rambling conversations the depth to which sheer ignorance and indifference about the EU characterized all these societies – with, of course, the UK standing out in its hostility and misperceptions.

A debate I organized at the University of Leeds in early June 2016, 'Is Britain Really a European society?', picking up on these works, saw Recchi (from EUCROSS) and Duchesne rather bleakly running through the basic quantitative and qualitative reasons why this was no longer a silly question.[2] Although nobody in the room truly believed it at the time (except perhaps the pugnacious, former supermarkets manager Phillip Davies, leading the Brexit argument), the event was sounding a death knell for Britain in Europe. While the well-meaning, and sympathetic Labour Member of Parliament (MP) Mary Creagh was outdebated by the drilled, common-sense focus of the Conservative Eurosceptic MP Davies, it was left to the nominally left-wing progressive David Goodhart to declare himself to be reluctantly voting 'remain', before giving ten minutes of eloquent reasoning why the EU had failed and why it was no longer good for Britain.

My own position is diametrically opposed to Goodhart's nationalism on Europe and on migration to Britain, to which he is vocally opposed as part of the 'Blue Labour' turn. My book on Europe, *Eurostars and Eurocities* (2008), is nothing if not the work of a post-national ex-British European citizen – now homeless, and apparently nomadic to the end. To those taking a first glance at this narrative portrait of the young mobile EU populations living and working in three prototypical Eurocities (London, Brussels, Amsterdam) in the mid-2000s, it might be easily supposed to be part of the naive idealism of that now long-past earlier era: the tale of 60 young Europeans (61, if you include the author), infused with the dynamism and apparently limitless opportunity of a Europa Endless, as it was, a Trans-Europe Express to a realizable cosmopolitan future.

But as Christian Joppke, Sophie Duchesne and Tim Butler all discern in their careful reviews of *Eurostars and Eurocities*, the storm clouds are certainly gathering in the pages as it progresses and the characters get older. The dream of the Eurostars will fail inevitably in the renationalization of everyday life and social relations around them, which asserts itself over the long run on social reproduction, welfare security, healthcare and inheritance in the lives of these ordinary middle classes on the continent. The two books that most influence the gloom of its later pages are, of course, *Die Welt von Gestern: Erinnerungen eines Europäers* (1942), Stefan Zweig's bitter memories of the lost pre–World War I cosmopolitan city of Vienna and the subsequent fall of Europe, written just before he killed himself on the run from the Nazis; and Mark Mazower's astonishing *Dark Continent* (1998), his macabre alter-history of twentieth-century European disaster, forgotten in the post-war period, in which fascism always lay at the end of the modernist tracks, not (our) Kantian utopia. So it is farewell again today to those Weimar liberal/social democratic hopes, squeezed now between the impossible totalitarian optimalities of neoliberal global capitalism (Friedrich Hayek), and the equally hopeless nostalgic version of nationalist socialism, now being parleyed by the likes of Wolfgang Streeck in Germany, and naive Corbynistas in the current UK democratic meltdown.

As regards democracy in the UK, what is next is anybody's guess. But, notwithstanding the strong evidence about Britain's incompatibility with Europe put forward in a number of the books discussed above, *Eurostars and Eurocities* paints a different, highly Europeanized, vision of London, before the fall. Fifty-two per cent – or to be more precise, the victorious 35 per cent or so of the British electorate who bothered to show up to vote 'leave' – is no more a verdict on the behavioural foundations of a society than it is an expression of truly democratic politics. Democracy, and Britain's extensive Europeanization, have both been silenced by a show of hands in a moronic inferno orchestrated by *Daily Mail* and *Daily Telegraph* headlines – democracy and the definition of Britain sitting in the crabby hands of a few Fleet Street editors.

For there was a paradox about British Euroscepticism all along – that, despite all the hostile public opinion measures of European identity, the clapometer polls and the portrait of the island UK that one might reasonably read, starkly, from decades of virulent anti-EU bile in the press, Britain was, on some measures, *profoundly* Europeanized in its everyday life, arguably more so than many of its neighbours.

It is another cliché, but fish-and-chip Brits have, of all European citizens, been among the most entrepreneurial in their use of European rights, what with their cheap airline holidays, sunbelt homeownerships and offshore, tax-dodging, financial gymnastics. Of course, the irony is that many Brexit voters, who enjoy their Costa del Sol breaks as much as anyone else, apparently think that all these benefits are founded in Great British colonial birthright – the national 'genius' Winston Churchill would say – not any legal European order. Or, as one such voter commented, blithely responding to an academic's web post about the consequences of losing European citizenship: 'Leaving the EU won't change anything, because British people have been able to travel and live anywhere they wanted in the world for more than three hundred years now'. Rule Britannia, indeed.

More significant, and more telling about the tragic global contradictions at the heart of 'Being British' in the early twenty-first century, was the fact that Britain had, despite itself, perhaps, become the most Europeanized, open, EU-integrated, labour market in Europe. London was the one place where the Four Freedoms came together and showed how Europe could indeed work. And European foreigners came in droves, in response to this demand, with market opportunities for the skilled, talented and desired, anchored in a genuine willingness to employ foreigners in all sectors of the economy on equal terms, and protected by still functioning labour laws and welfare rights, in labour markets far less rigid, parochial and nationally restricted than in France, Denmark, Germany and Spain. Before political reaction set in, Britain was transformed by waves of new migrations and mobilities that selected overwhelmingly at the top end, from Western Europe, and then increasingly from Eastern Europe.

Of course, these conditions were also why Britain was more attractive to other categories of less-privileged migrants from further afield, and these were equally part of the dynamics at the lower end of the labour market. But on that, Britain had an advantage, in that, as an EU member, it could rely on its neighbours to substantially protect its borders from the less economically desirable, notably refugees who would end up stalled by a UK national border located on French soil.

Coupled with its open migration economy, who also could doubt that Britain had also flourished, despite the doubters like Goodhart, under its proud image of dynamic superdiversity: its multicultural, multiracial, multinational mix putting it at the head of a global transformation of Europe that had slowly seen others – notably Germany – changing towards a more diverse future.

For sure, a sizeable percentage of Brexit voters were voting precisely against this changing Britain they saw around them. And on this they were voting as much against globalization as against the EU or the everyday Europeanization of their lives. Yet another part of the winning Brexit coalition was quite different in its attitude. In passing their verdict on global Britain in 2016, they were passing a quite different conceit – that Britain in fact did not need Europe for its open global positioning. There was some truth in this arrogant notion, channelled in the overconfident, braying national swagger of ex-public schoolboys such as Boris Johnson. One could see how young, free-moving Europeans – too many Spanish, Italian and Greek accents – might well be replaced by surfer boy Aryan Antipodeans on 'working holidays', somehow closer because they speak the same language; or by Americans who – with the falling pound – have never been so visible or felt so at home in London. The conceit may work then, until, that is, the reality of being shut out of regional and world trade deals becomes apparent.

But, as the fact that migrants keep coming shows, wherever they are coming from, the greatest lie of all – sold to those a disenfranchised, poorly educated social groups lumpen-proletariat, very deliberately left behind by the architects of the London boom and the divided society which sustained it – was that their leave vote was a vote against migrants and immigration. That the UK would somehow keep the same kind of global economy, pumping the same kind of Olympic games triumphalism, a quasi United States, yet without free movement, or at least without the people who move to fill the jobs.

In fact, EU membership not only protected the UK from the most difficult kinds of migrations – while helping filter the supply/demand dynamics to optimal selection dynamics – but it also ensured that a sizeable part of the migration driving the UK labour market was located in regulated, visible and taxable sectors of the economy. This was a sizeable achievement in a voracious, flexible global economy in which more than half of migration in the UK was still from outside the EU, and which also contained vast numbers of irregular, informal migrations in the 'dirty pretty things' category (to recall Stephen Frears's sordid 2002 film): the unquantified numbers of workers in the shadier parts of the hospitality and catering industries, in construction, or driving taxis, cleaning offices at night, servicing sex and security, washing cars.

Leaving the EU clearly will be a wild deregulation in this sense. The laughable smoke screen that the UK might be able to contain its migration demand by adopting an Australian or Canadian approach to immigration will soon disperse to reveal the reality. This is that the rip-off, neo-liberal, free-for-all of an independent UK open for global business will have less, not more, control over its borders, and this will mean importing everything that is bad and unacceptable about the United States as a society of immigration. That is: an economy structurally dependent on cheap labour and mass migrant ambition, yet wracked by violently racist anti-immigrant politics and policed by a draconian, arbitrary border-and-deportation regime, in which preferential selectivity on racial, ethnic and national grounds triumphs every time over rights; yet with borders that allow in, by the side door and around the fence, huge numbers of precarious exploitable workers, led by the organized crime partnership of *padrón* and *coyote*, and in which the entry regime is based on a alphabet soup of illogical, remote visa categories, supposedly controlling access, in which anyone who can, may pay their way in. Britain will become transnational in the same way the United States is, with transnationalism at the low end passing by the same dingy underpass across borders that allows British and global elites at the other end of the polarized global city to park their mobile money in London.

The rump of the EU, if it survives, may well conclude that the UK is welcome to its post-Brexit 'land of opportunities'. There are, of course, some scenarios of the capitalist future in which a fascist neo-liberal carceral Britain – a slightly more civilized Singapore, perhaps – turns out to be, as Johnson hopes, the triumphant model of independent life outside Europe. Our hope must therefore be that the centre of Europe – Germany – will hold, and that the variety of capitalism it may still offer will survive: an open, regulated, confident, migrant economy, with social protection and labour laws, a postnational commitment to Europe and some memory of the European past (something like what Gordon Brown was saying before the Brexit vote). There has to be a clearer and more powerful progressive political configuration somewhere, something better than the shabby, tattered, brave new island that Theresa May inherited this summer from the Brexit debacle.

Notes

1 http://www.eucross.eu/cms
2 The debate can be viewed online at: http://www.lssi.leeds.ac.uk/2016/06/22/videos-from-britain-and-the-eu-is-britain-really-a-european-society/.

CONTRIBUTORS

Stefan Auer is associate professor and programme director in European Studies in the School of Modern Languages and Cultures at the University of Hong Kong. Prior to this, he worked at University College Dublin (2001–2006) and La Trobe University in Melbourne (2006–2013). His books include *Liberal Nationalism in Central Europe* (2004), which won the UACES prize, and (with Nicole Scicluna) *Whose Liberty Is It Anyway? Europe at the Crossroads* (2012). In 2016, Dr Auer was awarded a Jean Monnet Chair.

Gurminder K. Bhambra is professor of sociology at the University of Warwick and guest professor of sociology and history at the Centre for Concurrences in Colonial and Postcolonial Studies, Linnaeus University, Sweden (2016–18). Her books include *Rethinking Modernity: Postcolonialism and the Sociological Imagination* (2007), which won the 2008 Philip Abrams Memorial Prize for best first book in sociology, and *Connected Sociologies* (2014). She is co-editor of *Silencing Human Rights* (2009); *1968 in Retrospect* (2009); *African Athena* (2011) and *European Cosmopolitanism: Colonial Histories and Postcolonial Societies* (2016).

Craig Calhoun is president of the Berggruen Institute, Los Angeles. He was previously director of the London School of Economics, having been president of the Social Science Research Council, university professor of the social sciences at New York University and director of NYU's Institute for Public Knowledge. His books include *Critical Social Theory* (1995), *Nations Matter: Culture, History, and the Cosmopolitan Dream* (2007) and *The Roots of Radicalism* (2012).

Colin Crouch, FBA, external scientific member, Max Planck Institute for the Study of Societies, is emeritus professor at the University of Warwick, where he was professor of governance and public management at Warwick Business School. He was previously professor of sociology at Oxford and at the European University Institute in Florence. His books include *Industrial Relations and European State Traditions* (1993), *Social Change in Western Europe* (1999), *Post-democracy* (2005), *The Strange Non-death of Neo-liberalism* (2011), *Making Capitalism Fit for Society* (2013), *The Knowledge Corrupters: Hidden Consequences of the Financial Takeover of Public Life* (2015), *Governing Social Risks in Post-Crisis Europe* (2015) and *Society and Social Change in 21st Century Europe* (2016).

Harry F. Dahms is professor of sociology, co-director of the Center for the Study of Social Justice and co-chair of the Committee on Social Theory at the University of Tennessee. He is the editor of the book series *Current Perspectives in Social Theory* and director of the International Social Theory Consortium (ISTC). He is the author of *The Vitality of Critical Theory* (2011) and editor of *Transformations of Capitalism: Economy, Society and the State in Modern Times* (2000).

Gerard Delanty is professor of sociology and social and political thought, Sussex University, Brighton, UK and founding editor of the *European Journal of Social Theory*. He is the author of various books, which include *Inventing Europe* (1995), *Formations of European Modernity: A Historical and Political Sociology of Europe* (2013), *The Cosmopolitan Imagination: The Renewal of Critical Social Theory* (2009) and (with Chris Rumford) *Rethinking Europe: Social Theory and the Implications of Europeanization* (2005).

Adrian Favell is chair in sociology and social theory at the University of Leeds and chercheur associé of the Centre for European Studies at Sciences Po, Paris. He is the author of *Philosophies of Integration: Immigration and the Idea of Citizenship in France and Britain* (2001), *Eurostars and Eurocities: Free Movement and Mobility in an Integrating Europe* (2008) and *Immigration, Integration and Mobility: New Agendas in Migration Studies. Essays 1998–2014* (ECPR); and editor, with Virginie Guiraudon, of *Sociology of the European Union* (2011).

Jonathan Hearn is professor of political and historical sociology at the University of Edinburgh. He is the author of *Claiming Scotland: National Identity and Liberal Culture* (2000), *Rethinking Nationalism: A Critical Introduction* (2006) and *Theorizing Power* (2012).

John Holmwood is professor of sociology at the University of Nottingham and a former president of the British Sociological Association. He is the author of *Founding Sociology? Talcott Parsons and the Idea of General Theory* (1996) and (with A. Stewart) *Explanation and Social Theory* (new edn. 1993). He edited *A Manifesto for the Public University* (2011) and is co-founder of the Campaign for the Public University.

Tim Oliver is Dahrendorf Fellow on Europe-North American Relations at the London School of Economics and currently visiting scholar at New York University, specializing in British, EU and transatlantic foreign policy. He has been writing and consulting substantially since 2013 about the prospect of the UK withdrawing from the EU, most recently in 'Brexit: What Happens Next?', LSE IDEAS Strategic Update, June 2016: http://www.lse.ac.uk/IDEAS/publications/Strategic-Updates/brexit_next.aspx.

William Outhwaite is emeritus professor of sociology at Newcastle University, UK and honorary professor at the University of Sussex. His publications include the following: *European Society* (2008), *Critical Theory and Contemporary Europe* (2012), *Social Theory* (2015), *Europe since 1989* (2016) and *Contemporary Europe* (2017).

Simon Susen is a Reader in Sociology at City, University of London. He is the author of *The Foundations of the Social: Between Critical Theory and Reflexive Sociology* (2007), *The 'Postmodern Turn' in the Social Sciences* (2015) and *Pierre Bourdieu et la distinction sociale. Un essai philosophique* (2016). He co-edited *Ciudadanía territorial y movimientos sociales: Historia y nuevas problemáticas en el escenario latinoamericano y mundial* (2010), *The Legacy of Pierre Bourdieu: Critical Essays* (2011) and *The Spirit of Luc Boltanski: Essays on the 'Pragmatic Sociology of Critique'* (2014). In addition, he edited special issues on the work of Shmuel Noah Eisenstadt, *Journal of Classical Sociology* 11 (3): 229–335, 2011, and on 'Bourdieu and Language', *Social Epistemology* 27 (3–4): 195–393, 2013.

Chris Thornhill is professor in law at the University of Manchester. His recent books include *A Sociology of Transnational Constitutions: The Social Foundations of the Post-National Legal Structure* (2015). He edited, with Mikael Rask Madsen, *Law and the Formation of Modern Europe: Perspectives from the Historical Sociology of Law* (2014) and is the author of 'The European Constitution and the *pouvoir constituant* – No longer, or never, sui generis?', in *The Self-Constitution of Europe*, ed. Jiří Přibáň (2016).

Martin Westlake, former secretary general of the European Economic and Social Committee, is senior visiting fellow at the Europe Institute, London School of Economics and visiting professor at the Department of European Political and Administrative Studies, College of Europe, Bruges. He is the author of *Kinnock The Biography* (2001), (with David Galloway) *The Council of the European Union* (3rd ed., 2004), (with David Butler) *British Politics and European Elections 2004* (2005) and *The European Economic and Social Committee* (2016).

Antje Wiener is chair of political science (global governance) at the University of Hamburg and the author of *'European' Citizenship Practice: Building Institutions of a Non-State* (1998), *The Invisible Constitution of Politics: Contested Norms and International Encounters* (2008) and *A Theory of Contestation* (2014).

INDEX

Lightning Source UK Ltd.
Milton Keynes UK
UKOW04f0509261017
311668UK00001B/22/P